MW00447968

11/23
STRAND PRICE
$5.00

◢ COLLEGE MADE WHOLE ◣

COLLEGE
MADE
WHOLE

Integrative Learning for a Divided World

CHRIS W. GALLAGHER

Johns Hopkins University Press
Baltimore

© 2019 Johns Hopkins University Press
All rights reserved. Published 2019
Printed in the United States of America on acid-free paper
9 8 7 6 5 4 3 2 1

Johns Hopkins University Press
2715 North Charles Street
Baltimore, Maryland 21218-4363
www.press.jhu.edu

Library of Congress Cataloging-in-Publication Data

Names: Gallagher, Chris W., author.
Title: College made whole : integrative learning for a divided world / Chris W. Gallagher.
Description: Baltimore, Maryland : Johns Hopkins University Press, [2019] | Includes
    bibliographical references and index.
Identifiers: LCCN 2018060103 | ISBN 9781421432625 (hardcover : alk. paper) |
    ISBN 1421432625 (hardcover : alk. paper) | ISBN 9781421432632 (electronic) |
    ISBN 1421432633 (electronic)
Subjects: LCSH: Education, Higher—Computer-assisted instruction. | Education,
    Higher—Aims and objectives. | Educational technology.
Classification: LCC LB2395.7 .G34 2019 | DDC 378.1/758—dc23
LC record available at https://lccn.loc.gov/2018060103

A catalog record for this book is available from the British Library.

*Special discounts are available for bulk purchases of this book. For more information, please
contact Special Sales at 410-516-6936 or specialsales@press.jhu.edu.*

Johns Hopkins University Press uses environmentally friendly book materials, including
recycled text paper that is composed of at least 30 percent post-consumer waste, whenever
possible.

It is institutions that help us to preserve decency. They need our help as well. Do not speak of "our institutions" unless you make them yours by acting on their behalf. Institutions do not protect themselves. They fall one after another unless each is defended from the beginning. So choose an institution you care about—a court, a newspaper, a law, a labor union—and take its side.

—Timothy Snyder, *On Tyranny*

CONTENTS

PREFACE

My college experience was . . . fine. I picked my school from a college guide in the public library because it was small, nearby, and affordable enough (with loans) if I lived at home. I liked some of my classes and disliked others. Some of what I learned stuck with me and some didn't. An English major (I'd always liked reading and writing) and political science minor (I'd always been interested in politics), I was not a great student, but I was diligent enough to earn decent grades. I made some friends and had some good times, but as a commuter student who held a job throughout college, I was not involved in campus life.

I did tutor at the Writing Center at the invitation of one of my English professors, and that experience, more than anything, lingers in my memory. Most of my classes are a blur, but I recall with utter clarity the moment Professor Al DeCiccio approached me in the basement of the student union—I was eating lunch with a friend—and asked if I would be interested in tutoring at the Writing Center. I remember with equal clarity the layout of the furniture and the wet-coat-and-pizza smell of the Writing Center, and even some of the sessions I had with fellow students there. And I remember long, coffee-fueled nights writing for and editing the literary magazine.

Otherwise, not much of my college experience sticks in my memory. A good Irish lit class. That cool co-taught postmodernism course (Professor DeCiccio again). A bio class that gave me fits. Arguing with my religion teacher—a priest—about purgatory (or was it limbo?). Listening to Echo and the Bunnymen and the Smiths on the ride in. That time my tire blew out on the highway. That party I left early.

Naturally, I matured intellectually and emotionally over my four college years. And I developed a firm enough grasp of American and British literature to perform adequately on the GRE and gain admission to a master's program in English—which I enrolled in, mostly because I didn't know what else to do.

▪ Danielle Murad Waiss's college experience has been, to use her word, "amazing."[1] She chose her university because of its strengths in global and experiential education and the quality of the faculty. She recognized in the school's experiential learning model—particularly its cooperative education program—an opportunity to connect and synthesize her learning inside and outside the classroom.

An excellent student with high marks, Danielle is a political science and international affairs combined major. She is involved in a wide variety of cocurricular and extracurricular activities, including the ballroom dance team, classes at Boston Ballet, and the Political Science and International Affairs Student Association, for which she has served on the executive board. She has co-led an alternative spring break trip to Texas; developed a service project teaching fitness to senior citizens; written for the *Political Review*; planned and led an honors seminar for her fellow students; completed three summer study abroad programs (one in Geneva, another in Japan, and a third in Germany, the Netherlands, Brussels, and France); studied abroad in London; interned for a member of Parliament; and completed two cooperative education experiences (co-ops)—one at the Massachusetts Attorney General's Office and the other split between the NATO Defense College in Rome and the International Institute for Counter-Terrorism in Israel. One of her most important achievements was choreographing and performing in a well-attended dance show called *Nizkor* for the university's Holocaust Awareness Week, an honor she earned as the recipient of a prestigious award from the Jewish Studies Program.

Even more impressive than these experiences themselves is the fact that Danielle understands and articulates them as part of a coherent, unfolding educational trajectory. She is deepening her understanding of political and diplomatic issues, of how various political (governmental and nongovernmental) institutions and organizations work, and of how she wants to contribute to that work. She sees herself developing as a more confident and competent reader, writer, and thinker as she moves across these different contexts and engages with different people and perspectives. In Parliament and at the NATO Defense College, she found herself in conversation with people who live and breathe the issues she had studied, and happily she found that "what I've learned in school has allowed me to follow along as if I had been working with them."

Danielle credits a range of mentors—faculty members, co-op employers, her family—who "have helped me tread my path and guide me and help me do what I need to get done and figure out who I am." She singles out her co-op advisor, "one of the most amazing people ever," who has "backed me up 100 percent. She really cares for me." Danielle's path is her own, but she has never felt on her own.

Now a senior, Danielle is undertaking a third and final co-op at the United Nations in New York. She says that the combination of her learning inside and outside the classroom "has helped me develop a lot of skills, and it's made me more confident in who I am and what I stand for. It's helped me shape my own opinions on things, but it's also opened my eyes up [to others' perspectives]." She is not sure what she will do upon graduation, but she is gravitating toward working in an international governmental organization or the Foreign Service. She already has a professional network that extends across several governmental organizations and nongovernmental organizations (NGOs).

▪ Two very different college experiences—but what is the key distinction, the difference that makes the difference? To be sure, Danielle and I have differing backgrounds: she identifies as a Mexican Canadian, Iraqi, Polish, Russian, Jewish woman and I as a white American man. We attended dissimilar institutions three decades apart. No doubt she's a far better and more accomplished student than I ever was. While I worked random retail and service jobs, her work experiences have been connected to her academic experiences and have not inhibited her ability to involve herself in a plethora of other co- and extracurricular activities. Her college experience has taken her to several countries, whereas mine was focused on campus. But the most important difference—the difference that distinguishes a "fine" college experience from an "amazing" college experience—is that Danielle is an integrative learner and I, for the most part, was not.

Integrative learners like Danielle connect and synthesize ideas, knowledge, and skills across learning experiences in different contexts. As they move across these contexts and interact with different people and groups, developing important relationships as they go, they build conceptual scaffolding that allows them to draw on prior knowledge and skills as they construct new knowledge and skills. They stand back from their experiences, reflect on them, connect them, and synthesize what they learn from them. They are highly intentional learners, choosing experiences that will help them develop their knowledge and skills, think through a problem, or learn something about themselves. For instance, Danielle uses her co-ops as opportunities to explore how governmental organizations and NGOs at different levels operate and where she might best fit. As Stanford design school professors Bill Burnett and Dave Evans (2016) might say, she is *prototyping*: trying out different ways to design her life.[2]

By contrast, I mostly rolled through college, taking my classes as they came. I experienced each course as self-contained, the curricula as menus of choices. I somehow made enough connections across my English courses to develop some understanding of American and British literary traditions, but otherwise I did not develop the reflective capacity necessary to be an integrative learner until well into graduate school. It's not just the passage of time that makes college mostly a blur for me—it's that I experienced college passively for the most part, never building the relationships, conceptual scaffolding, or reflective skills that would allow me to become an intentional, integrative learner.

But I got lucky. A few key things went right for me, and no doubt I benefited from being a white, cisgender man. I had a couple of professors who took an interest (in addition to Professor DeCiccio, shout out to Professor Kathy Cain), and I leaned heavily on these relationships. Those people taught something I was interested in and was pretty good at. I followed one lead, and it worked out. Thirty years later, even though

I spend most of my time in academic administration, I still think of teaching writing as my primary vocation.

Of course, Danielle is lucky too. She's blessed with brilliance, enormous energy, a supportive family, a wealth of educational opportunities, and more. But she's also an intentional, integrative learner, and that is making the difference. Maybe college will be a blur for her thirty years from now, but I doubt it.

Surely a good portion of what makes for an "amazing" college experience will always have to do with students and what they bring (or don't bring) to the venture. Danielle is—let's face it—a superstar. And it's not false modesty to say I was not. I'm sure I missed many opportunities that my college offered to me. (Possibly my grade school teachers' constant refrain "He doesn't apply himself" continued to describe me as an undergraduate.) But there are things that educators and institutions of higher education can do to make it much more likely that students will have "amazing" college experiences rather than just "fine" ones (or worse). They can design their classes, curricula, co- and extracurricular experiences, and educational models to help students develop as integrative learners. They can provide students with close mentorship every step of the way. And they can work to ensure access and opportunity to robust integrative experiences to all students who desire them—not just for four years after high school, but throughout their lives.

This won't be easy. Colleges and universities are not designed to promote integrative learning. That's because they are not themselves integrated. Even the very best of them have optimized parts of their operation without attending to the interdependencies of those parts. They attract star faculty in disciplines X, Y, and Z; set up world-renowned labs in research areas A, B, and C; develop an outstanding career services office or an excellent service-learning program. These are all good things to have, but as any student or parent who experiences the "[insert school name here] shuffle" can tell you, they typically remain highly compartmentalized and sometimes fractionalized operations. The predictable results are incoherence, inconsistency, and inefficiency—and, for most learners, an educational experience that is less than the sum of its parts.

The great challenge facing "traditional" (i.e., accredited public and nonprofit private) colleges and universities today is to offer an education that is more than the sum of its parts. For the first time in history, learning opportunities and credentialing options are readily available in convenient formats from a host of providers at rates much lower than college or university tuition. Federal financial aid is being freed up for these options, and regulations for non-accredited, for-profit, and non-institutional providers are being slashed. Unlike me, Danielle and her peers could decide to mix and match learning opportunities and credentialing options as they need them, without paying for everything that a college or university has to offer. Why shouldn't they? What do colleges and universities offer that other providers do not?

The short answer is *integrative learning*. The long answer is . . . this book. In the pages ahead, I argue that in order to survive what has been called "the great unbundling" of US higher education,[3] colleges and universities will need to offer learners more and more diverse learning opportunities in a wider variety of formats and modalities in more places over longer periods of time—all while becoming more, not less, coherent. In short, they need to integrate themselves in order to facilitate integrative learning.

A tough challenge, yes, but colleges and universities must rise to it. As I write in 2019, it does not seem an overstatement to say that the fate of our fragile democracy, and indeed the fragile world order, may hinge on our ability to help shape adaptive, integrative thinkers like Danielle. This book is devoted to advancing that goal and is dedicated to Danielle and her peers who, if anyone can, will show us how to achieve it.

ACKNOWLEDGMENTS

First and foremost, I want to thank the students of Northeastern University, particularly Danielle Murad Waiss, Riddhi Samtani, Martha Neuman, and "Elizabeth Zane." They inspired and shaped this book, and I am forever grateful to them for allowing me to share their stories.

I am also grateful to my many Northeastern colleagues who have read portions of the book or talked with me about the ideas in it, beginning with Beth Britt, Laura Green, and Uta Poiger. All three are invaluable colleagues, readers, and friends. Beth has read every word of this book and has shaped it in innumerable ways.

Thanks also to Northeastern colleagues Susan Ambrose, Susan Chang, Ellen Cushman, Amy Farrell, Natasha Frost, Jonna Iacono, Laurie Kramer, Neal Lerner, Jack McDevitt, Mary Mello, Mya Poe, Marc Rehmar, Joshua Roberts, Bruce Ronkin, Cigdem Talgar, Laura Wankel, Eric Winter, and Kate Ziemer, all of whom have taught me much and constantly remind me by their powerful example why we do this work. Same goes for Kristi Girdharry, Charles Lesh, and Kevin Smith, former Northeastern colleagues now making trouble elsewhere.

Susan Albertine, Maggie Britton, Jamey Gallagher, Peter Gray, Mike Kelly, Andrew Rusnak, and Shari Stenberg all provided invaluable insights at key moments in the project.

Thanks to Greg Britton, editor extraordinaire. What a warm, generous, and incisive reader. What a smart and dogged advocate for his writers. Who could ask for more? I also thank the two anonymous reviewers of the manuscript, whose feedback emboldened me to take the final needed step, and Juliana McCarthy and Merryl A. Sloane for their careful copyediting.

To the Boston construction workers who woke me up early every morning so I could get this book done, thanks a lot. Seriously. I know I'm just a pale light shining from a second-floor window to you, but I appreciate what you do.

Thanks to the National, Lord Huron, Miles Davis, and John Coltrane for drowning out the construction noise and providing the soundtrack for my writing and my life.

This book would not have been possible—or at least would have taken much longer—without a faculty development leave from Northeastern University.

Finally, thanks once again to Molly, Cady, and Erin for being the smart, courageous, and altogether inspiring women you are. You amaze me.

▊ Some of the material in chapter 6 first appeared in an earlier version in Chris W. Gallagher (2018), "College Re-Bound?" *Inside Higher Ed*, 13 June; https://www.insidehighered.com/views/2018/06/13/alternative -credentials-create-social-and-economic-inequities-and-shouldnt-be -seen.

◢ COLLEGE MADE WHOLE ◣

INTRODUCTION

THE FUTURE OF HIGHER EDUCATION IS INTEGRATION

The ravages of climate change. Nuclear proliferation. Network-based terrorism, both physical and cyber. Political disenfranchisement, disenchantment, and discord. Growing social and economic inequality. Threats to the pillars of democracy, including the separation of powers and freedom of the press. The emboldening of white supremacy and authoritarian populism. The impending automation of nearly half of the US workforce.[1]

Even as these challenges become more acute, calls grow louder for dismantling US higher education—our best, and perhaps only, hope of effectively addressing them. Public funding has been slashed and diverted from accredited colleges and universities to non-institutional, for-profit providers. Federal regulations are being cut and safeguards removed for students defrauded by shady operators. Robust academic curricula are being jettisoned in favor of online training modules in workplace skills. Professional faculty are being replaced by educational technologies and armies of semiprofessional part-timers. Degrees are being deemphasized in favor of "stackable" credentials. Dubbed "the great unbundling of higher education" (Craig 2015), these developments spell the literal dis-integration of higher education as we have known it.[2]

And not a moment too soon, judging by the eschatological titles of recent books on higher education: *The Fall of the Faculty, The Last Professors, The Toxic University, The Lost Soul of Higher Education, Zombies in the Academy, The End of College, College Disrupted, College Unbound, Fail U.*[3] These books are written from different perspectives, some by non-academics promoting a brave new world of "game-changing" reforms and others by academics bemoaning the corporatization of the university. But they are united in their conviction that the end times have arrived for higher education.

Yet this is far from the first time we have heard such pronouncements, and I doubt it will be the last. The 1990s brought *The University in Ruins, The Moral Collapse of the University, Imposters in the Temple*, and *Killing the Spirit*.[4] Clark Kerr (2001) reminds us that predictions of postsecondary doom were common even earlier.[5] The 1960s and 1970s saw *Academia in Anarchy, Chaos in Our Colleges, The Death of the American University, The Exploding University*, and *The Fall of the American University* (and that's just the beginning of the alphabet).[6] In fact, as I show in chapter 1, critiques like these go back more than a hundred years. Rumors of the death of this resilient and adaptive social institution have proven, again and again, to be highly exaggerated.

Wait—adaptive? Granted, this is not a word often associated with higher education, but in fact, the institution has constantly evolved over time in good ways and bad, and it must continue to do so. For instance, it has increasingly become a mechanism for reproducing and even expanding social and economic inequality, rather than the engine of social mobility many imagine it to be. Now, as inequality threatens the very foundations of our republic, fraying civic bonds and undermining political institutions, higher education must adapt in ways that interrupt and reverse this pattern.

Unbundling higher education—breaking institutions into multiple distinct providers of goods and services; courses and curricula into discrete modules; faculty into various instructional roles (content developers, instructional designers, success coaches, evaluators); learning into atomized skills and bits of knowledge; and degrees into smaller (micro, nano) credentials—is exactly the wrong solution to this problem. It will exacerbate stratification and inequality, leaving individuals who lack cultural and economic capital vulnerable to predatory practices in a deregulated market and undermining our collective capacity to confront the social, cultural, and economic challenges that beset us. Mixing and matching assorted credentials from random providers is hardly a recipe for producing the kind of integrative thinkers who can effectively address complex and dynamic challenges.

Today's rapidly changing social, political, and economic landscape demands thinkers who are comfortable working in the face of constant novelty and uncertainty—*and* who can slowly, patiently build a systems-based understanding of how the challenges developed and why. Thinkers who can develop new ideas, make new things, go off on wild flights of imagination—*and* who can produce sober analyses and considered judgments. Thinkers with specialized expertise about particular facets of the challenges—*and* with a general understanding of how larger forces and systems shape those challenges. Thinkers with a grasp of the affordances and limitations of technologies that can be brought to bear on the challenges—*and* an appreciation of how humans perceive, contribute to, and (one hopes!) ameliorate those challenges.

In truth, higher education as we have known it is not well designed to promote integrative learning and thinking either. But that's not because colleges and universities are too bundled—indeed, they're hardly bundled at all. Divisions between disciplines and between faculty produce courses and programs unrelated to each other, leaving students with lists of often incoherent major and general education requirements that they dutifully tick off. Divisions between campuses and communities produce the bogus conception that what happens at school is at worst divorced from and at best a simulated dry run for the "real world." Divisions between faculty undermine their pedagogical power and professional standing. Divisions between undergraduate colleges and continuing education or extension schools unhelpfully segregate "traditional" undergraduates seeking degrees and "nontraditional" adults pursuing lifelong learning opportunities. Higher education is only loosely bundled, and that's a problem.

It's tempting to respond to all this, as some have, with a call to "rebundle" higher education (Bass and Eynon 2016; Horn 2014; Jansson 2010; Large 2015).[7] But from my perspective, this isn't quite right. That *re-* appears to call for a move backward, a return to some previous moment when colleges and universities were appropriately bundled. It's true that unbundling has unfolded over time, but this does not mean that there was a golden era when colleges and universities were bundled just right. In fact, the metaphor of the bundle is itself unhelpful and has made higher education an easy target for champions of disintegration. A bundle is a collection of things tied or wrapped together. It doesn't add up to anything in particular or have a special function: a bundle of sticks is just a bunch of sticks.

Let's say a science department or college is interested—as many are these days—in unbundling their three-credit courses, creating instead a suite of one-credit offerings. The thinking is that the smaller courses will increase student flexibility and drive enrollments. The department chooses its most popular courses: on dinosaurs, asteroids, and volcanoes. If students take all three, the logic goes, they will have the equivalent of a traditional three-credit course. Arithmetic aside, will they? Are students getting the depth and intensity of learning from this bundle that they would in a three-credit course? Or are they getting the intellectual equivalent of bite-size snacks—tasty but neither filling nor nutritious? Bundling itself does not ensure meaningful learning, and it may even undermine it.

On the other hand, let's say the science department designs these one-credit courses as a connected set under the banner "adventures in scientific inquiry." The courses are still organized around dinosaurs, asteroids, and volcanoes, but now they are designed to help students learn how paleontologists, astronomers, and volcanologists do their work—perhaps how they go about answering the question "What *really* happened to the dinosaurs?" In this formulation, students have the opportunity and tools to integrate knowledge and skills across their learning experiences. Pretty filling, pretty nutritious: an integrative learning experience that is more than the sum of its parts.

Many institutions are experimenting with short-form courses, including pop-ups, as well as various forms of modularity, in which independent units, typically short in duration, are either embedded in larger experiences or offered as separate credit- or non-credit-bearing experiences. These initiatives are typically pursued under the goals of flexibility and customization. Those are fine goals, but institutions need to ask: Do these initiatives promote integrative learning or dis-integrative learning? They could provide opportunities for students to combine and synthesize learning experiences in ways that make sense for their learning journeys. Or they could lead to a menu of unrelated bits of content that students mix and match as they would from any provider.

Building a better bundle sounds like a laudable goal, but it still leaves us with simply a collection of things. Indeed, colleges and universities *do* often look and act as loose assemblages of assorted things, some of which bear no discernible relation to teaching, learning, or advancing knowledge. The unbundlers are right about that much. But the answer to this problem is not to turn to what is essentially a marketing strategy in which goods or services are tied together so consumers will buy more than they might otherwise from a single company.

In order to help shape the kind of integrative learning and learners that can confront the complex challenges of the twenty-first century, colleges and universities will need to be neither unbundled nor rebundled, but rather *integrated*. To integrate is to combine two or more things *so that they become a new whole.* The word's etymology traces to the Latin *integratus*, the past participle of *integrare*: to make whole. Integration is a creative process of bringing something new into the world, something that—unlike a bundle—is more than the sum of its parts.

As someone who has spent his entire adult life teaching and holding administrative positions in colleges and universities, I can tell you that integrating these institutions so that they function as cohesive and coherent wholes will be neither simple nor easy. Integrating the people, practices, and processes of these institutions runs up against the time-honored tradition that the great historian of American higher education Laurence Veysey (1970) called "patterned isolation."[8] Well-established and heavily guarded borders and boundaries will need to be traversed. Both the structures and the cultures of most institutions will need to change.

But this can be done, as the examples throughout this book demonstrate. These examples are drawn both from my firsthand experience and from my research into a variety of institutions across the country. Perhaps no college or university is perfectly integrated, but the innovative and hard work of institutional integration in the service of integra-

tive learning is well under way. I hope this book makes that work visible
and inspires others to join it.

Unbundling as Dis-integration

I use "unbundling" to name the current movement to dis-integrate higher
education. I call proponents of unbundling "unbundlers." This is not,
admittedly, a unified group: "edupreneurs," policy wonks, politicians, education journalists, and higher education leaders have differing perspectives and motivations. But they share an investment (often financial) in
breaking down aspects of higher education into their constituent parts
in the name of "efficiency." Throughout this book, my main interlocutors
are Kevin Carey (2015), the author of *The End of College* and director of
the Education Policy Program at the technology-oriented think tank
New America, and Ryan Craig (2015), the founding managing director
of the private equity fund University Ventures and author of *College
Disrupted: The Great Unbundling of Higher Education*. Published in the
same year, these two books have garnered a great deal of attention and
together lay out the case for unbundling higher education.

That case rests on a relentless critique of "traditional," "incumbent,"
or "hybrid" postsecondary institutions as maintaining a bloated, self-
satisfied, inefficient, archaic monopoly on higher education. Unbundlers depict colleges and universities as "country clubs" (Carey 2015,
240) where pampered students "sip sherry with the dons every afternoon" (Craig 2015, 119). I am not going to engage much with these silly
caricatures of posh universities with their stereotypical lazy rivers and
climbing walls. (I'm not sure how climbing walls became symbols of
opulence, but that's another matter.) It's certainly not worth defending
the few institutions that choose to spend money on extravagant ameni-
ties when the majority of college campuses are, if anything, underfunded. And while it's important to discuss the effects of big-time college athletics on the culture of college, this is not a book about that
either. This is a book about learning, and my concern is with the sub-
stance of unbundlers' arguments on that topic. In particular, I'm inter-

ested in their claim that because colleges and universities are trying to be too many things to too many people, they fail at their central goal of educating students.

Of course I'm also interested in the unbundlers' proposed remedy for what they see as moribund institutions: a deregulated market of unbundled products and services offered by a mix of nonprofit and for-profit providers and subsidized by federal financial aid dollars. Unbundlers conceive of education as a commodity—not unlike "the unbundled cable package where you're allowed to pick and choose your channels," in the words of education journalist Jeffrey Selingo (2013). As this metaphor suggests, unbundlers imagine students as customers who purchase only the skills and knowledge they need to qualify them for the job they desire. They understand the problems besetting higher education as business problems, and their solutions are business solutions. Unbundlers believe that "many of the challenges facing colleges and universities are best addressed—and will be addressed—through the involvement of the private sector" (Craig 2015, 175). This might involve outsourcing to private vendors previously "in-house" services and products, from food service and housing to advising and online course development. Or it might involve spinning off units (learning analytics teams, information technology departments, or even entire credential-granting programs) into free-standing companies, as University of Maryland University College and Southern New Hampshire University have done. The ultimate aim of the unbundling agenda, however, is to dismantle colleges and universities. In the unbundlers' worldview, we stand at the dawning of a new era of just-in-time, just-for-you education, freed from all institutional constraint. We are witnessing nothing less than "a complete educational remix" (Kamenetz 2015, x).[9]

The rhetoric of liberation and empowerment for all is common among unbundlers. They posit a post-university techno-utopia, in which MOOCs (massive open online courses), adaptive learning, digital credentialing platforms, and the like take the place of slow-footed institutions and the ineffective, not to mention expensive, faculty who inhabit them. Carey (2015), for instance, writes that the University of Everywhere will "liberate hundreds of millions of people around the world"

(4) and that "education that has historically been the province of kings and princes will be available to anyone in the world" (5). This idealism hinges on faith in the power of new and emerging educational technologies—the idea that we are on the verge of finding or creating the "killer app" (Craig 2015, 91) that will make higher education accessible and affordable to literally everyone.

For all its feel-good appeal, unbundling misconstrues the nature of higher education. It's sloppy thinking to assume that there is no difference between a TV watcher's relationship to a cable company and a student's relationship to the college or university they attend. As active participants in and, ideally, co-creators of their educational experiences, students should not be reduced to "customers" purchasing a product.

Indeed, unbundling operates from an exceedingly narrow understanding of the purposes of higher education. Unbundlers' "realistic" notion that higher education is only about preparing students for a job is historically and politically shortsighted. It ignores the long and continuing tradition of higher education as a public good. In light of the fundamental challenges our economy and our democratic republic is facing at the moment, this purpose is critical and must be reemphasized.

But even when we confine our attention to the purpose of preparing students for the workforce, unbundling misapprehends what employers want. While they constantly tout "employer-aligned competencies," unbundlers miss the fact that employers regularly report that they value broad education and a college degree, not narrow training and alternative credentials alone. Employers understand that in this fast-paced age of artificial intelligence and automation, many students will end up in jobs that do not even exist today. What people need is not narrow training for specific tasks, but a broad, integrative education that helps them develop the creative and critical capacities to thrive in challenging, rapidly changing environments.

Most unbundlers are not educators, and so perhaps it's not surprising that they also misconstrue the nature of learning. Learning involves more than amassing a set of skills and bits of knowledge through discrete, short-term engagements. Teaching involves more than packaging and distributing content over networks, as unbundlers sometimes suggest. Carey (2015), for instance, writes: "We can already, today, replicate much of what colleges are charging a great deal of money for and distribute that information electronically at almost no marginal costs" (102). Teaching and learning are complex social and cognitive processes, not technical problems of information transfer.

If the kind of do-it-yourself education unbundlers promote will work for anyone, it will be for students who already have a great deal of cultural and economic capital. As Randy Bass and Bret Eynon (2016) suggest, first-generation students, students of color, and students from economically disadvantaged backgrounds are most in need of integrated support and integrative learning environments (133). Ultimately, for all their bluster about liberation and empowerment for everyone, unbundlers' version of American rugged individualism for the digital age serves the interests of private companies looking to turn a profit on labor market volatility and the resulting scrambling for credentials. Unbundling will expand social and economic inequality, leaving our most vulnerable citizens prey to what Tressie McMillan Cottom (2017) calls "lower ed" and to purveyors of government-subsidized junk credentials.[10]

Unbundlers doubtless have varying motives, some of them laudable; however, we must understand unbundling as part of a decades-long, coordinated, libertarian campaign to undermine higher education as a "government monopoly." This is right out of the neoliberal playbook of creating austerity through disinvestment, sowing public distrust in public institutions, and then advocating privatization as the only viable option. The federal government is busily gutting safeguards against predatory for-profit education providers and rolling out a far-ranging deregulation agenda.[11] The Trump administration is questioning the value of degrees relative to shorter-term credentials, at least for low- and medium-skilled workers, despite clear evidence that those jobs will soon be performed by robots. None of this can come as a surprise in a cultural moment when expertise, evidence, science, reason, and even truth itself are cast by authoritarian faux populists as "elitist." But it doesn't look good for higher ed as we've known it.

Integrating Institutions for Integrative Learning

And here I come, calling for integrating institutions for integrative learning. Aren't institutions passé? Shouldn't we just blow them up? And isn't integrative learning an old idea?

I admit that integration is an old-fashioned and decidedly unsexy term. Perhaps compared to the nostalgic laments and the breathless prophecies that often constitute commentary on US higher education, this book's case for integration will strike many readers as moderate, maybe even conservative. Fair enough in one sense: I do believe that colleges and universities remain critical, even indispensable, to American culture and society. I regard them as social institutions of enduring value, worthy of both untiring nurturing and relentless scrutiny. I want to strengthen them, not blow them up.

Mine is not, however, an argument against educational innovation—far from it. In particular, I agree with unbundlers that higher education needs to be more flexible to allow for more personalized lifelong learning for a much broader swath of our society. But I think integrated institutions are best equipped to achieve that goal. What unbundlers are talking about is really mass customization, as if picking learning experiences were the same as picking iPhone colors. (Though even that "mass" is generous, since only those with economic and cultural capital are likely to benefit from unbundling higher education.) Customization provides the veneer of personalization by offering a highly restricted set of "choices" among prefabricated products that can be mixed and matched. This way, the customer feels some sense of power without the vendor having to learn anything meaningful about the customer. Institutions, by contrast, can offer truly personalized lifelong learning because they—their faculty, their staff, their students, their alumni—can get to know learners, forming relationships with them that extend beyond a one-time transaction for a one-off product. Integrated institutions marshal their resources to support self-directed learning: all parts of the institution work together to support the learner.

I will go one step further and say that integration, properly understood, is radical. Take the most common use of the term in education:

bringing together into the same school or school system children and adults of diverse backgrounds. This is itself a significant achievement, one that schools in many cities continue to struggle toward. But integration is not just a matter of assembling different folks in the same building. We might as well call that bundling. A truly integrated school is one in which the diverse perspectives, values, beliefs, and assets of the assembled students and teachers are confronted, engaged, and synthesized into a new whole. Not assimilated: integration does not require that constituent parts disappear or cease to have their own identity. They maintain their own integrity even as they are integral to the shared enterprise. Considered this way, integration is even more radical than the currently buzzy educational term *inclusion*, which promises only that diverse individuals and their backgrounds will be present and represented, not necessarily that they are integral to the creation of a coherent whole.

If we attend to the radical implications of integration, what I'm proposing is more "disruptive" than unbundling. As I've suggested, unbundling is an unimaginative solution (Privatize! Let the market rule!) to an inadequately defined problem (Workers need job skills!). It offers lazy thinking (Colleges are just like cable packages!) and fairy-tale narratives (Technology will liberate millions!). It amounts to outsourcing higher education to the private sector. Integrating institutions of higher learning, on the other hand, requires the hard work of redesigning colleges and universities as complex organizations operating within complex systems in a complex world.

Despite unbundlers' critique that colleges and universities are inefficient, they *are* organized according to the efficiency principle. That is, they are highly bureaucratic, hierarchical institutions designed to get the most output from their constituent operations with the smallest possible investment of resources. They are already only loosely bundled. The different parts of the organization—disciplines, academic units, programs, types of faculty and students, credentialing options—are not well coordinated and do not mutually reinforce each other. This is why in most institutions it's difficult to launch and manage even modest innovations across units, such as cross-listed and co-taught courses or joint faculty appointments. Indeed, institutional actors are typically engaged in a fierce internal competition for increasingly scarce resources. In this era of decreased public financial support for higher education, the efficiency principle has manifested in a variety of austerity measures, from program cuts to staff reductions to increased reliance on part-time teaching faculty. These actions may result in small savings in one part of the operation, but they undermine the enterprise as a whole.

This is precisely what happens when one tries to improve complex systems only by optimizing their component parts: the resilience of the system weakens, and it begins to function as less than the sum of its parts. Efficiency—rooted in Frederick Winslow Taylor's reductionist, standardizing scientific management—is fine for simple systems, but it's ill-suited to complex ones. If the goal is simply to move pig iron from one place to another (one of Taylor's famous examples), then it makes sense, from a management perspective, to reduce the task to its essential parts and then to devise the quickest way to accomplish it: the fewest number of movements by each worker, the optimum placement of those workers, and so on. But this kind of management does not work with complex systems in which multiple, interconnected components frequently interact, leading to unpredictable, nonlinear change.[12]

Institutional integration does not look to optimize the component parts of the organization; it looks to strengthen the interdependence of those parts so that the institution functions as a cohesive and coherent whole. Virtually everything about the structures and cultures of colleges and universities will need to change to pull off integration. In *The Uses of the University*, first published more than a half century ago, Clark Kerr (2001) famously described the modern American university as "a mechanism held together by administrative rules and powered by money" (15). A better term, he proposed, was "multiversity," by which he meant a host of competing and loosely associated communities: "the community of the undergraduate and the community of the graduate; the community of the humanist, the community of the social scientist, and the community of the scientist; the communities of the professional schools; the community of all the nonacademic personnel; the community of the administrators" (14). Even the word *community* might have been too strong: Kerr half-seriously joked that universities were "a series of individual faculty entrepreneurs held together by a common grievance about parking" (15).

Today, Kerr's joke hits a little too close to home. The widespread adoption of corporate language and practices has forced faculty into a perpetual entrepreneurial scramble to raise their own funds and build their unique brands. Meanwhile, colleges and universities are increasingly beholden to external constituencies, particularly those that provide much-needed funding in an era of reduced public support. Institutional fragmentation continues apace as colleges and universities struggle to remain relevant and useful amid rapid and bewildering social, cultural, and economic changes.

At the same time, some innovative colleges and universities are beginning to recognize their unique value proposition in an increasingly unbundled marketplace and are redesigning themselves to integrate different parts of the curriculum; the curriculum and the cocurriculum; liberal learning and professional learning; faculty roles; and degrees and alternative credentials. These institutions, some of which are featured in the chapters ahead, are leading responsible innovation in the higher education space. Indeed, they demonstrate that institutions with integrated expertise in teaching and learning, integrated learning infrastructures, and integrated educational missions are uniquely positioned to offer learners the kinds of integrative learning opportunities they need to thrive in a complex, rapidly changing world.

Here at the outset, I want to be clear about what I *don't* mean by institutional integration. First, I don't intend to invoke a nostalgic, vaguely Cardinal Newmanesque ideal of the university as a community of like-minded scholars imparting liberal education to homogeneous students with the luxury of devoting themselves to the life of the mind in splendid isolation from the real world. (Not least because that caricature is unfair to Newman, but that's another story.)[13] Institutional integration is forward-looking, not backward-looking, and it promotes the porosity of boundaries within and beyond institutions.

While it prizes porosity, integration is also not an attack on disciplinarity or specialization. It's not an excuse for administrators to consolidate their power and break apart and take over academic departments and programs in the name of "synergy." Divisions of knowledge—like distinctions between the curriculum and the cocurriculum, between liberal learning and professional learning, and so on—are not themselves insidious, and indeed they can be useful. Disciplinary expertise is more vital than ever in our rapidly changing, technology-saturated, "post-truth" world. The challenge is to organize our institutions so that faculty and students have regular opportunities to integrate knowledge, perspectives, frameworks, and methods from multiple fields and spheres of activity. What is to be avoided is not specialization, but fractionalization and the strict compartmentalization of expertise. Different institutions will find different ways to organize themselves, but disciplines and their faculty should find themselves strengthened, not threatened, by such arrangements. The trick is to design the institution to allow disciplines to mutually reinforce each other, at once retaining their integrity and becoming an integral part of the enterprise as a whole.

And what about integrative learning? Hasn't that idea been knocking around for some time? Well, yes. Depending on whom you ask, its roots trace back to John Dewey or even to Plato, and it has been a popular concept in recent decades. A frequent subject of symposia, conferences, special issues of journals, and academic books, it has received considerable attention from organizations and funders, including the Association of American Colleges and Universities, the Carnegie Foundation for the Advancement of Teaching, the William and Flora Hewlett Foundation, the Teagle Foundation, the Andrew W. Mellon Foundation, and the National Science Foundation. It's promoted by professional accreditors like the Accreditation Board for Engineering and Technology. It's an important feature of national and international higher education initiatives, such as Project Kaleidoscope; the scientific thinking and integrative reasoning skills framework; the program Integrative Learning: Opportunities to Connect; and the Degree Qualifications Profile. It's a term of art at many colleges and universities, some of which house centers, institutes, or programs devoted to integrative or integrated studies.

Yet, for all the good work and hard thinking about it, we might say of integrative learning what Gandhi is reported to have said of Western civilization: it would be a good idea. If higher education really took integrative learning seriously, colleges and universities wouldn't be designed as loose confederations, and unbundling wouldn't have gained the traction it has.

Part of the problem is that the term *integrative learning* is sometimes used loosely: to refer to the mere juxtaposition of two majors, say, or as a synonym for "interdisciplinarity." Some of its proponents claim that *all* learning is integrative, while others insist that only "outside-the-classroom activity" counts.[14] In this book, integrative learning is what happens when *learners connect and synthesize ideas, knowledge, and skills across contexts and over time.*[15] It's similar to the concept of "learning transfer," although learning theorists and researchers debate the appropriateness of this term (some object that learning necessarily transforms as it moves from one context to another, so "transfer" isn't quite right), and they have identified different kinds of transfer—near and far, low-road and high-road, and so on.[16] In general, *transfer* names what happens when learners draw on prior experiences as they construct knowledge and develop skills in a new context. This process does not need to be conscious or intentional. Integration does. As Rebecca Nowacek (2011) suggests, integration always involves transfer, but not all forms of transfer rise to the level of integration.[17] Moreover, most discussions of transfer direct attention to the way learners apply or transform learning from context A *to* context B. Integration, by contrast, considers how learners construct new learning *across* and *from* contexts A *and* B (and C and D . . .). Integrative learning is what happens when learners step back, reflect on their learning in two or more contexts, and arrive at new understandings.

The key to integration is that it's not merely juxtapositional or additive; it combines ideas, knowledge, and skills from two or more contexts into a new whole. It's what allows learners to be intentional about their learning, to articulate (in both senses of that word) their learning across what would otherwise be disparate experiences and episodes, and to craft coherent learning journeys. It is learning made whole. It is what we need to integrate colleges and universities *for*.

Who Should Read This Book?

This book is written for four audiences. First, it's for my faculty colleagues, especially those—the majority, I find—who are worried about the state of higher education and want to understand better the threats and opportunities we face and what to do about them. As I discuss throughout the book, faculty are critical to the achievement of integrated institutions and, I believe, to the survival of any form of higher education that lives up to that name. In particular, I hope this book is a wake-up call for faculty who wish only to be left alone to teach their classes and conduct their research—a prod to become involved, or more involved, in their institutions and in conversations about the future of higher education.

Second, this book is for academic administrators. They too must understand the threats and opportunities higher education faces, and they too will be key players in the colleges and universities of the future. In order to survive, every institution must craft an ambitious, clear-eyed educational vision and plan that articulates its unique value proposition. I hope this book helps administrators, in collaboration with their faculty and students, to do just that.

Third, I've written this book with educational policy makers in mind. I understand the attraction of unbundlers' promise to make higher education faster, cheaper, more efficient, and more responsive to a rapidly changing job market. My goal is to convince policy makers that the unbundling movement can't deliver on its promises and that only integrated institutions can prepare students for a complex, ever-changing social and technological landscape and for the rigors of democratic citizenship. I hope policy makers will be inspired by this book to provide institutions with the resources and support they need.

Finally, this book is for anyone with a stake in the future of US higher education. I think this group includes all of us who inhabit this fragile republic (and planet). But I will settle for the subset of folks who take an active interest in colleges and universities, perhaps especially parents and students confronting an unprecedentedly complex and perplexing higher ed landscape. I am the parent of two college students, and I hope this book helps my peers and their kids think through the kinds of higher learning experiences they need and want as we face together the opportunities and challenges of this exhilarating, terrifying time to be alive.

How the Book Works

Chapter 1 lays the conceptual and historical foundation for the other chapters by investigating the purposes of US higher education historically and today. Unbundlers argue that we are stuck with a late nineteenth-century hybrid-university model that tries to do too many things at once, and they want to narrow the purpose of higher education to job training and career advancement—a private good that individuals and families should purchase in a deregulated market. However, the historical record shows that colleges and universities from the early national period to today have been shaped by multiple purposes, both public and private, and that this multiplicity has allowed this social institution to be adaptable and resilient. Today we are in danger of losing sight of the public good of higher education—in part because unbundlers and other neoliberal "reformers" treat it as a private commodity rather than as a public trust. The first chapter proposes that the health of our democracy and our ability to confront the complex problems we face in this era of rapid social and technological change hinge on an integrated mission for higher education: serving whole individuals in ways that simultaneously serve the whole society.

Chapter 2 goes to the heart of the teaching and learning enterprise of higher education by asking *what* students are supposed to be learning in college. Traditionally, colleges and universities have sought to impart general knowledge while engaging students in the concentrated study of a particular subject. The quest to balance breadth and depth has led to the familiar curricular model: major + general education + electives = degree. Unbundlers criticize this model for requiring students to take courses unrelated to their career aspirations, and they advocate segregating, streamlining, and/or jettisoning general education in favor of industry-aligned vocational education. But the chief problem with the traditional M+GE+E=D model is that those parts of a traditional undergraduate curriculum don't add up to a coherent, holistic educational experience. In this chapter I propose designing curricula and courses to allow students to integrate generalized understanding (breadth) with specialized expertise (depth). This could involve new forms of general education that integrate with majors, or it could involve dispensing with the traditional formats altogether. In any case, only an integrated curriculum that guides students to learn and think both as experts and as informed and curious non-experts can prepare them to confront complex, systems-embedded problems.

Chapter 3 takes up the question of *where* students learn—an increasingly important and vexed topic as higher education embraces both experiential learning and online technologies. Unfortunately, many colleges and universities have merely added experiential and online learning options. Students can take advantage of an internship or study abroad, or they can take an online course or two to gain flexibility in their schedule, but these opportunities are not integrated seamlessly into their learning journey. Moreover, learning in these alternative physical and digital contexts is often framed as "direct," "authentic," or "real-world," rendering classrooms unreal and thus divorced from those other learning contexts. Unbundlers take this logic a step further, arguing that online technologies allow us to realize the slogan "learning happens everywhere" and finally jettison classrooms and campuses altogether. But while learning *does* happen everywhere, the conclusion should not be that place doesn't matter. The problem with the way experiential learning and online education are often practiced is that they don't pay enough attention to the particularities of learning contexts or to students' integration of ideas, knowledge, and skills across those contexts. In this chapter I propose integrating institutions to help students integrate classroom learning with learning elsewhere, including in digital spaces. This will involve developing new tools and methods for reflecting on and articulating learning across a multitude of learning contexts. In our networked society, in which information and people are becoming ever more mobile, it's critical that higher education empower students to chart their own pathways, navigating diverse physical and digital contexts with confidence and competence.

Chapter 4 turns to *why* students learn, addressing and seeking to transcend the pernicious dichotomies that frame much of the discussion of US higher education: STEM (science, technology, engineering, and math) vs. liberal arts; practical education vs. learning for its own sake; hard skills vs. soft skills; and so on. These binaries have led to unhelpful debates about the relative value of different majors, jockeying by various disciplines for increasingly scarce resources, and the segregation of liberal learning from professional learning. Unbundlers, some of whom pay lip service to the value of liberal education in the abstract, ultimately promote narrow, industry-aligned higher education. For them, a college education requires students to take too many courses that don't lead directly to a job. But if we understand liberal education as engaging students in the study of culture and society in order to equip them to think for themselves, to exercise their independent faculties, and to arrive at their own considered judgments, then not only is it immensely practical, but it is critically important to and ultimately inextricable from professional learning. As the social and cultural landscape is rapidly changing, so too are industries and professions. In this chapter I propose integrating colleges and universities to promote the integration of liberal learning and professional learning. This will involve breaking down the traditional institutional barriers between and among the liberal arts, STEM, and the professions. This task is particularly critical as robots increasingly make inroads into the workforce, putting a premium on liberally educated professionals, especially those who can successfully navigate the human-technology interface.

Chapter 5 takes up the question of *from whom* students are learning, advancing the theme of the human-technology interface by examining evolving faculty models in the context of new and emerging learning technologies. The combination of the adjunctification of college faculty and the advent of online educational technologies threatens the extinction of the full-time, tenured or tenure-track faculty member. Higher education is increasingly employing technologically reliant, distributed labor systems in which faculty roles are unbundled (or disaggregated) and performed by paraprofessional and professional staff: instructional designers, web designers, coaches, tutors, contracted assessors, and others. While unbundlers view this system as a means of achieving efficiencies, it has not been shown to lower costs—or to improve learning. Indeed, it fragments learning, undermines faculty expertise and professionalism, and robs students of what we know is the most important contributor to learning in college: meaningful relationships with faculty mentors. Once responsible for the holistic education of students, faculty have been progressively relieved of student-related service/administrative duties, research faculty have been severed from teaching faculty, and teaching faculty have seen their instructional responsibilities distributed across a range of staff and technologies. In this chapter I argue that students confronting an increasingly complex and dangerous world need the disciplinary and pedagogical expertise of faculty mentors more than ever. I propose an integrated faculty model that features predominantly full-time, professional, diverse faculty members; the integration of teaching, research or creative activity, and service/outreach; and the integration of faculty expertise and learning technologies.

Chapter 6 offers a consideration of *when* students learn. As the workforce continues to evolve in response to the new economy and particularly to automation, people will increasingly require education throughout their lives. Already, alternative credentialing is big business, and a quarter of Americans hold a nondegree credential.[18] In the main, colleges and universities have been slow to respond to this demand, continuing to focus primarily on four-year degrees for students just out of high school. Unbundlers favor nondegree credentials—at least for students who cannot afford a traditional education or are not "college material." But given the continuing, and indeed increasing, value of degrees in the wake of the Great Recession and the coming automation of much of the workforce, a two-tiered higher education system is a recipe for growing social and economic inequality. It forces the most vulnerable among us to take on the risk of financial debt by entering into relationships with for-profit entities whose very purpose is to capitalize (on) people's frustrated ambitions and desperation (McMillan Cottom 2017). What is needed instead is a concerted effort to expand access to degrees *and* to alternative credentials for all who desire them. We need high-quality, reputable options for those who don't desire degrees, but these options cannot replace degrees and should not be used as an excuse to ignore the inequities that lead us to believe that we know who deserves education in the first place or that desiring a college degree is a purely personal and unfettered choice. In this chapter I suggest that accredited colleges and universities are positioned to lead the way toward the integration of degrees and lifelong learning opportunities through responsible innovation. Accredited colleges and universities have an opportunity to leverage their disciplinary and pedagogical expertise, their unique teaching and learning mission, and their learning infrastructure to offer people the kind of integrative, cohesive learning experiences they need throughout their lifetimes.

This is a frightening and exciting time for colleges and universities. Threats are legion, but so are opportunities. Indeed, it's a frightening and exciting time for all of us, and if we are going to thrive in the turbulent years ahead, we will need integrated postsecondary institutions more than ever. The brief conclusion to this book dramatizes that need, pulling together (integrating) my arguments through the eyes of Esther, a high schooler who aspires to be the first person in her family to attend a US university. We cannot let smart, ambitious learners like Esther down. She needs us.

And we need her.

CHAPTER 1

THE MANY AND THE ONE

Integrating Higher Education as
a Public Good and a Private Good

◼ Riddhi Samtani is from Sint Maarten, a small island country in the Caribbean. She came to the United States for college because she "wanted to experience the American culture and an American education." She wanted what she calls "that whole breadth of experience" that comes with college: "You mature a lot with college experience—the independence, the freedom, the ability to balance work and play." She was passionate about climate change and environmental protection: "I come from an island that is susceptible to climate change. Sea-level rise could really inevitably hurt our future, my parents, our livelihoods. That issue is really important to me, and I want to make a difference on that."

An international affairs major with a minor in environmental studies, Riddhi has tailored her undergraduate career to her concern for the environment. She has taken courses and conducted research with scientists, policy makers, and economists who share her interests. The question that has come to preoccupy her is, "How do we get the private sector to participate in sustainable investment?" She shaped this question through her coursework and her first co-op, a full-time, six-month employment experience at an environmental agency, and she pursued it directly during her second co-op at an investment firm, where she helped develop a corporate social responsibility (CSR) program. She has also completed a summer research project studying the effects of climate change on coral reefs in her home country and completed a service trip to South America to study and participate in efforts to rebuild barriers to protect against coastal flooding. Together, Riddhi says, these various experiences have helped her to remain "curious and open to learning" and to remember that "learning doesn't stop."

Riddhi is currently on her third co-op, having returned to the investment firm to continue work on the CSR program and to further the company's ongoing efforts to meet and exceed global standards of diversity, inclusion, and sustainability. As she approaches graduation, she is committed to helping to change the culture of the investment industry, and she intends to work in the private sector as part of what she sees as a generational movement to "make Wall Street green." She sees herself working to push investors and companies to move past glib branding and to make measurable progress toward sustainable, environmentally responsible practices. This, she says, is her passion and her life's work. ■

The college experience is living up to Riddhi's hopes. She is indeed getting a "breadth of experience," pursuing her passion inside and outside the classroom. She is learning, maturing, and shaping her personal and professional goals. As she puts it, "I had a passion. Being [in classes] gave me the technical expertise to fulfill it. Then the co-ops have given [me] the professionalism that goes with it." She feels her unique combination of personal background, scientific expertise, and policy and corporate experience has prepared her well to pursue her personal and professional ambitions.

Riddhi's experience demonstrates that higher education is an individual, private good. She is clearly the beneficiary of her educational experience. At the same time, note the range of public goods that appear even in this brief profile: primary scientific research on coastal erosion, policy work at a federal agency, community and youth organizing, and environmental advocacy in the private sector. Riddhi's work, even as an undergraduate, is contributing to the public good: it redounds to the benefit and well-being of all members of society. There can be no doubt that we are all better off by having her in the world, working professionally on the complex challenges associated with climate change and environmental sustainability.

Higher education in the United States serves private *and* public goods, contributing to both individual and societal advancement and well-being. As Riddhi's example shows, these goods can be mutually reinforcing: we all benefit when she benefits. Unfortunately, however, recent decades have witnessed an erosion of the idea that higher education is a public good. Instead, higher education is associated strictly with professional preparation and advancement and measured solely in terms of an individual's return on investment. Because public funding has been slashed, students and their families are forced to finance college, often by taking on unsustainable debt loads. Meanwhile, increasing amounts of federal aid are subsidizing private education companies, which profit from social inequality and economic insecurity (McMillan Cottom 2017).[1]

Unbundlers are stoking these developments. They offer relentless critiques of outmoded "hybrid" institutions stuck in some gauzy, nineteenth-century notion that college can be everything to everyone, and they advocate opening the higher education market to private providers and offering government subsidies in the form of federal financial aid. While they purport to be promoting flexibility and personalized education for individuals without access to higher education, they are pushing a privatization agenda that promotes the interests of companies and investors.

Riddhi's example shows that "traditional" higher education—she is obtaining a bachelor's degree from an accredited university—can be highly personalized and flexible. It also shows that the power of her educational experience lies in its integrated, holistic nature: under the guidance of disciplinary and pedagogical experts, she has integrated her learning across disciplines, across classrooms and other learning contexts, and over time. I take up these aspects in later chapters. This chapter is concerned with the fundamental question of what higher education is for, its purpose. I consider what happens when we unbundle the public good from the private good—and what becomes possible when we integrate the two, when higher education serves individuals in ways that simultaneously serve society as a whole.

Before I move forward, I begin with a look back.

Multiple Missions from the Beginning

The principal target of unbundlers is the hybrid university, which took shape in the nineteenth century in response to three distinct goals: practical training (represented by the Morrill Land-Grant Acts), liberal education (represented by the classical colleges and the ideas of Cardinal Newman), and research (represented by the German university tradition). According to Kevin Carey (2015), "instead of choosing, American universities decided to do all three things at once, with consequences that last to this day" (29).[2] Carey largely blames Harvard's Charles William Eliot, who in the last quarter of the nineteenth century set the mold for the comprehensive modern American university with its research and teaching missions; graduate and undergraduate schools; disciplinary divisions; majors and electives; and so on. While society has changed a great deal in the past 150 years, the argument goes, the modern university has not. Worse yet, isomorphic tendencies in higher education mean that all kinds of institutions have taken on the trappings of the modern university, essentially remaking themselves in Harvard's image. And so US higher education is defined by this "deeply flawed, irrational institution designed to be bad at the most important thing it does: educate people" (Carey 2015, 36).

Focusing on one historical moment—the late nineteenth century—and offering up this simple story, unbundlers claim that US higher education has too many missions, is too isomorphic, and is impervious to change. Unbundlers believe that the sole purpose of higher education is to promote individuals' professional prospects—to provide a narrowly defined private good. Carey (2015) is explicit on this point: "people don't borrow tens of thousands of dollars to merely acquire the knowledge and skills taught in college. They pay for the keys to a lifetime of educational opportunity and financial reward" (185). In the unbundlers' view, "for more than a century, the hybrid university has had a government-backed, culturally reinforced monopoly on the sale of increasingly valuable credentials" (185–86). Credentials are commodities sold in a "human capital marketplace," to use Ryan Craig's term (2015, 105).[3] The tragedy of the fateful "great compromise" 150 years ago is that the hybrid university lost sight of this purpose, allowed it to get bundled with other purposes, and then became the gold standard for all of higher education in the United States down to the present day.

Unfortunately for unbundlers, the historical record is more complicated than they claim, and it does not support their arguments. In fact, US higher education's embrace of multiple missions—from its early days, not just at the dawn of Eliot's modern university—has been the secret of its success and ensured this social institution's resilience and adaptability. Education historian Charles Dorn (2017) explains:

> As a number of prominent historians in the field, including Laurence Veysey, Frederick Rudolph, and Christopher Lucas, have noted, the genius of the American university ultimately rested neither solely in its stated commitment to the common good nor in the worth it assigned scholarship nor exclusively in the commercial advantage students gained from occupational preparation. Instead, the capacity to sustain multiple commitments concurrently enabled these institutions to meet the demands of a variety of constituents, thereby gaining the support necessary to flourish in the decades following the Civil War. (131)[4]

Through case studies of eleven diverse colleges and universities, Dorn demonstrates with archival evidence that these "multiple commitments," aligning with both public and private goods, have shaped US higher education from its inception to the present day.

This is not to say that these commitments have gotten equal billing throughout history; as Dorn (2017, 3) notes, "socially widespread preferences and attitudes" have affected the relative value placed on each commitment. Roughly, Dorn shows that the early national period was associated with civic-mindedness, the antebellum and Civil War years with practicality, the Reconstruction period through World War II with commercialism, and the postwar era with affluence. Each historical era had a dominant social ethos, but it's important to recognize that each ethos was operative in each time period; this is not a matter of old preferences and attitudes giving way to new.

In other words, the formation of the hybrid university did not mark a radically new bundling of the purposes for higher education, nor is the history of US higher education a story about a social institution moving from a public-good status to a private-good status. Dorn (2017) again:

> Throughout [its history], amidst dramatic institutional reform and adaptation, American higher education remained committed to

the public good. The form this commitment took surely changed over the years and college and university officials undoubtedly employed the rhetoric of the public interest while simultaneously advancing policies and practices that did little to advance it. Nevertheless, the archival record informing this study reveals a broad array of higher-education institutions demonstrating a continuing dedication to the common good even while broader social, political, and economic forces undermined, if not directly opposed, that aim. (4)[5]

For example, the Morrill Act in 1862 reflected a shift in the country's social ethos from civic-mindedness to practicality, but it did not signify a repudiation of civic-mindedness. To be sure, in many institutions of that time, classical curricula gave way to more utilitarian pursuits. But this should not be understood as an abandonment of the public good: the goal was to improve an industrializing society and to open the doors of higher education to agrarian and poor people. Nor was civic-mindedness displaced entirely: at places like the Agricultural College of the State of Michigan (now Michigan State University), faculty and students rebelled against a proposed reduction of the four-year academic curriculum to two years and the excising of the liberal arts (88). The "new universities" were devoted both to "liberal" and "practical" studies because there was a broad recognition that both were needed in order for an individual to function effectively in an era marked by rapid social and economic changes.

Each institution Dorn studied across the span of US history was founded on and sustained multiple missions. Women's colleges, such as Smith, prepared women to work outside the home *and* to become civically active. Historically black colleges and universities, like Howard, defined racial uplift in terms of preparing students to participate in public life *and* to participate in commercial ventures, like the on-campus building-block company or the blacksmith shop. Community colleges from their early twentieth-century beginnings have served both as academic junior colleges *and* as vocational schools for working-class students while serving the economic and social needs of the communities in which they are located. In all cases, the public good and the private good have been viewed not just as important, but as mutually reinforcing. Individuals and society are improved by increasing access to education for women, people of color, and the working class. Individuals learn, grow, and obtain jobs, *and* a more diverse, educated populace spurs economic and social progress.

Like all good histories, Dorn's *For the Common Good* (2017) demonstrates that there is nothing new under the sun—and that change is constant. In the early twentieth century, debates raged in the public press about the value of going to college (122), complaints were lodged about the corporatization of the university, and students were excoriated for coming to college only to be trained for jobs.[6] Sounds familiar. At the same time, the history of US higher education is a history of change. While corporate influence on higher education is nothing new, the past few decades have seen colleges and universities devote more and more of their energies and resources to patents, licenses, copyrights, corporate partnerships, and tech transfers—in other words, to the commercialization and commodification of research and teaching.

From the early national period to today, colleges and universities have adapted to meet the changing needs and desires of society. Entirely new kinds of institutions—quite different in form and function from Eliot's Harvard—have emerged. This has happened in a decentralized fashion, largely by adding new layers to accommodate new groups of students (women, African Americans, the working class). This stratification has its downside: it allows higher education to expand while preserving exclusivity at the top, which means that even as higher education becomes more accessible, it becomes more inequitable (Larabee 2017; Newfield 2011).[7] But it demonstrates that unbundlers are simply wrong to suggest that US higher education is monolithic and unchanging. As Dorn (2017, 233) shows conclusively with archival evidence, "especially in form but also in function, higher education in the United States has undergone dramatic transformation over the past two hundred years." That adaptability is rooted in higher education's institutional diversity and ultimately in its manifold mission. While we have yet to realize that mission with anything approaching inclusive excellence, the mission itself is not a weakness, but rather the source of this enduring social institution's great strength.

Who's Afraid of the Public Good?

The educational benefits extended to service members returning home from World War II through the Servicemen's Readjustment Act of 1944 (the GI Bill) were intended to assist individuals who had served their country, but they also represented a massive investment meant to stimulate economic growth and strengthen democratic citizenship. As had been the case throughout the history of US education, there was no clear dividing line between higher education as a public good and as a private good. Here is how the 1947 Truman Report, *Higher Education for Democracy*, described the role of education in a democratic society:

> It is a commonplace of the democratic faith that education is indispensable to the maintenance and growth of freedom of thought, faith, enterprise, and association. Thus the social role of education in a democratic society is at once to ensure equal liberty and equal opportunity to different individuals and groups, and to enable the citizens to understand, appraise, and redirect forces, men, and events as these tend to strengthen or weaken their liberties. . . .
> . . . [Education's] role in a democratic society is that of critic and leader as well as servant; its task is not merely to meet the demands of the present but to alter those demands if necessary, so as to keep them always suited to democratic ideals. Perhaps its most important role is to serve as an instrument of social transition, and its responsibilities are defined in terms of the kind of civilization society hopes to build. If its adjustments to present needs are not to be mere fortuitous improvisations, those who formulate its policies and programs must have a vision of the Nation and world we want—to give a sense of direction to their choices among alternatives. (4–5)[8]

Today, such a statement seems almost quaint. Higher education is now assumed by many to be strictly a private good, a benefit only to individuals who enroll in it. State funding has been slashed. Federal funding is being diverted to for-profit providers (something that happened with GI Bill funding as well). Public discourse focuses entirely on preparing students for jobs.

Why have Americans—unlike most of our European counterparts—come to think of higher education as an exclusively private good, the costs of which should be borne primarily by the individuals who happen to be enrolled at any given time, rather than by society as a whole?[9] It's not as though colleges and universities have stopped promoting the public good. On the contrary, they continue to advance human understanding; produce socially useful research and products; provide educational experiences for and financially support their local, state, and regional communities; and model democratic life by teaching civic engagement and civic discourse. Higher education in the United States is also an unrivaled creative force: among the things and ideas created or discovered at universities are lasers, bar codes, radar, transistors, superconductivity, DNA sequencing, artificial intelligence, election polling, the theory of cognitive dissonance, game theory, social mobility, and social networks.[10] At the same time, higher education performs an indispensable critical role in and for society: it is a place set aside for the rigorous, evidence-based examination of ideas and theories, no matter how unpopular or politically unpalatable (Cole 2010, 378). Our economic, social, and political systems are to a large extent shaped by and even made possible by higher education. So why don't we treat higher education as the public good that it is?

There is some evidence that the retreat from public responsibility for higher education is racially driven—that as the college-going (or at least college-aspiring) population has become more racially diverse, white Americans have withdrawn their support for publicly funding higher education.[11] The GI Bill itself had a disparate impact on minority students, particularly African Americans, who were often underprepared in underresourced segregated high schools, were banned from some colleges and universities, faced all manner of discrimination from college and university officials and program officers, fell prey to exploitative for-profit providers, and were directed to woefully underresourced historically black colleges and universities, many of which turned returning GIs away by the thousands. For a brief period in the 1960s and 1970s, African Americans and Hispanics began enrolling in larger numbers, but that trend began to reverse during the 1980s when President Ronald Reagan, framing college students as "freeloaders," drastically cut Pell grants and shifted responsibility for funding higher education from taxpayers to individuals and families with federal loans.[12] Since that time, our preoccupations with the "war on drugs" and "law and order" have diverted public funds from education to incarceration, laying the school-to-prison pipeline.[13]

The 1980s saw the consolidation of neoliberalism, an economic and social agenda that pairs market fundamentalism—the idea that markets are the best arbiter of value in all matters—with the privatization of public goods and services.[14] Under neoliberalism, austerity rules, and cash-strapped public institutions are forced to adopt business practices rooted in corporate efficiency. Meanwhile, public funds for education, environmental protection, prisons, health care, and so on are diverted to private, profit-extracting enterprises and used for military buildups and tax cuts for the wealthy. Neoliberalism is at root an attempt to effect a massive upward redistribution and concentration of wealth.[15]

Under neoliberalism, we have seen significant and accelerating public disinvestment in higher education. Forty-five states spent less per student in 2016 than they did before the 2008 recession—and state funding had already been falling.[16] While funding for many other social programs has rebounded since the recession abated, this is not so for higher education. In some states, public universities are public in name only. The state of Colorado supports only 3 percent of the University of Colorado's operating budget, and Texas's support for its state university has dropped from 50 percent in the 1980s to 12 percent today (Davidson 2017, 175–76).[17] The share of the University of Virginia's operating revenue provided by the state dropped from 35 percent to 10 percent during that same period.[18] As a result, colleges and universities are ever more reliant on tuition dollars and external sources of funding, including governmental and corporate research sponsors and philanthropists.

While external funding is not a problem per se, it can create conflicts of interest while undermining the perceived need for public funds (Newfield 2011). Put simply, colleges and universities should not be doing the bidding of external individuals or groups that happen to have capital. Their first responsibility is to the truth, wherever it may lead. While the vast majority of academic researchers work hard to maintain their integrity, it's nonetheless the case that the more an institution is reliant on external sources of funding, the less likely it is to bite the hand that feeds it.

Meanwhile, colleges and universities are run more and more like traditional businesses, complete with strategic planning, outcomes assessment, budgeting based on responsibility center management, outsourcing, reliance on revenue-producing entrepreneurial activities, cost-cutting measures, aggressive branding and marketing, and labor casualization (i.e., increasing reliance on part-time, per-course instructors, rather than full-time and tenured or tenure-track faculty). The idea, of course, is to make colleges and universities more efficient, but these measures have not been shown to significantly bring down costs. Adopting private-sector salaries and staffing structures in public institutions may even *increase* costs.[19]

In any event, if there are cost savings, they do not make up for the decreases in public funding, and because costs are passed on to "consumers," the price of higher education continues to rise. Data from the College Board indicate that published tuitions and fees have increased steadily and significantly for all types of institutions, tripling or more in constant dollars since the mid-1970s.[20] As a result, many working- and middle-class families and individuals are forced to take on risky debt.[21] Some are seduced and defrauded by fly-by-night for-profit operators. Many non-wealthy students who begin college do not finish, most often for financial reasons.[22] Economic stratification leads to educational stratification and vice versa—a vicious circle if ever there was one. This social institution, which we imagine as an engine of social mobility, has become instead an agent of continuing and widening social inequality, with the best indicator of college graduation remaining what it long has been: parents' income.[23]

Treating higher education as a private good means that prospective students and their families bear the onus of "affordability," as Sara Goldrick-Rab (2016) has shown so brilliantly in *Paying the Price: College Costs, Financial Aid, and the Betrayal of the American Dream*. Given high prices and the ready availability of loans, the question has shifted from "Can I pay for this?" to "Will this pay off for me in the long run—that is, is this a good investment?" The answer is often yes. Students are willing to take on risky debt—not to mention paying considerable opportunity costs, such as not being able to support their families while they pursue a degree—because they feel they have no other good option. College education is viewed as necessary to make a good living in today's economy. And indeed, a college degree does continue to be a good "investment": despite stories of baccalaureate baristas and burger flippers, the college graduate wage premium is at an all-time high.[24]

Conceiving of higher education as a private good purchased in a deregulated market has opened the door to for-profit institutions, which have successfully lobbied for alternative accreditation standards and for federal financial aid eligibility. Millions of students are enrolled in for-profit colleges and universities, or what sociologist Tressie McMillan Cottom (2017) calls "lower ed." This is the subsector of higher education that exploits social inequality without making any contribution to the public good other than "the assumed indirect effect of greater individual human capital" (111–12). For-profit colleges and universities, as McMillan Cottom notes, are not new. But the scale and scope of these institutions *are* novel: they are now giant, multinational corporations enrolling millions of students in a wide range of programs. And because they receive financial aid money, they are publicly subsidized. In the context of an unstable labor market, rising health-care costs, and weakened social safety nets, for-profit institutions are (re)training workers, largely at the workers' expense and subsidized by taxpayers. McMillan Cottom describes this as a "negative social insurance program," distinguishable from an actual social insurance program (such as Social Security) by the fact that it "doesn't actually make us more secure" but rather "makes our collective insecurity more profitable" (181).

Compared to their peers in public two-year and four-year colleges, students in for-profit colleges and universities have lower completion and graduation rates, have higher debt loads and loan default rates, and are less likely to be employed after graduation.[25] They are taught boxed curricula by untrained instructors, most of whom work on a course-by-course basis. Even the people at the very top of these institutions sometimes lack proper academic credentials.[26] Yet these schools are not cheaper than nonprofits; in many cases, they are exponentially more expensive than community colleges and public universities (McMillan Cottom 2017, 97). Even judged by very narrow metrics, McMillan Cottom shows, these institutions fall far short: "for-profit colleges do not have employment or wage returns that justify their costs to either students or to our public system of financial aid" (67).

Yet, while enrollments in for-profit institutions have taken a hit in the wake of fraud and predatory lending scandals,[27] the continuing need for higher education combined with the Trump administration's deregulation agenda will likely boost enrollments in the years ahead. And because the federal government is increasingly willing to waive regulatory requirements governing financial aid even for non-accredited, non-institutional providers, we are likely to see more of them enter the market as well.[28]

Here, of course, unbundlers perceive an opportunity. As I mentioned in the introduction, Ryan Craig (2015, 175) argues that solutions to higher education's problems lie in the private sector. He notes approvingly "the emergence of *EdSurge*, an online news resource that covers [the] financing of private education companies" and particularly "the aptly named KA'CHING section of its weekly newsletter" (176). He points out that there are huge untapped markets for online education not only in the United States, but around the world, especially in China. Craig's *College Disrupted* is essentially a primer for edupreneurs looking to edge their way into these markets; its subtitle may as well be *How to Make a Killing on the Great Unbundling*. Like other unbundlers, Craig blames "overregulation" for what he sees as the slow pace of change. (Craig was writing before the 2016 election.) He chastises the federal government for "hustling" the country in order to protect the monopoly that colleges and universities have in the higher education market (196). The remedy, of course, is deregulation.

Michael B. Horn and Andrew P. Kelly make the unbundlers' case for deregulation in a 2015 American Enterprise Institute policy paper:

> Amid a chorus of concerns about quality and cost in American higher education, a range of new postsecondary models has emerged as an alternative to the traditional system. In particular, entrepreneurs have asked why the ability to provide college-level courses should be reserved for only colleges. Digital content and smart people are abundant, and advances in technology have made it possible to deliver that content and assess learning at far lower costs and without respect to geography. In response, organizations have developed modular—or unbundled—offerings powered by technology that target both adult and traditional college-age learners. Although these models cannot deliver all of what a traditional college or university does, they can provide affordable options that are more flexible, targeted, and customizable. (1)[29]

This is a classic problem-solution analysis in unbundler style. It opens with a swipe against "traditional" higher education, moves to an expression of sympathy for the entrepreneurs who are victims of a monopoly, and then posits that superior technology-enhanced solutions exist. For all that the authors pack into this first paragraph, they have nothing at all to say—here or elsewhere in the paper—about the *purpose* of higher education. In this way, the paper is actually atypical: unbundlers usually offer platitudes about opening the gates of the ivory tower to the masses or increasing the national or global stock of human capital. Horn and Kelly, however, have a clear constituency: the beleaguered private providers that are shut out of the higher education market. The authors present the regulatory system as a relic designed to protect outmoded institutions and degrees, but they never discuss what that system, much less the institutions it regulates, is for. Each policy option they explore—ensuring transparency and outcomes, leveraging private financing to shift risk, recognizing a new accreditor that would be more open to non-institutional providers, decoupling accreditation from financial aid, letting the market sort itself out—is treated solely as a business proposition. Their only concern is opening up the market to entrepreneurs.

The first clause of the last sentence of the paragraph quoted above from Horn and Kelly (2015)—"Although these models cannot deliver all of what a traditional college or university does"—might read like a hedge or a note of modesty, but it's a critical part of their "disruption" argument. Because they view education as nothing more or other than a content delivery service provided by "smart people" with advanced technology, Horn and Kelly are free to treat higher education as if it were a market like any other. And this is how disrupted markets work: alternative providers edge into a market with products that are cheaper but not quite as good as the ones already available. As they gain a foothold, they improve and eventually push out the more expensive, less efficient, and now outmoded products or services.

The classic disruptive innovation example is the computer industry, which Apple edged into with relatively cheap and, at first, not very powerful or useful computers. As Apple's devices improved, personal computers eventually pushed out the expensive and complex-to-operate mainframes and mini computers that had previously defined the market. In their policy paper, Horn and Kelly (2015) take the analogy one step further, invoking Dell's disruption of Apple and IBM with its modular devices, which were assembled from parts purchased from multiple manufacturers.[30]

The Dell example works as an unbundling argument because the company allowed consumers to mix and match parts to create their own customized machine. But Horn and Kelly (2015) never do the conceptual work to establish the link to higher education. Is a college education really enough like a mix-and-match computer that we can simply assume a one-to-one correspondence? Only in a world in which we imagine higher education strictly as a private good on an open market. But a college education is not a product; it's a set of experiences and the relationships and resources that make those experiences possible. It asks more of students than to be consumers and more of colleges and universities than to package a commodity. Moreover, higher education is not just for individual students. As a society, we ask colleges and universities to educate people for work and for citizenship at home and globally. We ask these institutions to produce research that is socially useful and that pushes the boundaries of knowledge. We ask them to incubate innovation and entrepreneurship. We ask them to engage—and financially support—their local, state, and regional communities. We ask this and much more.

Yet despite their glib and false analogies, unbundlers are gaining traction, in no small part because edupreneurs, who control a great deal of wealth, have put significant pressure on the federal government to relax regulations concerning the use of financial aid. In 2011, venture capitalists invested $429 million in educational companies.[31] In 2014, US educational technology firms raised $1.4 billion in venture capital and private equity (S. Gallagher 2016, 16). Every day, it seems, brings new learning management providers, "online enablement firms," credential technology firms, learning analytics and tracking companies, and more.

While privatizers like Horn and Kelly (2015) argue that the private sector can assume the financial risks associated with delivering higher education on a mass scale, what they are really calling for is more of what McMillan Cottom (2017) describes in the existing for-profit subsector: public subsidies for profit-extracting companies, a "negative social insurance program" that commoditizes social inequality and economic insecurity. Anyone who thinks that it's a good idea to put higher education in the hands of private companies whose goal is profit rather than teaching and learning needs to read McMillan Cottom's devastating book. She shows convincingly that the poor outcomes for the students of these institutions—who are disproportionately women, people of color, and people living in poverty—are not a bug but a feature: they are what happens when companies' first priority is to turn a profit. And it's what we will get in spades if unbundlers have their way.

Unbundlers' idea that smart people with advanced technology can deliver higher education to the masses at a fraction of the cost of traditional higher education is a sham. First of all, it's becoming increasingly clear that online education is not necessarily cheaper than face-to-face instruction (Davidson 2017, 20–21). Second, if higher education were only about "delivering content," as unbundlers insist, then MOOCs would have been the salvation that many of their champions claimed they were. They turned out not to be because these classes alone cannot offer what a comprehensive university can offer to students: meaningful relationships with faculty who know how to shape learning experiences; close mentorship on engaging work over time; and guided integrative learning that allows students to chart an intellectual pathway. MOOCs and other online experiences can certainly be part of a robust and integrative educational experience, but they cannot replace institutions.

Educating people well is expensive.[32] Doubtless, some colleges and universities could reduce costs. Some presidential salaries are exorbitant, and some institutions spend too much money on nonessentials meant to lure wealthy students. Maybe some savings could be found by rethinking credit-hour requirements or accelerating degrees—though I have yet to see any such models that go beyond tinkering or that save significant amounts of money while ensuring educational quality. Maybe as educational technologies progress, the costs of technology infrastructures will come down. Ultimately, though, higher education worthy of that name is expensive because it involves deep, time-intensive human relationships. It's not just a product that can be produced on the cheap.

Despite perennial breathless exposés about wasteful, bloated universities, most postsecondary institutions are underfunded. Tenured and tenure-track faculty make decent but by no means lavish salaries—certainly not the kinds of salaries other professionals, such as lawyers and doctors, make on average—but now the majority of faculty are part-time adjunct instructors who make a per-course pittance, often less than minimum wage when calculated hourly (and often without benefits or job security; see chapter 5). The overwhelming majority of campuses bear no resemblance to the well-appointed, lazy-river-sporting exceptions that draw the attention of journalists and reformers. Indeed, many campuses, especially those of public institutions and most particularly of community colleges, are in desperate need of updating; some buildings are even unsafe.[33] On many of those campuses, academic and administrative units are understaffed. While administrative staff overall have grown in recent years relative to faculty positions—a fact that is often used to accuse institutions of "administrative bloat"—that growth has been spurred largely by increased support services for students and by matters beyond institutions' control, such as increased state and federal reporting requirements.[34] In any case, this is not a place where major cost savings are to be found. Finally, most of the growth in the cost of attendance in recent years has not even been in tuition or fees, but rather in non-tuition costs, including books, supplies, and especially living expenses, which account for two-thirds and sometimes even more of total costs (Goldrick-Rab 2016, 77).

There is no magic bullet for bringing down college costs—not without sacrificing educational quality. But there is a way to bring down the *price* of college for students and their families, and that is to increase public funding for it. This would mean recommitting ourselves to the idea that higher education is a public good. This is not pie-in-the-sky idealism or nostalgia; indeed, there are some important voices today calling for public reinvestment in higher education. During the 2016 election campaign, candidates Bernie Sanders and Hillary Clinton announced their support for free tuition at community colleges. Some states, including Minnesota, New York, Oregon, and Tennessee, and some cities, including Chicago, San Francisco, and Tulsa, are considering or have already passed legislation supporting free college programs (typically two years at a community college). Sara Goldrick-Rab (2016), who has conducted extensive research into college affordability and the financial aid system, supports an incremental "first degree first" approach in which public subsidies would pay for associate's degrees, which would be offered by all public colleges and universities, and then a first degree of any kind at any public college or university.[35]

The idea of free college as a public good obviously took a hit in the 2016 national election, but the cities and states that have already taken action provide some measure of hope. We must remember that when people say free college is "unaffordable," they are expressing less an economic fact than a political and moral choice. We find a way to pay for military buildups and for tax cuts and loopholes for our wealthiest corporations and citizens. We find a way to pay for hurricane disaster relief (at least for some). We need to recognize that the costs of *not* paying for high-quality higher education are also disastrous. Our economy suffers and so too does our democracy.[36] Education, as Cathy Davidson (2017, 192) has argued, is "our main bulwark against the forces of disorder and ruin" and is "the best investment we can make as a nation, not only for the sake of younger generations of students but also for all of us facing an unsettling and unsettled future."

Investing in Students, Investing in All of Us

While Davidson (2017) asks us to think of the well-being of students as yoked to the well-being of us all, the hard truth is that many people don't see students as worthy of public investment. A cottage industry has grown around depicting college students as lazy, entitled, selfish, and mercenary. One popular book calls students "excellent sheep": compulsive overachievers and soulless conformists who couldn't care less about learning or making a difference in the world. They just want their birthright: high-paying jobs.[37] Another book—which turns out to be a serious ethnographic investigation of how higher education perpetuates inequality—bears a title that reduces higher education to one particular social activity: *Paying for the Party*.[38]

Much of the student bashing is based on a toxic mix of anecdote, nostalgia, and bad science—like the problematic study that informs the sensationalistic *Academically Adrift*, which dropped a bomb on higher education in 2011 with its claim that 45 percent of students showed no significant gains in critical thinking, complex reasoning, or writing skills during their first two years of college.[39] The authors' methodology and extrapolations from the data have been roundly criticized.[40] Subsequent studies have reached different conclusions.[41] But this has not stopped people looking for ammunition against students and colleges from seizing on the study's explosive headline.

Unbundlers are happy to join this chorus. They are particularly fond of portraying college as an unserious place—a playground, a party, a country club—for the spoiled children of privilege. Ryan Craig (2015) punctuates his book with narratives of his own college-boy high jinks as a Yale undergrad. The upshot of these stories is that college was a waste of time: "I feel I owe little to college itself. I came to Yale reasonably literate and motivated and left four years later much the same (except four years older)" (213). This morality tale is meant to underscore the notion that students go to college for the fun and games, not to learn. (One might wish Craig had learned at Yale not to generalize from an *n* of one.) Kevin Carey (2015) agrees: he describes students as "slacking through late adolescence in a haze, confident that social connections and inertia will see [them] through" (6). Since the coming University of Everywhere creates a global competition for jobs, he intones, the "message for all students should be: Put down the bong and get to work" (245).

Are college students as lazy, entitled, and uninterested in the world beyond their own noses—or beyond their own earning potential—as the unbundlers claim? That's certainly not my experience. For more than two decades, I have taught at a two-year college, three state universities, a small private college, a large private university, and a law school. The vast majority of the thousands of students I have encountered have been hard-working, invested in learning, and committed to making meaningful contributions to their families, their communities, and the world.[42] They are engaged in a variety of activities on campus and off, and many of them, like 70 percent of their peers nationally, work.[43] I'm now at the age when many professors begin to complain about the "students today," who fail to live up to their more studious (or respectful or other-directed or whatever) predecessors. But the students I encounter today are so smart and engaged that I can't slip into that kind of lament. To be sure, some students party, take their studies less seriously than they should, and rebel against college authorities—as has always been the case.[44] And most students want good-paying jobs and financial security—as has always been the case. But these are neither moral failings nor inconsistent with other goals, including contributing to the public good. If anything, I find that students today—on both my campus and those I have visited—are more socially and politically engaged than students I taught earlier in my career (and certainly more so than when I was a student).

It's true that surveys show that today's college students are "increasingly placing a premium on the job-related benefit of going to college." More and more students cite "to be able to get a better job" and "to make more money" as important reasons to go to college.[45] This should come as no surprise in a country that is obsessed with money and wealth, beset by a volatile economy, and insistent that a college education is the key to stable employment. (Remember, most of these students are already working; getting a better job and making more money are for many of them pressing daily concerns.) Besides, we should not assume that because students cite "to be able to get a better job" and "to make money" as reasons to go to college that they don't have *other* reasons for attending as well.

This is precisely what we have found among the twenty students my research assistants and I have been interviewing each semester since the fall of 2014 at Northeastern University.[46] Their answers to the question "Why did you come to college?" are varied and complicated. These are students majoring in the social sciences and humanities, and so we might expect more diversity in their answers than we might get from students in professional majors (though note that at Northeastern, economics and criminal justice are in the College of Social Sciences and Humanities). But they are also students enrolled in a "co-op school" well known for providing students with full-time work experiences while they are enrolled. Almost all of these students cited the co-op program as a factor in their decision to attend Northeastern. As well, Northeastern is highly selective; these students are strivers. They are on the whole just the sort of students we might expect to be all about jobs, jobs, jobs.

But that's not the case. Eleven of the twenty students explicitly mentioned jobs or careers in their responses. I am using "explicitly" generously here, counting those who said things like "I wanted to figure out what to do with my life." This means that almost half of our participants did not even mention jobs or careers when asked why they decided to attend college. One student mentioned *only* a desire to determine what to do as a career; every other student—nineteen of twenty—mentioned at least one other reason for attending college.

What were those reasons? To learn, to enjoy learning, to change the world, to grow socially, to take advantage of new opportunities / try new things, to take classes unlike the ones available in high school, to be "kicked in the butt," to meet friends, to find their passion, to learn how to live on their own, to travel, to experience American culture and American education (that's Riddhi), to experience independence and freedom, to learn how to balance work and play, to meet people from different places, to work with great professors, to experience college in Boston, to study abroad, to get involved in campus organizing, to build community relationships, to immerse themselves in their fields of study, and to improve their writing skills. Twelve students—more students than mentioned careers/jobs—explicitly mentioned learning, separate from learning about a career or learning what they wanted to do with their lives. In short, while careers are important to these students—and why wouldn't they be?—they also want to learn about themselves, about others, and about the world. They want to grow and mature and become more responsible. And they want to make a difference in their communities and in the world. These desires are not contradictory; ideally, they are complementary.

Northeastern is a highly selective university, and one might object that these students have the luxury to think about things other than their careers. What about nontraditional students and students at non-elite colleges? It would be a mistake—and a patronizing one at that—to assume that the spectrum of reasons these students have for attending college is any narrower. Sara Goldrick-Rab (2016) reports that among students from low-income families in her study of Pell grant recipients, "getting ahead" was a primary reason for attending college, but nearly 70 percent cited a love of learning as a "very" or "extremely" important factor as well. As Goldrick-Rab puts it, "learning for its own sake was important to students in this sample" (167). Students in her study also wanted to support their families, be role models for their siblings, and contribute to their communities.

Consider too the seven-minute video *I Am Going to College Because...*, produced by City University of New York student Estefany Marlen.[47] The students in the video are diverse in every way imaginable, including country of origin, and many of them are nontraditional and first-generation students. Some of these students articulate professional goals, but overwhelmingly they are interested in making contributions to their families, communities, countries, and the world. One student captures the spirit of all of them when she says she wants to "become someone who is more independent, open-minded, and is able to help herself, others, and the communities she lives in." Professor Cathy N. Davidson (2017) at CUNY glosses the students' answers this way:

> I want to do something I love; I want to help others; I seek equality and social justice; I care about people and want to serve others; I am a woman and want to see more women in STEM fields; I am the first person in my family to be able to write my own name and I want to write it proudly and for good; I want to be useful to myself and everyone else; I want to help children; I want to contribute to my community; I want to make my family proud; I want a more successful future. (251)

We should also not assume that students who attend for-profit colleges have any less complex or diverse reasons for attending college. In her study of this subsector, McMillan Cottom (2017, 21–22) shows that these students have the same aspirations as students who attend traditional institutions—though they often have fewer options for acting on them. The majority of these students don't even know they're attending a for-profit college or university (59), so we should not think that their reasons for attending would be any different from those of other students.

It's clear that many students see no contradiction between making a better life for themselves and contributing to the public good—and they're willing to work for both. In fact, they see these goals as mutually reinforcing: they are striving to improve themselves *in order to* improve their families, their communities, and the world.

Conclusion

Who benefits from US higher education? Whose interests does it serve? To be sure, the individuals who are fortunate enough to gain a college education benefit in numerous ways: they earn valuable employment credentials; they are socialized into adult life or into professional cultures; they learn to live and work with diverse others; they are given opportunities for intellectual, emotional, and social growth; they build their personal and professional networks; and much more. At the same time, we all benefit when individuals are well prepared to contribute to our economic, social, and political systems. Our automating economy increasingly demands highly skilled and innovative workers. Our embattled democracy is in dire need of informed citizens and wise leaders. Our civil society, not to mention this planet of ours, cannot survive without a renewed commitment to solving complex local and global problems together.

When we factor in the innumerable contributions that colleges and universities make to everything from local and regional economies to medical advances to new product development to how we understand the human condition, it's absurd to think of higher education as exclusively a private good, the cost of which should be borne entirely by the individuals (and their families) who are enrolled at any given time. More than that, it's dangerous to restrict postsecondary education to those fortunate enough to have families that are able to pay outright for college or to those willing to take on large amounts of debt. What if that next life-saving medical breakthrough or life-enhancing technology or life-affirming cultural product hinges on nurturing the talents and insights of a child who happens to be born to parents without means? Or on developing the talents and insights of an adult with neither the time nor the money to invest in their education? Even people without sympathy for these personal tragedies of unrealized potential must understand the economic, social, and cultural costs of not investing in these individuals.

At its best, higher education promotes individual advancement in ways that simultaneously promote social advancement. The private good and the public good are not in conflict; in fact, they should be understood as mutually reinforcing. This has been the case historically, and it must be the case as we move deeper into this troubled century.

The challenge faced by higher education is to design educational experiences that promote both individual and collective well-being, that serve the whole person and the whole society. The chapters that follow make the case that this challenge is best taken up by institutions designed to promote integrative learning. I start with how institutions can promote the integration of the breadth and depth of learning.

CHAPTER 2

DEPTH AND BREADTH

Integrating Specialized Expertise
and Generalized Understanding

◣ To say that Martha Neuman was not looking forward to her required statistics course would be an understatement. She dreaded it. A human services major, Martha thought of herself as a social justice organizer and advocate. She had been active on campus as a peer health educator with the university's Sexual Health, Advocacy, Resources, and Education group; completed a co-op with a feminist social justice organization in Washington, DC; and studied public health issues in Zambia and India. Her social justice work, as she saw it, was about working closely with flesh-and-blood people, not nameless, faceless numbers, and so she was, in her words, "fairly opposed to statistical analysis." She harbored a human services practitioner's suspicion of what she perceived as academia's bloodless and distanced approach to studying human populations and movements. She felt "really grounded" in the reproductive justice movement, which she thought of as "scrappy grassroots, . . . very radical, outside the system."

Something strange was happening in her Gender and Reproductive Justice class, however. Martha was finding that "there was a ton of really interesting research and scholarship around the reproductive justice phenomenon." She was particularly surprised and excited to learn about academic research on health issues for women, especially women of color and pregnant women, in private prisons. She was beginning to see how empirical and even quantitative research and scholarship could inform—and be a form of—advocacy.

This experience motivated Martha to conduct her own research for her research methods course, using what she was learning in the Gender and Reproductive Justice class and also—to her astonishment—in the statistics course. She interviewed and surveyed classmates and friends about their perceptions of identity in relation to the sexual education they had received. "I thought it was going to be boring and dry," Martha recalls, "but it was not. It was so interesting." Even the statistical analysis was fascinating: "correlations and regressions, things [she] knew nothing about" helped her to see the data more clearly and to draw connections between her own research and the studies she was reading for Gender and Reproductive Justice.

Martha then was able to use her new research skills to build on the research she'd conducted in the Gender and Reproductive Justice and research methods courses in subsequent classes, including Women in World Politics, Policy in Practice, and her capstone course, in which she analyzed gun violence through a reproductive justice lens. Martha says that being able to pursue her passion for gender and health across her classes made all the difference in her undergraduate career. She appreciates "the way that my classes . . . unknowingly interacted to let me spend all semester talking and writing about the same thing." She credits her professors who gave her "autonomy and freedom" to write about what interested her. Martha says this gave her "a way to create trends [in her] academic career." She now has "a body of [her] own work all relating to [her] interest in sexual education and LGBTQ identity formation."

Martha parlayed this integrated body of work into presentations to campus and community audiences on sexual education and health. She continued to draw on it in job interviews. She says she draws on it even now in her role as a campaigns and fundraising organizer for a state coalition of progressive political and advocacy organizations. ◣

Trends across an entire academic career, a body of one's own work: this is what integrative education looks and sounds like. Martha connected and synthesized ideas, knowledge, and skills across her courses and across disciplinary domains that students often experience as discrete. Her college education was more than the sum of its parts.

Martha is a remarkably able and passionate learner, but surely some of the credit for her successful college experience can be ascribed to the coherent and cohesive human services major. Drawing on both their practitioner and academic expertise, the program's small, tight-knit faculty have designed an educational experience that offers students "the theoretical and skill-based background necessary for practice and research."[1] Faculty routinely encourage and guide students to connect and synthesize their learning across their courses and between their courses and their co-ops and field experiences.

But notice that even for Martha, this coherence is difficult to discern. She says her classes "unknowingly interacted." She praises her professors for letting her research and write about what interested her, but she perceives herself as having carried the burden of integration. She approached the statistics course, at least initially, as a dreaded general education requirement, an obligation she needed to tick off rather than an opportunity to advance her ongoing investigations of questions, problems, and topics that were important to her.

Ultimately, the statistics course played an important role in Martha's development as a researcher and practitioner. She integrated the knowledge and skills it offered into her repertoire, and this allowed her to expand and deepen her body of work. This is rare. Most students in most colleges and universities experience most of their courses as self-contained units and the different parts of the undergraduate experience—majors, gen ed, electives—as distinct, even unrelated. Even students who adore their courses and learn a lot from them often experience their learning as fragmented, disjointed. The result: an education that is less than the sum of its parts.

This result is virtually assured by a pervasive formula in US undergraduate education: M+GE+E=D (major + gen ed + electives = degree). The idea is that students get some depth through their majors and some breadth through their gen ed and elective courses, and these add up to a well-rounded, well-educated graduate. At most institutions, general education courses are taken before major courses, theoretically laying a broad foundation upon which specialized studies may be built. This sounds logical enough, but it's not generally what happens. Instead, most students view gen ed requirements as a nuisance and a distraction from the work they are interested in. To be sure, students benefit from early academic exploration, but loading up requirements in the first year or two makes genuine exploration *less* likely, and it sends the message to students that specialization is what really matters.[2]

Unbundlers are critical of the depth-plus-breadth model for being too broad and not keyed closely enough to employer-aligned competencies, and they propose fully unbundling majors from general education. But the fundamental problem with the undergraduate curriculum is that it's already unbundled—indeed, fragmented—and needs to be integrated. Students should develop an area of specialized expertise *and* a generalized understanding of the contexts—social, cultural, economic, technological—in which they live, learn, and work. But effectively addressing complex problems in rapidly changing contexts requires something more: the integration of specialized expertise and generalized understanding. Without a generalized understanding of the contexts in which problems have taken shape and now persist, specialized expertise could easily be misdirected, misapplied, or even dangerous. By the same token, without specialized expertise to bring to bear on the problems, generalized understanding of its contexts may give some insight into the problems but will not be enough to intervene in them.[3]

In this chapter I am concerned with the integration of courses and curricula. At the outset, I want to be clear that my goal is not to advance a particular curricular scheme. In particular, I am not interested in promoting what is sometimes called integrated studies or integrative studies. While programs going by these names may be excellent, they are sometimes merely interdisciplinary courses or curricula. *Interdisciplinary* and *integrative* are not synonyms. Integrative learning can happen *within* disciplines (across courses or across classrooms and other learning contexts), and it might not happen in so-called interdisciplinary learning experiences, which could just be another way of packaging content. The challenge for colleges and universities is to develop curricular models in which students are guided to connect and synthesize knowledge and skills across their courses and programs.

The Breadth-then-Depth Model

"What's your major?" It's the first question college students often hear upon meeting a stranger. The major is baked into our understanding of what a college education *is*. The same is true of its trusty counterpart: gen ed. Sprinkle in some electives for flavor, and voilà: the traditional recipe for an all-American college education. The M+GE+E=D curricular model is so common that it's rarely questioned or even commented on. But this model is not natural or inevitable. It has a history. Indeed, it's the result of an uneasy compromise resulting from a debate that's almost as old as American higher education itself.

This is not the place for a comprehensive history of higher education curricula, but standard academic accounts offer a helpful thumbnail sketch.[4] The American college, from the colonial era through the early nineteenth century, was dominated by a prescriptive classical curriculum based on the seven liberal arts: the trivium (grammar, logic, and rhetoric) plus the quadrivium (arithmetic, geometry, astronomy, and music). The Yale Report of 1828, which offered a steadfast defense of the classical curriculum, especially the study of Greek and Latin, was a response to a growing sentiment that higher education should prepare undergraduates for professional work.[5] That sentiment intensified throughout the nineteenth century with the growth of industrialization, professions and specialized disciplines, and land-grant colleges and universities. These developments led to more curricular choices for students and to more "practical" education. They also led to what historian Laurence Veysey (1970) called "patterned isolation" among disciplines and to curricular fragmentation. The post–Civil War period saw the rise of the German-inspired research university and the wide adoption of the elective system first developed at Harvard (by the unbundlers' bête noire, President Charles Eliot), where required subjects were gradually whittled down to only two: rhetoric and modern language for first-year students. The elective system had its critics, especially among academics who claimed that it lacked coherence and was too "vocational." Throughout the early to mid-twentieth century, debates raged between those who supported general, liberal education and those who favored specialized, practical education. In 1945, a Harvard faculty committee produced the famous *Red Book*, officially titled *General Education in a Free Society*, which argued for a balance between general and specialized education and recommended a mix of required entry-level courses and distribution requirements.[6]

This sketch simplifies a complicated history, but it underscores a few important points. First, curricula are the result of ongoing debates about the purpose and function of higher education, which I took up in chapter 1. Second, those debates tend to revolve around the perceived relative value of liberal or classical studies and practical or professional studies, which I take up in chapter 4. Third, and most relevant to this chapter, the state of play from the Cold War to today is more or less captured in Harvard's *Red Book*: almost every US postsecondary institution has struck a compromise resulting in some (alleged) balance between depth and breadth.

The most common manifestation of this compromise—the M+GE+E=D formula—is sometimes called the Cold War curriculum (Menand 2010; Schneider 2010).[7] A major, typically representing one-third to one-half of undergraduate coursework, allows students to develop considerable depth in a subject area, while general education and electives allow them to gain broad understanding and to explore other subjects. Debates rage over whether or how much one's major matters in terms of earning potential, and some institutions allow individualized, double/dual, or combined majors—but the major remains a sturdy feature of the college experience. General education, meanwhile, takes a variety of forms, including core models that feature shared courses or course sequences and distribution models in which requirements in certain knowledge domains (humanities, arts, natural sciences, and so on) are fulfilled by any number of identified courses. Some institutions have created hybrids of these models, and the content of these programs is hotly debated both on campuses and beyond them,[8] but like the major, general education is a nearly ubiquitous feature of the undergraduate experience. Louis Menand (2010, 29–30) calls it "the most modern part of the modern university."

As a curricular scheme, M+GE+E=D has commonsense appeal: sure, every student should gain some depth and some breadth of learning. But does it actually provide these? And does it promote the kind of integrative learning students need to confront a complex world?

An integrative major-and-gen-ed curriculum would provide opportunities and encouragement for students to connect and synthesize ideas, skills, and knowledge (1) within their majors (that is, across courses in their majors), (2) within their general education curriculum (that is, across courses they take to fulfill their gen ed requirements), and (3) between their majors and their gen ed courses.

Within Majors

This should be a no-brainer: a major is by definition a course of study leading to a degree—a credential in that subject. Students should deepen, extend, and refine their knowledge and skills as they move through the major, and by the time they complete it, they should have specialized expertise in that subject. In practice, this is more easily accomplished in some majors than in others. No major is entirely straightforward and uncontroversial, but in general, majors associated with relatively stable forms of technical expertise (mechanical engineering, say) are more amenable to tighter, progressive curricula than are majors associated with a wider range of activities, methodologies, and frameworks, which do not necessarily build in a linear way upon each other (English, for example).

There are a host of other issues that may affect the design of a major curriculum: accreditation standards (or lack thereof), resident faculty expertise, the will of the faculty to engage in regular updates of the curriculum, the point in students' undergraduate careers when they tend to declare their major, and many more. In any case, majors are not always designed to promote integrative learning. In fact, curricula are often reflections of what faculty want to teach, not what the faculty have determined students should learn. As new faculty are hired, their courses—often excellent in their own right—may be simply added to a list of requirements. Course rotations and faculty availability end up determining what gets taught.

When faculty do put thought into designing curricula, a vague goal of content "coverage" often prevails, leading to majors that aren't very deep after all. To take my own field as an example, the English major at many institutions is little more than a list of requirements with no obvious connection to each other.[9] It's not uncommon to see English curricula with complicated sets of distribution requirements, some by historical period, others by nation (American lit, British lit), and still others by disciplinary field (literature, writing). And those requirements can be fulfilled with a variety of courses that often seem to have little in common.

There are of course exceptions, and indeed we are seeing movement toward more coherent and cohesive majors as disciplines move away from coverage models and toward curricula organized around themes, theories, frameworks, and methodologies. This is partly a function of the desire to dispense with dead-white-guy canons, partly a function of the growing influence of learning research in colleges and universities, and partly a function of the recognition that in an era when there are more than 28,000 peer-reviewed journals,[10] there is simply too much to know even within relatively narrow fields of study. Program assessment, while no academic's idea of a good time, is also playing a role in helping faculty articulate the knowledge and skills they want their majors to acquire. In many institutions, professors are coming out of their individual classrooms to work with their colleagues to forge shared visions of student learning across the major. They are designing their courses with specific visions in mind, helping their students build on prior knowledge and preparing them to build on their current learning. This is all exciting to see, but even within majors, it's still not the norm.

Within General Education Programs

Theoretically, general education programs should have some measure of coherence: they are, after all, the faculty's answer to the question, "What should all students know and be able to do by the time they graduate?" At a minimum, they should add up to some coherent whole: a body of knowledge and skills that represents an institution's vision of a well-educated graduate. In practice, though, gen ed programs typically represent less a coherent vision than a hodgepodge of requirements and courses that reflect the outcome of highly contentious jockeying by faculty.

Anyone who has been involved in a general education overhaul, as I have (at two different institutions), understands how challenging and messy this process can be. Getting a small group of faculty to agree on where to have lunch is hard enough; getting the *entire* faculty (or at least the majority of those who vote) to agree on the common goals for all students and how those goals will be met is almost impossible. Most faculty would rather teach courses to students who choose to study with them, rather than those who end up in their courses because they are fulfilling a general education requirement—but they also want their areas of expertise well represented in the overall scheme. Cue the passive-aggressive, and sometimes aggressive-aggressive, turf battles. Arguments can rage sometimes for months and even years over whether to adopt a core model (specific courses fulfill requirements), a distribution model (requirements dispersed across knowledge domains), or some hybrid of these. Then come the arguments about how many requirements there should be and of what they should consist. Then about how the requirements will be approved. How they will be implemented. How they will be monitored. Assessed. Reported. And at each stage, programmatic coherence tends to be sacrificed to implementational realities. This is not to say that there are no defensible and even exciting general education programs, but the tendency in these negotiations is toward the production of a set of poorly described curricular requirements that have little obvious relation to each other.

Some, no doubt, will defend the hodgepodge. Isn't it a *good* thing that students are required to try out a bunch of different kinds of courses? What if that science-minded student would never have taken a humanities course? But forcing students to march through a grab bag of requirements does not, in my experience, promote exploration. It promotes resignation at best, hostility at worst. As a humanities professor, I believe that requiring students to take a humanities course for the precise reason that it's outside of their declared interests is counterproductive. Exploration is not the opposite of connection; connections make exploration more meaningful, even if through contrast. Students are much more likely to explore in good faith if they are invited to consider how the humanities frame and pursue important questions vis-à-vis how the sciences do. But this is not how gen ed programs are generally designed. Instead, that science-minded student is much more likely to have to sit through a major authors class or world history or an intro philosophy course because that course showed up on a (for all the student can tell, random) list of humanities classes fulfilling the gen ed requirement—and of course because it fit their schedule. Those courses may be well conceived and wonderfully taught, but this is likely to be lost on students under these conditions.

Across Majors and General Education Programs

If majors and general education programs on their own rarely promote integrative learning, we should not expect to find integration *between* them. And indeed we don't. Carol Geary Schneider (2010), a former president of the Association of American Colleges and Universities, suggests that the Cold War curriculum's supposed balance of breadth and depth does not deliver on that promise and actually hinders attempts to implement integrative education programs:

> In this now-standard model, breadth—to be attained in the first two years of college—is the glue that connects the so-called transfer curriculum in community colleges with the work of the four-year institutions. Depth, which is supposed to come later, is seen as the centerpiece of the advanced curriculum. With general education to be "gotten out of the way as soon as possible," as students everywhere are still advised today, there is no intention of and certainly no game plan for helping students make their general studies serve as a *context* for their major studies. The entire design fosters specialization rather than integration, and critics have complained vehemently about exactly that design flaw ever since "breadth" began to gain steam.

For Schneider, the $M+GE+E=D$ model provides only lip service to breadth, in effect promoting specialization because it fails to integrate the two parts of the model: gen ed does not serve as a "context" for majors. Instead, these two components of the undergraduate experience are kept separate—indeed, are held in tension with each other, competing for students' time and energy. They are supposed to add up to a well-rounded education, but they are rarely made whole.

In my experience, most students, reasonably enough, do exactly what Schneider (2010) says they do: they look for the least painful way to get gen ed requirements out of the way so they can get on with their "real" (read: specialized) courses. As Schneider notes, many community college transfer curricula essentially *are* the gen ed requirements for the target transfer institutions. At many four-year institutions, students are able to complete the majority—sometimes all—of their gen ed requirements before they set foot on campus, through advanced placement (AP), international baccalaureate (IB), dual or concurrent enrollment, and/or transfer credit. Institutions have an incentive to design generous policies in this area—students are more likely to enroll if they come in with significant amounts of credit—and there is today a great deal of pressure to accelerate students through their gen ed requirements. Without wading into the pitched debates on transfer and credit policies, I will note that the debates themselves reflect the dis-integrative nature of the undergraduate curriculum. Of all the questions being hotly debated—How many credits can students transfer from another institution? Is an AP or IB test score a good indicator of college-level knowledge and skills? Is it appropriate to fulfill college requirements in a high school setting? and so on—we rarely ask how general education integrates with students' majors. Gen ed is by definition a thing apart. This state of affairs naturally undermines gen ed, which becomes perfunctory, but it also represents a significant missed opportunity to make the undergraduate experience more coherent and meaningful.

What's Next?

Unbundlers see the failures of the M+GE+E=D model as endemic to and emblematic of the excesses of the hybrid university. They see colleges and universities as trying to do too much—in this case, preparing students for employment (their definition of depth) and offering them a liberal arts education (their understanding of breadth). Jeffrey Selingo (2014) offers the following solution:

> To reduce the tension between providing the vocational training that employers demand and a traditional liberal-arts education, the bachelor's degree should be split into two parts: a one-year program focused on a general education, followed by separate programs of varying lengths, depending on the particular needs of an academic field. So after that first year, the credential for a computer-science major might take three years, but history or English majors might take just one.[11]

There is, in my view (I'm an English professor, remember), much wrong with Selingo's proposal, but the central problem, for the purpose of this chapter, is that it doubles down on the segregation of general education and majors. Not only is "breadth" given short shrift, as Schneider fears, but majors are reduced to credentials for vocational training.

From here, it's only a half step to the conclusion that maybe gen ed isn't necessary at all. After all, unbundlers believe that curricula should be tightly "matched to job descriptions" (Craig 2015, 87). For Ryan Craig, curriculum design is a matter of "mak[ing] a direct connection between an available job and a training opportunity" (136). In this worldview, breadth is irrelevant, an extravagance that traditional institutions push on students to jack up the price of admission. Monica Herk (2015) of the Committee for Economic Development (a policy organization promoting free enterprise) argues that it's "unfair and inefficient to require middle-income and poorer families to go into debt to purchase a 2- or 4-year degree consisting of many classes that are largely irrelevant to their goal of obtaining a job."[12] Herk is quick to note that "the liberal arts aspects of postsecondary education" are not "unimportant or lacking in value"; she is only saying that "much of what students spend their 4 or 2 years studying may be largely unrelated to the skills and knowledge that employers are seeking."

There is an appealing populism to claims like this, but do they hold up? Are students really paying for things—those frilly "liberal arts aspects"—that employers aren't looking for? No. Employers continue to value college degrees precisely because they represent more than a solely technical education. In a 2014 National Association of Colleges and Employers survey, employers identified ten attributes they value most highly in employees. Topping the list were items like "ability to work in a team structure," "ability to make decisions and solve problems," "ability to communicate verbally with people inside and outside the organization," and "ability to plan, organize, and prioritize work." "Technical knowledge related to the job" came in seventh, just above "proficiency with computer software programs." The message is clear: employers value both broad, general skills *and* narrow, technical ones—but they view the former as more important.[13] Other surveys of business and nonprofit leaders similarly find that employers want candidates who can "think critically, communicate clearly, and solve complex problems," particularly "with people whose views are different from their own," and that "employers overwhelmingly endorse broad learning and cross-cutting skills as the best preparation for long-term career success" (AAC&U 2015).[14] Employers understand that the jobs that will not be automated in the coming years will require significant creative and critical capacities; narrow, task-oriented training will not be sufficient.

Even more evidence that employers favor holistic education comes from the testimony of corporate leaders. Pete McCabe, vice president of global services organization for GE Transportation, insists that in today's world "the problems that are going to change outcomes fundamentally, whether it be in productivity, or health care, or wherever else, are going to be systems problems. It's the interconnection points of all the discrete problems inside a function [that matter]. . . . [T]he exponential value is delivered when you start connecting the dots" (quoted in Aoun 2017, 35–36).[15] Based on interviews with business leaders, Northeastern University president Joseph E. Aoun (2017) concludes that "domain-specific training—even in high-demand domains like data sciences—is not enough. . . . Holistic, systems thinking is a quality needed in any complex operation" (37). This is why Google hires "generalists" based largely on their analytical reasoning abilities. Aoun notes that in the era of automation, the jobs remaining for humans in virtually *all* industries will require "mindsets rather than bodies of knowledge—mental architecture rather than mental furniture" (41). Yes, people will need to master specific bodies of knowledge and skills, "but that alone will not be enough when intelligent machines are doing much of the heavy lifting of information. To succeed, tomorrow's employees will have to demonstrate a higher order of thought . . . [and] comprehend and act on a broad perspective" (41).

Alumni also say that a narrow education in technical knowledge and skills is not enough. In the 2014 Gallup-Purdue Index Report, alums reported that they were more likely to be engaged at work if their college experiences had featured the following: a professor who cared about them; applied learning; involvement in extracurricular activities and organizations; and projects that took more than one semester to complete.[16] Sustained and meaningful relationships plus intellectual work, not technical skill building, are what prepare students to engage deeply in work even after they graduate.

So even if we limit ourselves to the idea that the exclusive purpose of college is to prepare students for jobs, sacrificing breadth is a bad idea. But I've shown that "balancing" breadth and depth, à la the M+GE+E=D model, leads to disjointed undergraduate experiences. What to do?

The only way to prepare students properly for a complex, rapidly changing world is to design educational experiences that facilitate the *integration* of breadth and depth. To unpack this claim, we need to step back and think about what depth and breadth really mean.

In today's information-rich world, in which the pace of knowledge production is breakneck, it's not enough to say that depth means knowing a lot about something and breadth means knowing a little about many things. We need to take a holistic approach in which specialized expertise (domain-specific knowledge and skills) and generalized understanding (contextual, systemic awareness) are dynamically integrated. The world will keep on changing, and graduates will undoubtedly find themselves in a multitude of unfamiliar, as-yet-unimagined contexts, so the goal must be to teach students *ways* of learning and knowing that will allow them to contribute meaningfully to the professional, civic, and personal endeavors they engage in throughout their lives.

In order to gain specialized expertise, one must learn not just content but also, and perhaps more important, *how to think* like an expert in a particular field, whether academic or professional. Domain-based knowledge and skills are always shifting in response to internal and external developments, so the key to an expert's success is not what they know at any given moment, but rather their ability to learn and think the way experts in that field do.

If depth means learning how to be an expert, breadth means learning how to be a *non*-expert. This might sound strange, but the same logic applies. There is simply too much to know, and what's worth knowing is constantly shifting. To be sure, faculty should teach content they deem important, but the point is not to fill students with all the information they could need—an impossible goal. The purpose of general education should be to allow students to try on and try out different ways of learning, knowing, and thinking. In addition to gaining new insights, they should also come to recognize the *limits* of their own perspectives and expertise and to value the perspectives and expertise of others. Curious, informed, responsible non-experts are as important as experts in complex and ever-changing social contexts—including and especially democracies. For instance, people who say "Well, everyone has their own opinion" about climate change or the benefits of vaccination are ignoring—at the peril of all of us—the expertise of the vast majority of scientists and doctors. Likewise, if a team is planning to build a bridge across a river in the Amazon, it's critical for the soil experts, engineers, anthropologists, and local residents to bring their expertise to the project *and* to recognize the limits of that expertise and the value of each other's expertise. A structurally sound bridge in the wrong location is just as useless as a structurally unsound bridge in an ideal spot.

In an academic context, we often associate depth with disciplinarity and breadth with interdisciplinarity, but we should avoid these conflations. Disciplinarity does not necessarily lead to fragmentation, and interdisciplinarity can lead to increased fragmentation. Indeed, as Jerry A. Jacobs (2013) has shown through citational analysis, most disciplines, at least in the arts and sciences, tend to be porous, dynamic, collaborative—and quite broad. Many disciplines are highly internally differentiated, and if they are presented to students as a grab bag of unrelated courses, as Gerald Graff (2004) has argued they often are, then students will be unable to develop much depth. By the same token, interdisciplinary studies can be quite deep and specialized. Ironically, interdisciplinarity can result in increased siloing and isolation, as faculty and students work in the tiny overlapping spaces of the Venn diagrams of the constituent disciplines.[17]

The ultimate goal is for students to be able to size up an unfamiliar situation or problem, identify and activate their relevant expertise, determine what they will need to learn, and go learn it—all while recognizing and valuing both the limits of their own expertise and the extent of others' expertise. They must understand themselves as experts *and* as non-experts and know when to exercise their specialized expertise and generalized understanding. They must connect and synthesize different ways of learning and thinking into a holistic understanding of themselves as learners and thinkers.

Students need the opportunity, encouragement, and motivation to connect and synthesize knowledge and skills across courses and experiences in their majors, across courses and experiences in their general education program, and across these two parts of their educational careers. Or perhaps it's time to dispense with the concepts of majors and general education altogether. What if students were allowed to design their own field and focus areas? What if they could choose a home (inter)discipline and two collateral fields? Or a pathway with milestones that indicated both depth and breadth of knowledge? The M+GE+E=D formula is so taken for granted at most institutions that these questions are almost unthinkable. But colleges and universities need to ask themselves if the current design of their curriculum is promoting or hindering integrative learning. Does the education they offer add up to more or less than the sum of its parts?

If the answer is not "more," then why shouldn't students piece together their postsecondary learning experiences and credentials from the quicker, cheaper unbundled options in the higher ed market? Maybe in the past, the answer to that question was, "Because we're Brand X University, and our name *means* something." Possibly for a very small group of elite schools, reputational value propositions continue to hold sway, but for the rest of us, and soon for all of us, that answer will not—and should not—fly. It's time to innovate for integration.

Fortunately, some institutions are showing the way. Bennington College, Hampshire College, and NYU's Gallatin School of Individualized Study have indeed eliminated majors in favor of personalized courses of study.[18] More commonly, institutions retain majors and general education but redesign these components of the undergraduate experience in ways that promote integrative learning across them.

Champlain College, for instance, has designed the Integrative Interdisciplinary Core, a "vertical" general education program featuring theme-based seminars during each of the four undergraduate years.[19] These discussion-based core courses explore broad questions from multiple disciplinary perspectives.[20] They culminate in a capstone course, co-taught by one faculty member in the professional division and one in the core (liberal arts) division, in which students develop a project "that integrates the knowledge [they have] acquired in [their] major, [their] learning in the Core and contemporary issues in professional ethics."[21] Instead of imagining gen ed as separate from and preparatory to majors, Champlain incorporates it across the full span of the undergraduate experience, which allows students to shuttle back and forth between being an emerging expert in a field and being an informed non-expert who can draw on their domain expertise to inform discussions and projects in interdisciplinary contexts. Teachers of core courses are asked to be mindful of students' expertise—which they themselves might not have—and to leave room in their courses for students to bring it to bear. In the capstone class, students are asked to integrate their deep learning as experts (in their major courses) with their broad learning as non-experts (in their core courses).

LaGuardia Community College not only builds integration into the curriculum, but also puts the tools for integration in students' hands. Its electronic portfolio program guides students to integrate what they learn in their majors with "core competencies [inquiry and problem solving, global learning, integrative learning] and communication abilities [oral, written, digital]" (LaGuardia Community College 2017, 23).[22] These general education competencies and abilities are introduced in first-year seminars, which are taught within disciplines so students can explore their majors right away (an important goal in a two-year institution), and they are incorporated into subsequent courses in majors as well, serving as touchstones for students as they move through their programs. The ePortfolios allow students to collect, reflect on, and showcase their work. In the words of Professor Justin Rogers-Cooper, they allow students "to make sense of their learning personally, across disciplines, over time" ("LaGuardia Community College" 2017, 23). By the end of their career at LaGuardia, students have a digital professional and personal portfolio that they can use to display the depth and breadth of their learning to prospective employers, colleges and universities to which they wish to transfer, or family and friends. The result, as anyone who browses the online ePortfolio gallery can easily see, is active, intentional, integrative learning.[23]

My institution, Northeastern University, has developed a general education program that eschews both core and distribution models. NUpath is designed around student learning goals in eleven areas, such as engaging with the natural and designed world, exploring creative expression and innovation, conducting formal and quantitative reasoning, employing ethical reasoning, and integrating knowledge and skills through experience. While at first glance these might look like distribution requirements, the learning goals can be achieved in any discipline and at any level of the curriculum. For example, students could complete the "analyzing and using data" requirement in the Technologies of Texts course in the English Department or meet the "employing ethical reasoning" requirement in a cyberlaw class in the College of Computer and Information Science. The curriculum is flexible enough to allow students to fulfill general education requirements when they're ready to, at the level of the curriculum that makes sense for them, and in a disciplinary area that will contribute to their intellectual development. They shuttle between being emerging experts and being informed non-experts, "integrat[ing] core learning into their individual educational journeys."[24] The general education requirements are understood not as a foundation but rather as a series of markers along a learning path that students chart for themselves. Ultimately, NUpath is meant to encourage students to consider their majors and gen ed as seamless parts of their holistic, integrated educational paths and intellectual biographies.

These are just a few examples of colleges and universities working to integrate breadth and depth of learning. Institutions of various kinds are rethinking the relationship between majors and gen ed with the goal of helping students integrate what they learn across courses and curricula. In the end, students must be the ones who integrate their learning, but this does not happen automatically or by collecting discrete credentials from a grab bag of providers. There is much that institutions and faculty can do to ensure that students' educational experiences are more than the sum of their parts.

What Institutions Can Do

The most important thing colleges and universities can do to support integrative learning across courses and curricula is to design programs and curricula to provide opportunities for students to connect and synthesize their learning. Perhaps this sounds circular or simplistic, but it would require institutions to move away from the time-honored practice of simply adding new courses, majors, minors, or gen ed programs with little regard for the coherence of individual experiences or for the integrity of the holistic student experience. For too long, institutions have relied on a fuzzy notion of "curricular pluralism," which holds that simply exposing students to different viewpoints through a wide range of course experiences will promote critical thinking (Graff 2004, 63). While bright and able students will always be able to make some connections between and among their courses and programs, deep and sustained integrative learning does not happen on its own. It needs to be cued.

Specific actions that institutions can take to promote integrative learning across courses and curricula include the following:

- *Design coherent curricula that promote holistic educational experiences.* The M+GE+E=D formula may be a convenient expression of curricular pluralism, but it does not ensure a coherent educational experience. Curricular pathways and "signature work" of the sort promoted by the AAC&U might (Peden, Reed, and Wolfe 2017). Core competencies that extend across majors and gen ed might. Doing away with majors altogether and having personalized courses of studies might. The specific model is less important than that each institution design an integrated curriculum that regularly invites students to connect and synthesize their learning across the courses and programs. Interested parties should be able to take a quick look at a college or university's curriculum and understand immediately how the pieces fit together to create a coherent whole. If they can't, the institution still has work to do.
- *Set the expectation that all courses and curricula must prioritize integrative learning.* Courses must give students opportunities to connect and synthesize their learning with other courses within and beyond the major. Curricula must encourage students to connect and synthesize their learning within the courses in the curriculum and then in other courses, curricula, and learning experiences. These expectations could be criteria for course and curriculum approvals. They could also carry through to the curriculum planning (course scheduling) stage, where too often faculty preferences alone determine what classes are actually offered. Of course faculty expertise and teaching preferences must be taken into account, but the student experience must be the paramount consideration.
- *Motivate and reward faculty to learn about integrative learning.* While most faculty work hard and have their students' best interests at heart, few of them were trained to teach and fewer still know how to design learning environments and experiences that promote integrative learning. They must be afforded the time and incentives, financial and otherwise, to develop this expertise. There are many

ways to provide such opportunities, including workshop series, inquiry groups, and learning communities, all of which could be supported by small grant programs or other forms of professional recognition. Teaching and learning centers staffed by learning experts can organize many of these activities.[25]

- *Motivate and reward faculty collaboration.* Moving past curricular pluralism will require faculty to relinquish what I have called the "teacher in private practice" model and to design courses and curricula together (C. Gallagher 2007).[26] I see this happening on my own campus and on those I visit. True, a small number of faculty cling to a misinterpretation of the principle of academic freedom by claiming that their classrooms are inviolable spaces and they should not have to work with their colleagues. But many more are beginning to see the value and intellectual excitement that comes from collaborative course and curriculum design and planning. They correctly see no conflict between their right to teach without political interference and collaborating with colleagues to provide high-quality, coherent learning experiences for their students. But make no mistake: this is work, and it takes time. Institutions must be prepared to create opportunities and to provide incentives to make it happen. Ideally, *all* faculty learning opportunities would be collaborative, and many of them would involve faculty working together across departmental boundaries.

- *Incorporate integrative learning into assessment programs.* Student learning assessment is now broadly (if not always enthusiastically) accepted as a fact of academic life: accreditors require it, university and college administrators prioritize it, and more and more department leaders and faculty are coming to see the value of it.[27] Assessment is typically done at the program level. Each program specifies the knowledge and skills it desires for its graduates and expresses them as learning goals. Institutions should encourage programs to incorporate integrative learning into their assessments. The AAC&U's integrative and applied rubric can be a useful discussion tool and starting place in departments and programs undertaking this task.[28] Institutions should also design methods for assessing integrative learning *across* programs. Electronic port-folios of the sort used at LaGuardia Community College—which has developed a robust assessment program around the ePortfolios—can be helpful for this purpose.

What Faculty Can Do

The most important thing faculty can do to support integrative learning is to work with their colleagues to design courses and curricula that provide students with regular opportunities to connect and synthesize their learning. Specifically, faculty members can do the following:

- *Actively participate in curriculum design and planning with colleagues.* Too many faculty leave curriculum planning to others, concerning themselves only with their own courses. For students to get the most out of their educational experience, they need to be able to connect and synthesize what they are learning in one course to what they are learning or have learned in other courses. Exercises like curriculum mapping—collectively reviewing the curriculum to determine where and when the knowledge and skills associated with student learning goals are introduced, taught, and reinforced in the curriculum—can help faculty understand how students experience their courses. These exercises often result in faculty making their student learning goals more explicit and central to their courses.
- *Participate in program assessments.* If many faculty are reluctant to engage in curriculum design and planning, many more are down-right allergic to assessment. Most come by this allergy honestly: assessment is often treated as a cynical compliance exercise, and some institutions misuse data to surveil and punish faculty and departments. Meaningful assessment should be led by faculty: they are the ones setting the learning agenda, and they are the ones teaching the students, so they should be the ones figuring out what's working and what's not working. And that's really

what program assessment should be: gathering information about a program in order to support student learning. Higher education accrediting bodies are most interested in making sure that assessment processes happen and that the information gathered through them is actually used for program improvement. If assessment is only a machine feeding the institutional beast, or if the data from assessment are being misused, then faculty should demand that assessment be placed in their hands, where it belongs. Without assessment, it is impossible for faculty to know how, to what extent, and under what conditions students are able to integrate their learning within and beyond their programs. That is critical information to feed back into curriculum design and planning.

- *Teach for integration.* Here, I'm adapting a common phrase in the learning sciences literature: "teach for transfer." I follow Rebecca Nowacek (2011) in thinking of integration as necessarily conscious and positive, whereas transfer can be unconscious and take negative forms (as when a learner misapplies a concept that holds true in one context but doesn't hold true in another context).[29] Transfer encourages us to think in linear terms: learners apply or transform learning from context A *to* context B. Integration directs our attention to ways in which learners construct knowledge and skills *across* and *from* multiple contexts (A and B and C and D . . .). Teaching for integration means being mindful of the many learning contexts students traverse and designing opportunities for them to step back and reflect on how their learning is cohering across those contexts and experiences. It means helping students articulate (in both senses of that word) their learning in the here and now with their prior learning, with learning they are currently doing elsewhere, and with learning to come. As I suggested in the introduction, there is a robust literature on integrative learning, and faculty can avail themselves of that. Many teaching and learning centers provide workshops, inquiry groups, and the like devoted to integrative learning. Here are some simple strategies for encouraging integrative learning across courses:

- Early in each semester, engage students in self-assessment and goal setting, drawing on previous courses to determine what they know and are able to do as well as what they would like to know and be able to do by the end of the course. Help them place the course in their arc of intellectual development.
- During class discussions, prompt students to incorporate what they are learning or have learned in other classes. Throughout the semester, solicit from students their relevant specialized expertise and generalized knowledge.
- Design assignments—from informal blog posts or weekly written reflections to more formal research projects—that explicitly ask students to draw on what they are learning or have learned in other courses, including courses outside their major.
- Help students understand the "conditions of applicability" of what they are learning (Ambrose et al. 2010).[30] When and in what contexts does the concept or principle or skill under discussion obtain—and when and where does it not?
- Offer students reflective activities that help them solidify their knowledge and skills and make them available for future use, including crafting their learning journeys and intellectual biographies. These activities are particularly important at the end of the semester. For instance, I often ask students to design a concept map that reflects their current understandings of what they learned in the course—and then to draw a larger map of their learning journey in which this course is one location. Alternatively, I ask students to write letters of introduction to future teachers or employers telling their learning story and outlining the knowledge and skills they currently possess as well as those they hope to learn.

These are just a few ways to teach for integration; Ambrose and colleagues' *How Learning Works* (2010) provides many more. The key is to help students connect and synthesize ideas, knowledge, and skills across courses and curricula. As they move through their undergraduate experience, they will gain an understanding of their evolving specialized expertise and their generalized understanding. Just as important, they will begin to see the applicability and limitations of both, as well as what those around them bring to the table.

Conclusion

In an integrated college or university, the institution and faculty take responsibility for students' learning across courses and across curricula. To be sure, students are also responsible for their learning, and ultimately we want them to become self-directed learners. But it is the responsibility of institutions and faculty to design the opportunities and environments in which students can learn to be self-directed. The good news is that this is happening in all kinds of institutions.

In the next chapter I broaden the discussion of integration across courses and curricula to consider the integration of classroom learning and learning in other contexts. In chapter 4 I consider both forms of integration in light of the stubborn and pernicious dichotomy between the liberal arts and professional education.

CHAPTER 3

INSIDE AND OUTSIDE

Integrating Classroom Learning
and Learning in Other Contexts

◼ Elizabeth Zane (a pseudonym) began her six-month co-op at a global change-making organization in Mexico with confidence. She had taken courses in global social enterprise and entrepreneurship on her way to a global social enterprise minor, which would complement her international affairs major and Spanish minor. Her courses had been taught by a business professor she describes as "very business-oriented and extremely blunt." His approach seemed like good preparation for her work on the team that would interview and develop proposals for candidates to be part of a social entrepreneurs network. Her job would be to apply the organization's criteria to each candidate and make an evidence-based case to the organization's board for or against their candidacy. She thought her professor's emphasis on efficiency and effectiveness in methods, policies, and procedures would serve her well in evaluating candidates.

And it did—to a point. What she had learned in class gave her a foundation for assessing "entrepreneurial capability," one of the five criteria against which candidates were judged. But she soon learned that the organization's understanding of entrepreneurship was very different from the one she had learned in class. Instead of looking for clear-cut, measurable skills, her colleagues were talking about "initiative" and "drive"—"all that really big stuff," as Elizabeth describes it, "that's harder to pinpoint." Compared to her professor's no-nonsense business approach, she found the organization to be "touchy-feely and emotional."

Over time, as Elizabeth worked with her team to evaluate candidates and develop profiles of them for the organization, she remained somewhat critical of the organization's criteria, which she thought were too vague. But at the same time, she came to see the value of the more holistic, subjective judgments her team was making. Qualities like "leadership" are not entirely amenable to objective measurement after all, and the work of social change involves more than good business sense. The vetting process, she decided, "doesn't have to be so black and white and so business-focused."

Returning to campus, Elizabeth found that she was more critical about what she was taught in her courses as a result of her experience at the change-making organization. She was no longer a "sponge for information," she jokes, but rather "a sponge for information with a critical eye." Reflecting on her coursework for her minor and her work in the field, she says, "The two experiences have allowed me to find a middle ground for myself with my own understanding." ◣

In this chapter I expand my discussion of integrative learning to the integration of knowledge and skills across classrooms and other learning contexts. Elizabeth's experience illustrates several features of this form of integration that are important to keep in mind. First, it's bidirectional: Elizabeth integrated her learning from classrooms into her co-op and from co-op back into classrooms. Second, that learning, as it travels across these contexts, changes. Elizabeth did not mechanically apply knowledge and skills she already had; she extended, refined, challenged—in a word, reconstructed—her learning. Third, that type of reconstructing is a matter of recontextualizing.[1] She revised her knowledge and skills as she experienced different contexts and different places.

It's critical that students learn to integrate knowledge across a variety of contexts on and beyond campus and in both physical and digital spaces. As they move across contexts, they begin to see how things fit together, how systems work. They engage with others who view and experience the world differently than they do. They learn the arts of democratic citizenship—how to learn and live and work with diverse others. At the same time, they become observers of their own learning: they come to see how what they learn in one context may be applied, extended, reinforced, revised, or challenged in another. They become integrative learners and integrative thinkers who can take on the challenges of complex and rapidly changing social, cultural, political, and economic landscapes.

None of this happens naturally or easily: simply being placed in a context does not necessarily allow one to learn from it, much less to connect and synthesize that learning with what one learns in other contexts. Completing an internship, for instance, might give students some work experience, and taking an online course may allow them to learn in a different modality—but these experiences take on meaning and force only when they are integrated into larger learning trajectories. For that to happen, students need to develop the capacity to recognize, value, and analyze each experience, no matter where it occurs, as one among many that comprise their unfolding learning journey.

The phrase "no matter where is occurs" is important. It's now widely accepted that learning happens everywhere. This helps explain why so many colleges and universities are turning both to experiential learning and to online learning, neither of which is tethered to physical classrooms and campuses. Unfortunately, many institutions have merely *added* experiential and online learning opportunities. As any parent or prospective student who has recently been on a college tour can tell you, almost all colleges and universities today boast about their internships and study abroad programs. Many also trumpet their online offerings as opportunities for students to gain flexibility in their schedules. But if one were to ask how these opportunities relate to each other or how students are guided to integrate them into their educational experiences, the tour leaders would likely have no answer. These are typically one-offs, items on an extended menu, evidence of the disintegrated nature of most postsecondary institutions. Even worse, some parents and prospective students come away from these campus visits wondering why, if all these *other* experiences are so exciting, they should spend time on campus or take classes at all. It's a fair question, and every college and university should be prepared to answer it.

Meanwhile, unbundlers opportunistically exploit the "learning happens everywhere" mantra to argue that online technologies allow us to jettison classrooms and campuses altogether. They claim that the "University of Everywhere" (Carey 2015),[2] enabled by digital learning, renders "place-bound" institutions obsolete. But while learning *does* happen everywhere, it doesn't follow that place doesn't matter. The problem with the way experiential learning and online education are often practiced is that institutions do not pay enough attention to the particularities of learning contexts. Mixing and matching discrete, unbundled credentials from a variety of providers beholden to their bottom lines will only exacerbate the discontinuity and fragmentation of learning. The task ahead is to integrate colleges and universities to help students integrate classroom learning with learning elsewhere, including in digital spaces. In our networked society, in which information and people are ever more mobile, higher education must empower students to craft coherent learning pathways and to navigate diverse physical and digital contexts with confidence and competence.

Experiential Learning, Classroom Learning, and Integrative Learning

Learning by doing.[3] Learning by applying knowledge and understanding to "authentic" problems in the "real world."[4] Learning through "direct" experiences outside of the classroom.[5] Experiential education, it seems, is all the rage in higher education. But while these common institutional definitions of experiential learning, drawn from institutional websites, commendably position students as active learners, they do not help students integrate their learning across contexts and may even hinder integrative learning. What binds them together is a binary opposition between classrooms, which are positioned as inauthentic or unreal contexts where only indirect or theoretical learning takes place, and the real world, which is authentic and where direct and practical learning takes place. Certain kinds of experience are endowed with an inherent status—real/unreal, direct/indirect, authentic/inauthentic—that does not hold up to scrutiny and, more important, undermines students' ability to integrate learning across contexts. Students are left to think that the learning they do in classrooms is wholly unrelated to the learning they do in real contexts or—best case—that even though classrooms aren't real, they correspond closely enough to real-world contexts that students can apply some of what they've learned. In either case, classroom learning is devalued: the real action is elsewhere. This is not a recipe for integrative learning.[6]

Champions of experiential education as "learning by doing" often cite John Dewey as the progenitor of experiential learning. But this slogan does not capture the complexity of Dewey's thinking and may even distort it. For Dewey (1916, 86), while education is the "continuous reconstruction of experience,"[7] not all experiences—not all forms of "doing"—are educative, and some experiences can even be miseducative. Dewey's (1938) two criteria for evaluating the quality of an experience are *continuity* and *interaction*. By "continuity," he meant the ways in which experiences are connected to and shape one another. Experiences can be miseducative in many ways, but one of the principal ways is that they "may be so disconnected from one another that, while each is agreeable or even exciting in itself, they are not linked cumulatively to one another," thus leading to habits of mind that are "dispersive, disintegrated, centrifugal." Learners become unable to control their future experiences and begin to take their experiences "just as they come" (Dewey 1938, 11–12). For Dewey, then, experiences are not educative unless learners are able to integrate what they learn from them with what they learn from other experiences.

By "interaction," Dewey (1938, 25) meant that experiences are defined by an individual's engagement with the immediate physical and social environment. Dewey understood educators to be expert shapers of experiences. They shape experiences by making use of the physical and social affordances of the learning context, what Dewey termed "the conditions of the local community, physical, historical, economic, occupational, etc." (23). Educators exploit these affordances so as to create the conditions for educative experiences—that is, experiences that build meaningfully on prior experiences, that are worthwhile in their own right, and that lead to further educative experiences.

For Dewey (1938), the classroom is very much a place where real experiences take place. Indeed, one of his chief critiques of traditional education was that it treated classrooms as practice spaces for real life, rather than as part of it. He warned his fellow progressive educators that it was "a great mistake to suppose, even tacitly, that the traditional schoolroom was not a place in which pupils had experiences" (12). The problem with traditional education—in Dewey's day and ours—is that it offers the wrong sort of experiences: experiences that do not promote continuity and interaction.

Deweyan experiential learning *is* integrative learning. It's not only about learning by doing inside or outside the classroom—it's about connecting and synthesizing learning across experiences, and therefore across contexts, including classrooms. It's highly attentive to the present learning experience both on its own terms and as it connects to learners' prior and subsequent learning experiences.

Deweyan experiential learning is also highly attentive to context as a shaper of experiences. It recognizes what situated learning theory has made clear: learning cannot be meaningfully separated from where and how and with whom it takes place.[8] While situated learning theory insists that every learning context is different, it also insists that learning can be transferred or integrated across contexts. Indeed, knowledge and skills become most meaningful and usable when learners recognize where, when, how, with whom, and under what conditions they are relevant. This is why situated learning theorists call for models such as "cognitive apprenticeships," which "embed learning in activity and make deliberate use of the social and physical context."[9] All knowledge, according to this theory, is constructed in contexts of use. A concept or skill constructed in one context will need to be reconstructed in another context because no two contexts are exactly the same. Knowledge, skills, and learners themselves all change—transform in ways subtle and profound—as learners integrate knowledge across contexts.

So yes, learning can happen anywhere—but place matters *even more* when students learn in more than one context. The affordances and limitations of place shape students' learning while they are engaged in that internship, co-op, study abroad, or service program, and then again when they enter a new context—say, a classroom—and reconstruct their knowledge and skills. For example, Elizabeth's understanding of social entrepreneurship was first shaped by learning in a classroom from a business professor with a particular black-and-white view of entrepreneurial capability. She largely adopted his perspective through the course's evaluation of cases he introduced. As she moved into the nonprofit space and engaged in the messy, subjective process of evaluating and selecting candidates with her colleagues, who had different views from her professor, her knowledge and skills were transformed—though not entirely—by the experience and by her co-op employer's broader perspective on entrepreneurial capability. Reentering coursework, she engaged with her professors and peers on campus and was able to integrate what she had learned in her previous coursework *and* her co-op experience, constructing a new perspective, which she claimed as her "middle ground." This new, integrated understanding became possible for her not because place doesn't matter, but because it does.

This way of understanding experiential learning has important implications not only for how colleges and universities design experiential learning opportunities for their students, but also for how they approach the thorny issue of how they award academic credit for learning that happens outside of their institutional boundaries. Prior learning assessment (PLA) is a large and complex topic, and I cannot do it justice here. But one thing is clear: as the mantra of "learning happens everywhere" takes hold, colleges and universities will increasingly be called on to evaluate and validate learning from a wide range of on-ground and virtual experiences beyond their walls, from workplace experiences to military training to civic activities.[10] Some institutions, under pressure from the acceleration and completion agendas or from less than reputable institutional and non-institutional educational providers that are more "generous" with their credit-awarding policies, will be tempted to take shortcuts. In the name of ease and flexibility, they might not uphold rigorous academic expectations for documenting, reflecting on, and demonstrating learning. This would be a mistake, again raising the question of why students shouldn't just turn to cheaper non-institutional providers. Reputable colleges and universities need to keep in mind what Dewey teaches us: it's not the having of an experience that matters; it's our ability to learn from it and to integrate that learning with what we learn in other contexts. Care must be taken that students are not *given* credit for experiences they've had, but instead *earn* credit for integrating prior learning into their educational pathway. Indeed, when PLA is done right, place matters doubly. First, it shapes the original learning experience, and second, it shapes the current learning experience as the learner represents that prior learning in the context of their ongoing learning trajectory. Understood in this way, PLA could be a lever for institutional integration and a tool for integrative learning.

Online Learning, Classroom Learning, and Integrative Learning

The slogan "learning happens everywhere" is a key thrust in unbundlers' attack on the monopoly they claim colleges and universities hold on higher education. Unfortunately, they misconstrue this truism to mean that place doesn't matter. They posit the University of Everywhere as a solution to the problems created by "place-bound" colleges and universities (Carey 2015, 135). The University of Everywhere, freed from the constraints of place, is literally a utopia—a *nowhere*.

It's a techno-utopia, to be precise. Unbundlers imagine a great digital nowhere, an infinitely open virtual space unencumbered by physical constraints. Kevin Carey (2015), for instance, announces that massive open online courses (MOOCs)

> are accelerating seismic forces that threaten colleges that have stood, largely unchanged, for decades or more. These historic developments will liberate hundreds of millions of people around the world, creating ways of learning that have never existed before. They will also upend a cornerstone of the American meritocracy, fundamentally altering the way our society creates knowledge and economic opportunity. Whether they know it or not, Harvard and MIT are helping build a new and unprecedented institution: the University of Everywhere. (4)

Carey arrived at this prophecy after his experience of a MOOC called Introduction to Biology, which he completed through MIT. (For a fuller discussion of the rise and fall of MOOCs, see chapter 5.) The centerpiece of *The End of College*, this experience convinced Carey (2015) that MOOCs can replace in-person, campus-based education. Indeed, they may even be an improvement: "Live and taped lectures aren't the same. Live lectures are definitely worse" (173). He believes that his experience was roughly equivalent to that of the students who enrolled in Introduction to Biology on campus: "part of me was a little jealous that I couldn't join the after-lecture colloquy. But not so much that I would have paid $5,000 in tuition for the privilege. Whatever value relationships with the TAs [teaching assistants] and professor might have yielded, I was able to get a good grade without them" (174).

Like Ryan Craig discussing his experiences at Yale, Carey is willing to generalize from an *n* of one, using his "successful" completion of this one course as a blueprint for an education revolution. It's quite a leap from one well-off American middle-aged college graduate completing a single online course to the liberation of millions of people around the world. And it's a particularly implausible leap, since Carey fits the profile of the very small percentage of people who actually complete MOOCs: he already has a degree, is employed full time, and lives in a developed country.[11] He doesn't much care about the accoutrements that the resident MIT students get, including intimate, sustained engagement with professors and peers, as long as he gets the grade. But he doesn't stop to consider that what works for him (by his narrow metrics) might be insufficient for people with less cultural and economic capital. Because he is writing about a nowhere—and perhaps because he is a well-off white man unable to appreciate fully his own privilege—Carey is able to imagine that anyone anywhere could get the same experience he did.

This is of course not true on several counts. There is first of all the issue of access: many parts of the world, including parts of the United States, still lack reliable internet service. Moreover, people who enroll in MOOCs, or any online course, are not floating in a digital nowhere: they are interacting in and across physical and virtual spaces. Because *all* learning is situated learning, where and how and with whom people learn is always critical. The online learner remains a physical being occupying a physical space. Is she housed? Is she fed? Is she well? Does she have a safe and comfortable workspace? Who else is around, and do they help or hinder her learning? Can she rely on her computer? Or can she get to a library to use one? (Are the machines working today?) Does she need to run an errand? Bring her kid to the doctor? And on and on.

The online learner is simultaneously occupying a digital space. Is the platform designed to be accessible to her, even if she has a disability? Can she understand how to navigate it, even if she is unfamiliar with online learning technologies? Does it require ways of interacting with others that make sense to her? Who else works in this digital space, and do they help or hinder her learning? Is she the kind of learner who will take the initiative to log on when she needs to, manage her own time, and keep herself on track—all without the encouragement and support of a teacher and peers she knows personally? Does she have adequate technical support if she needs it, and does she know how to access it? And on and on.

The point is that Carey writes as if his supposedly disembodied experience can be universalized, when in fact online learning is an embodied experience in which learners must navigate physical and virtual spaces. Dewey's principles of continuity and interaction apply to both kinds of learning context. As learners move in and across these contexts, it's critical to account for the affordances and limitations of both. As with experiential learning, place matters *doubly* in online learning.

Unbundlers fail to account for another reality as well: online learning is not for everyone, certainly not all the time. (Surely this partially explains the astonishingly low completion rates of MOOCs.)[12] Different learners learn differently. Moreover, individuals learn different things in different ways, so even those who do take to online learning may also need and want on-ground learning. In the years ahead, some learners will choose wholly face-to-face higher education experiences and others will choose wholly online experiences, but the most successful purveyors of higher education will be those that seamlessly integrate the physical and the digital. They will offer a variety of modalities—face-to-face, online, and hybrid—and assist their students in integrating knowledge and skills across their diverse on-ground and online learning experiences.

While online education will continue to play an important, and likely increasing, role in higher education in the years ahead, we should not imagine that the day will come when online learning fully replaces face-to-face learning in physical spaces. Indeed, there is a certain irony in the unbundlers' argument that digital technologies render physical spaces for learning moot, given that the tech companies that have been most instrumental in developing those technologies, such as Google, have built extensive campuses. The Mountain View Googleplex alone consists of more than three million square feet of space for work and—famously—for recreation and wellness. The company works closely with architects to design spaces that promote meaningful interaction, leading one California newspaper to muse that Google is as interested in remaking physical landscapes as it is in remaking digital ones.[13] It has also developed a set of Google for Startups campuses around the world—including in London, Madrid, São Paulo, Seoul, Tel Aviv, and Warsaw—where entrepreneurs can gather in meeting rooms and class-rooms to generate ideas for start-ups, engage in mentoring, code, meet with potential investors, and the like.[14] In 2017, Apple unveiled Apple Park, a nearly three-million-square-foot circular architectural marvel in Cupertino. Apple's chief design officer, Jony Ive, insists that the technical achievement is not the point; the achievement, he says, "is to make a building where so many people can connect and collaborate and walk and talk."[15] Even IBM, which led the "telecommuting revolution," has begun bringing thousands of its employees back into workspaces. These tech companies have come to understand the "power of presence" and the fact that some work is best accomplished when individuals and teams gather and interact in a physical place.[16]

College and university classrooms and campuses are particular kinds of physical places. They are places where disciplinary and pedagogical experts, staff, and students gather to pursue, share, and advance knowledge both for the sake of the individuals assembled and for the broader public good. They are places where theories are formulated, discoveries are made, products are developed, and ideas are hatched. Places where students learn how to learn, how to become experts, and how to become informed and curious non-experts. Places where young people are socialized into adult life and people of all ages are provided opportunities for intellectual, emotional, and social growth. Places where people learn to live and work with those whose perspectives and experiences differ from theirs. They are special places, and they are worth preserving and enhancing.

There is certainly a conversation to be had about *how much* time college students should be expected to spend in classrooms and on campuses. As I discuss in chapter 6, there is nothing magical about 3 credit hours per course, fifteen weeks per semester, or 120 credit hours for graduation. We need to experiment in particular with course lengths. Shorter-term, pop-up courses can allow faculty and students to address quickly unfolding events. Longer-term seminars can offer more sustained engagement with complex, slower-moving issues and phenomena. If there are better ways to organize learning while still ensuring academic quality and integrity, colleges and universities should explore them. But the question they should keep front and center is, "How can we organize time and space in ways that promote deep, meaningful, and integrative learning experiences?"

If all that faculty are doing in classrooms is offering canned lectures that could just as easily be watched in video form, then the time and space *are* being wasted. If the goal is merely content delivery, then by all means, package it and deliver it over a network. Carey might even be right in this case that a taped lecture is superior to a live one. But this is far from the only, or even the predominant, mode of interaction in today's college classrooms. On any day on any campus, students are engaged in discussions, debates, simulations, group projects, labs, peer teaching, peer review of each other's writing, and much more.

There is also something to be said for the much maligned and hopelessly unfashionable live lecture. We know too much about the importance of active learning for long-term retention and use of knowledge to think that traditional lectures should ever be the sole or even the predominant pedagogical strategy in any course,[17] but we should not deny that an effective lecture can be intimate, interactive, and even inspiring in a way that a recording never can be. Skilled lecturers don't merely deliver content; they perform. That performance is a shared experience between the lecturer and students, irreducible to mechanical or digital reproduction. A good lecture provides information, but it also models a way of understanding, a way of thinking, a way of building an argument. Effective lecturers can read the room, responding to learners' enthusiasm, confusion, or resistance. They can pause to take questions, test students' developing understandings, or garner reactions. They can use the physical space of the room to project their voices, walk up and down the aisles, display a video on a screen, use props, or just let a moment breathe. I am not a particularly good lecturer, and I rarely lecture in my own classes, but as a classroom observer, I have witnessed dozens of performances like this. I have seen students light up with new understanding. I have seen them literally flinch at the revelation of hard truths. I have seen them nearly jump out of their seats to respond to something they didn't even know they cared about.

No matter how powerful an individual learning experience might be, however, what ultimately matters is that learners are able to integrate learning across contexts. Mixing and matching isolated experiences from unbundled providers will lead to fragmented, discontinuous learning. So will simply adding internships, study abroad, service-learning experiences, and online courses to a traditional undergraduate experience. Mobility across physical and digital spaces is not enough.

On the other hand, an integrated college or university can function as a sort of learning home base to which students continually return to work with mentors and peers as they craft their learning journeys. Or, perhaps better, we can think of a college or university as a central node in a student's learning network—one that helps them identify, navigate, and connect the other nodes. It can be a place where they plan, reflect on, evaluate, and adjust their learning network and pathways. A place of interaction, continuity, integration.

Integrating Institutions for Integrative Learning across Contexts

Learning *does* happen everywhere, and it's to the good that today's college student is presented with a wide range of learning opportunities beyond courses on campus: internships, service-learning programs, study abroad, lab- or community-based research, online courses, and much more. But the point of higher education is not to collect opportunities; it's to select, reflect on, and connect learning experiences, weaving them into a coherent learning journey. Making a variety of learning experiences available to students is only the beginning; the real task is to integrate these institutional components to promote integrative learning.

Fortunately, colleges and universities of various kinds are engaged in just this sort of integration. As one might expect, given their public mission, many community colleges are national leaders in experiential education. The best among them embed experiential learning within the academic program, allowing students to integrate their knowledge and skills across learning contexts. For instance, Guttman Community College, a part of the City University of New York system, is a "model of high-impact, evidence based experiential education supported by campus-wide infrastructure" (City University of New York 2016, 13).[18] All Guttman students begin with a summer bridge program that features several "field experiences" to explore New York City as well as a group research project and presentation focused on the city's neighborhoods.[19] Throughout their time at Guttman, students remain connected to the communities and industries of the city through a variety of initiatives, including a first-year experience focused on thinking critically about the city and "community days" in which students, staff, and faculty engage in a wide range of civic engagement activities. Various offices and programs on campus lend support to the college's experiential learning model, including the Office of Partnerships and Community Engagement, and Global Guttman, which oversees study abroad and campus-based global learning opportunities. No matter their major— Guttman offers programs in business administration, human services, information technology, liberal arts and sciences, and urban studies— students are urged to use the city as a learning laboratory that extends and enhances the classroom experience.[20]

Like Guttman, Hendrix College, a small liberal arts college in Arkansas, has embedded experiential learning—which it calls "engaged learning"—into its academic program. Its signature program is called Odyssey, which requires students to complete a minimum of three experiential projects in areas such as artistic creativity, global awareness, professional and leadership development, service to the world, and undergraduate research. Students complete projects through preapproved courses or cocurricular activities or by designing their own projects under the guidance of a faculty member or administrator. The preapproved courses come from across the disciplines and generally involve a service-learning or community-based research component. Cocurricular opportunities include theatrical productions, study abroad, service-learning trips, internships, peer tutoring, mock trials, and more. Examples of student-initiated projects include restoring an antique ceramics kiln, completing a medical internship in Zanzibar, studying racial tension at World Cup soccer matches, and working on an organic farm in Ireland.[21] The college has built a robust infrastructure for the Odyssey program. Funding is available to students; awards are given annually; forums have been created for sharing projects; Odyssey professorships provide faculty with the time required to work intensively with students on their projects; an extensive guide has been generated; and so on. According to two faculty members teaching in the program, the current focus is on "weav[ing] the Odyssey ethos even more snugly into both co-curricular and curricular programs" and helping students make more intentional links between their classroom learning and learning in other contexts (Fleming and Schantz 2010, 80).

Institutions are also experimenting with integrating online and face-to-face learning. Hybrid and blended courses are increasingly popular. For instance, we are beginning to see the use of MOOCs to supplement in-class learning. Whereas Kevin Carey saw his MOOC experience as substitutable for an on-ground course, Masato Kajimoto, a professor of journalism and media studies at the University of Hong Kong, sees his MOOC, Making Sense of the News, as part of his on-ground courses on campus. He uses lectures he recorded for the MOOC to flip the on-campus course, allowing his students to get the content outside of class and to use class time for active learning. Kajimoto also crafts lectures for his in-class performance, using local, timely examples. He reports that this format leads to "better activities, engagement, and quality of discussion," and students' end-of-course evaluations corroborate his view that it supports their learning.[22] There are signs that this kind of integration of MOOCs and on-campus learning may become a bigger part of the higher education landscape. As I discuss in chapter 6, for instance, MIT and other universities are developing "micro master's" degree programs in which students complete MOOCs and then apply that credential to a traditional master's degree on campus. Here, MOOCs are refashioned from one-off learning opportunities to part of a holistic learning experience that asks students to integrate their learning across digital and physical contexts.

One final example operates at the nexus of experiential, digital, and integrative learning. My institution, Northeastern University, is developing a next-generation experiential learning approach called self-authored integrated learning. SAIL is a conceptual framework and digital platform for choosing, creating, reflecting on, visualizing, and above all integrating learning experiences, wherever they occur, across contexts and over time.[23] Students are encouraged to view *all* of their experiences—courses, research projects, co-ops, clubs and organizations, service opportunities, workshops, athletic participation, and so on—as opportunities to learn. Anyone in the Northeastern ecosystem, including students, can add a learning opportunity and map it to the SAIL framework. Students document learning "moments" and are guided by the SAIL framework to mine their experiences for meaning and to see connections between them that they might not have otherwise. The framework includes five dimensions—intellectual agility, global mindset, civic consciousness and commitment, professional and personal effectiveness, and well-being—each of which is associated with a set of skills (e.g., computational thinking, information literacy, systems thinking, civic-mindedness, inclusivity/inclusive action). The digital platform allows students to generate an at-a-glance data visualization of all their experiences as well as a timeline. SAIL's visualization and goal-setting tools help students assess where they are as learners and where they want to take their learning next. Students can also connect with their advisors and with other learners in the system to share reflections on learning experiences, receive or offer recommendations, and the like. The most important aspect of SAIL, however, is not the app; it's the way in which it mobilizes the entire university—students, faculty, staff, and administrators—to be explicit and intentional about learning in an effort to help students craft their own learning journeys.

Each of these institutional examples moves beyond merely adding an experiential opportunity or online course and instead shapes learning environments in which students are encouraged to integrate learning across a range of physical and digital contexts. When they transcend the additive approach to developing learning opportunities and commit to integration, colleges and universities offer models of interaction and continuity—Dewey's two criteria for educative experiences—that no unbundled provider could hope to furnish. They need to seize this strategic advantage.

What Institutions Can Do

As the examples in the previous section suggest, colleges and universities seeking to facilitate integrative learning across courses and other learning contexts will need to design new physical and digital infrastructures. Embedding experiential and digital learning into traditional academic programs disrupts academic business as usual. Building links among the curriculum, cocurriculum, and extracurriculum fundamentally changes the nature of each. People who had operated independently in their own spheres of activity now must work together to design courses, programs, and learning ecosystems that promote these connections. As we have learned at Northeastern, the success of SAIL rests not so much on developing a killer app as it does on developing new structures and cultures that promote integrative teaching and learning.

Specific actions that institutions can take to promote the integration of classroom learning and learning in other contexts include the following:

- *Thoughtfully design physical and digital spaces to promote integrative teaching and learning.* I have described campuses as special places devoted to advancing learning, but many are poorly designed for this purpose. They are a collection of buildings, consisting mainly of offices and traditional classrooms, complete with chalkboards or whiteboards at the front of the room and rows of student desks. Spaces shape interactions, and these classroom spaces are designed to promote one-way communications. Campuses that promote active, integrative learning are designed as cohesive ecosystems consisting of flexible, multi-use spaces that promote various modes of interaction and continuity. Some traditional classrooms may remain, but such campuses also have open spaces, digital commons, studios, maker spaces—a panoply of formal and informal living and learning options that facilitate many modes of human engagement and are thus inclusive of and accessible to many kinds of learners. The same is true of institutionally sponsored digital spaces. Some learning management systems and online course templates are little more than digital reproductions of traditional physical classrooms. That's because they are designed around the same assumptions about who does what in the pedagogical relationship. Digital spaces, no less than physical spaces, must be designed for interaction and continuity.

- *Cultivate reciprocal relationships with community and employer partners.* In addition to not necessarily promoting integrative learning, simply sending students out into the community or to workplace settings is ethically suspect. Students who descend on a community without an understanding of its history or its contemporary challenges and dynamics, or who are dropped into a nonprofit organization full of missionary zeal, can do more harm than good. From the other direction, employers can easily take advantage of cheap or free labor without contributing to students' educational experiences. These are just a couple of the many land mines strewn across the landscape of these partnerships. Care must be taken to avoid patronizing or exploitive relationships. Colleges and universities must cultivate partners who understand their teaching and learning mission and must work with them to develop the learning experiences, match students to those experiences, set expectations, evaluate student performance, help students deepen prior learning and make current learning available for future use, and much more. Often a centralized office—perhaps an Office of Service Learning or a Center for Community Engagement—can take the lead, but infrastructural support will be needed from both the academic affairs and student services arms of the institution. No matter how an institution pursues these partnerships, the key questions for all parties to ask are, "How will this experience contribute to students' academic, professional, civic, and personal growth?" and "How will students make positive contributions to the organization or agency and to the broader community?"[24]

- *Provide professional development opportunities for faculty and staff to learn about integrative experiential learning.* Most faculty are not accustomed to making space in their courses for students to integrate their learning with learning they have done elsewhere or to working extensively with students outside the classroom. They can learn how to do so in workshops, inquiry groups, seminars, fellows programs, and the like—perhaps coordinated by a teaching and learning center staffed by experts in integrative experiential learning. And don't forget staff, who typically aren't accustomed to thinking of themselves as educators. As I have discussed, culture shifts require mindset shifts as well as new sets of skills. If everyone on a campus—from the dining hall workers to the campus police to the administrative staff in the Physics Department— plays a role in educating students, then those employees will need to learn how they can promote students' integrative learning. Opportunities to do so can be provided through workshops or town hall sharing sessions or through mentoring by senior staff members.

- *Offer recognition and rewards for integrative learning.* Integrating classroom learning with learning in other contexts does not come naturally or easily to most students. Providing forums for students to be recognized for this work—whether it's a showcase, an awards ceremony, or peer-to-peer workshops—can help model and motivate integrative learning. Guttman holds a Global Learning Summit, at which students share and are recognized for their global learning experiences.[25] At Northeastern, we host well-attended student poster sessions and run an annual Coolest Co-op contest. Hendrix College offers awards for Odyssey projects.

- *Create an adequate and appropriate technological infrastructure.* Students engaged in integrative learning across classroom and other contexts will need to be able to locate potential learning experiences on and beyond the campus. An electronic database, at a minimum, is necessary. In most cases, institutions will want to incorporate communities and communications features in their platforms to facilitate interactions with partners. As the institutional examples above demonstrate, tracking and visualizing or displaying student learning also may involve other digital platforms, such as learning dashboards, electronic portfolios, or digital coaches. The key, as always, is to make sure the technology aligns with and facilitates the kinds of intellectual work and interactions desired.

What Faculty Can Do

While some faculty might see the "learning happens everywhere" mantra as a threat, it's really an opportunity. Students enhance and amplify their classroom learning when they integrate it with learning in other contexts. As this chapter's opening example of Elizabeth shows, integrative learning allows students to arrive at their own understandings, making learning their own.

Faculty can work both inside their classrooms and beyond them to promote integration across classrooms and other learning contexts. When designing classroom activities and assignments, it may be helpful for faculty to keep Dewey's two experiential criteria in mind and ask themselves:

- Is this classroom experience designed to assist students in connecting and synthesizing what they are learning here with what they have learned, are learning, or might learn in contexts outside the classroom? (continuity)

- Is this classroom experience designed to engage students in meaningful ways with the immediate physical and/or digital environment? (interaction)

Asking these questions can help faculty design classroom experiences that alert students to possible connections to other learning experiences and simultaneously to find the immediate experience meaningful and educative.

Faculty might also keep in mind the pedagogical strategies I discussed in chapter 2, slightly tweaked:

- Engage students in self-assessment and goal setting early in the semester.
- Prompt connection to other learning contexts during class discussions.
- Design formal and informal assignments that ask students to make explicit connections to what they are learning or have learned in other learning contexts.
- Help students understand the conditions of applicability of what they are learning.
- Offer students reflective activities that help them solidify knowledge and skills and make them available for future use.

Conditions of applicability take on particular significance here, though perhaps I should call them conditions of applicability *and transformation*. As I have suggested, learners do not simply carry learning, unchanged, from one context to another. Each context is unique, and because contexts shape learning, knowledge and skills must be reconstructed in each new learning context. If learners do not account for the shaping influence of learning contexts, whether physical or digital—if they take them as somehow "natural" or given—they risk developing passive habits of mind, taking experiences "just as they come," as Dewey put it.

To this end, faculty can prompt students to reflect on the affordances and constraints of the learning contexts in which they find themselves. How is the space designed, that is, how is it organized and laid out physically or digitally? What technologies and tools are available? What learning objects are present, and how are learners expected to interact with them? Who else is interacting in the space? What are the modes, norms, and rules of interaction between participants? When and how can learners enter and interact in the space? How does the space support certain kinds of learners/learning and hinder others? The key is not to hold out for a "perfect" learning context—no learning context will suit all learners equally well—but rather to be mindful of how the affordances and constraints of *any* learning context shape learning.

Faculty can also facilitate the integration of classroom learning and learning in other contexts by forming learning collaborations with partners in the institution. Colleges and universities are full of potential mentors for students: academic advisors, co-op or internship coordinators, debate team coaches, health professionals, study abroad advisors, service-learning coordinators, resident assistants and residential life leaders, career services specialists, student group leaders and faculty sponsors, athletic coaches—the list goes on and on. Faculty can reach out to these folks (or be open to their overtures) to explore ways that the knowledge and skills that students are learning in classes can be applied or transformed in other institutional contexts. In some cases, faculty might collaborate with these partners on a shared educational project or program. Who knows—maybe a conversation over coffee between a volleyball coach and a sociology professor teaching Gender and Society could lead to an academic study of Title IX issues on campus, which could eventually lead to a Sports and Society program involving multiple academic departments, the Title IX and other diversity professionals on campus, and the entire athletics program.

Of course, students also interact with and learn from people outside the institution, and those people are also potential partners. Faculty can reach out to or be open to invitations from external partners, including internship or co-op employers, leaders of nonprofits for which students volunteer, community organizers and leaders with whom students interact, or alumni looking to remain connected to the institution. Who knows—maybe a lunch meeting of a computer science professor and a start-up software company's CEO could lead to a joint effort to teach computer scientists "soft skills," which could eventually lead to a full-blown Cultural Agility in the Tech Sector program involving multiple companies, several departments on campus (including, for instance, communications), the Internships Office, and the Career Services Office.

The idea is to help students experience classroom learning not as an isolated phenomenon, but rather as part of a coherent whole: a higher education experience that is more than the sum of its parts.

Conclusion

We live in a world in which content, including educational content, is ubiquitous and easily accessible to most of us. Advances in information, communication, and educational technology allow us to deliver this content and interact around it virtually anywhere, anytime. Some colleges and universities view this state of affairs as a threat to their sustainability, but in fact it represents an enormous opportunity for them. Properly understood, the slogan "learning happens everywhere" is a declaration of unmet demand. As the 2016 elections clearly demonstrated, there is a lot of bad information out there and plenty of bad actors willing to exploit people's naïveté. The blooming, buzzing confusion of information overload only increases the need for what higher education teaches: how to frame smart questions, create and test hypotheses and solutions, gather and evaluate evidence, formulate logical conclusions and arguments, and much more.

But colleges and universities can no longer think of their campuses as the exclusive zones where this work happens. Campuses are special places, yes, but they exist as part of the "real world," not set off from it. The college and universities that will thrive in the years ahead will integrate their physical and digital infrastructures to offer the sorts of experiences that can only happen there (Dewey's principle of interaction). At the same time, they will design into those experiences opportunities for learners to connect and synthesize what they learn there with what they learn elsewhere (Dewey's principle of continuity). Each institution will do this differently, but do it they must. Integration is *the* value proposition of postsecondary institutions in the digital age.

CHAPTER 4

A LIFE AND A LIVING

Integrating Liberal Learning
and Professional Learning

■ Growing up in India as the son of two American entrepreneurs, Jackson Golden loved the Red Sox. He felt most connected to the United States when he was watching his beloved team on TV at 5:00 a.m. When the time came to apply to college, he set his sights on Boston.[1]

Jackson chose to study anthropology at Northeastern University. That major allowed him to hone his cross-cultural understanding while preparing to follow in his parents' footsteps and start his own business. He says, "Training in anthropology helped me leverage my unique position as a product of two cultures. My coursework and work experience at Northeastern equipped me with tools to build a business that creates cultural fluency and mobility through sport." While he values his coursework in business, particularly a class called Entrepreneurship, he cites three anthropology courses as particularly influential: Consumer Cultures; Global Markets and Local Cultures; and Sport, Culture, and Society. These courses helped Jackson to gain an understanding of the dynamic relationship between economics and culture in different global contexts—a connection he doesn't think he would have made "from a strictly business perspective"—and how economics and culture shape and are shaped by sports. These classes also connected him with faculty mentors, including anthropology professor Alan Klein who, Jackson says, "showed me that professors here aren't just speaking from an abstract space on the sidelines, but from the thick of it, actively involved in making a difference in the world."

These courses and mentors gave Jackson the conceptual foundation and the confidence to create his own co-op and, in the process, his own business: Grand Slam Baseball, a youth development organization that works with schools to promote baseball in India; hosts the New Delhi Little League; and organizes local, national, and international baseball tournaments.² He laid the groundwork for this new organization during his first co-op to India, and he built it into a thriving enterprise during a subsequent co-op, for which he hired two other co-op students.

Jackson graduated in 2015 and continues to run Grand Slam Baseball with a business partner. He describes himself as a proponent of "sports diplomacy," a term coined by Richard Verma, a former US ambassador to India. Jackson credits his study of anthropology with helping him achieve this goal: "Studying the role and importance of culture helped me recognize the unique niche for people like me who grew up between cultures. I want to continue cultivating cross-cultural spaces that give youth fluency and tools to navigate the currents of globalization to their benefit." ⌐

Stories like Jackson's are not as rare as they once were. It seems that everywhere one turns, one finds stories about liberal arts majors being hot commodities in business and particularly in the tech industry; about rich and successful people who have liberal arts degrees; about how liberal arts majors make as much money in the long run as—and sometimes more than—their STEM counterparts; and about high-profile businesspeople, such as Mark Cuban and Jonathan Rosenberg, predicting that the future of the workforce will belong to liberal arts majors.³ The titles of four books published in 2017 all echo this theme: *The Fuzzy and the Techie: Why the Liberal Arts Will Rule the Digital World*, *Sensemaking: The Power of the Humanities in the Age of the Algorithm*, *A Practical Education: Why Liberal Arts Majors Make Great Employees*, and *You Can Do Anything: The Surprising Power of a "Useless" Liberal Arts Education*.⁴ These are not, as one might expect, defenses offered up by beleaguered, possibly desperate liberal arts professors. These books were written by, respectively, a venture capitalist, a founder of a business strategy consulting firm, a professor of business who writes about Silicon Valley, and a contributing writer at *Forbes*.

As a humanities professor, I am grateful for the respite from derisive depictions of the liberal arts as the longest, most expensive route to becoming a burger flipper or barista. I am more than happy to take a break from claims that the humanities are experiencing a "crisis of massive proportions and grave global significance" (Nussbaum 2010, 1).[5] At the same time, I doubt we have seen the end of "the end of the liberal arts." Crisis discourse tends to be cyclical. Nor am I convinced that it's a good thing for the liberal arts that their value is being reduced to graduates' marketability or earning potential or attractiveness to Silicon Valley. One of the virtues of the liberal arts is that they *aren't* reducible to the skills associated with a particular profession: they teach knowledge, skills, dispositions, and habits of mind that are broadly applicable to an array of professional and life experiences.

While the crisis discourse is often overblown, there is no doubt that shrinking student enrollments in liberal arts majors represent a significant challenge for these disciplines.[6] Data from the National Center for Education Statistics show decreases in humanities majors such as language, literature, linguistics, philosophy, and religious studies, and increases, some of them significant, in majors such as computer and information sciences, engineering, and the health professions.[7] The recent spike in positive press for liberal arts degrees may go some way toward stanching these trends, but we will have to wait and see.

But as much as I would like to see more liberal arts majors, I don't believe that producing more of them is the answer to the world's problems. Moreover, this business of counting degrees in order to tabulate wins and losses for the liberal arts is counterproductive. It leaves in place, indeed reinforces, a set of pernicious dichotomies: "fuzzies" vs. "techies," liberal arts vs. STEM, liberal education vs. professional education, soft skills vs. hard skills, and learning for learning's sake vs. practical learning. These dichotomies reinforce and are in turn reinforced by strict institutional divisions in colleges and universities. I am not talking here about disciplinary distinctions, which are not themselves insidious; we *want* specialists who know more about their subjects and how to study them than others do and who are certified by their peers as experts in their areas. The problem arises when we sort those disciplines into mutually exclusive, often competing categories. In most institutions large enough to have divisions or colleges, for instance, liberal arts disciplines and faculties are cordoned off from STEM and professional faculties not only structurally, but also culturally. The tacit—and sometimes explicit—notion is that some of these disciplines teach students how to get a job while others teach them how to be better, more refined, more well-rounded people.

Unbundlers and others exploit these dichotomies to argue that liberal education is a luxury we can no longer afford. Recall Monica Herk's (2015) argument, introduced in chapter 2, that while "the liberal arts aspects of postsecondary education" are not "unimportant or lacking in value," it is "unfair and inefficient to require middle-income and poorer families to go into debt to purchase a 2- or 4-year degree consisting of many classes that are largely irrelevant to their goal of obtaining a job."[8] Kevin Carey (2015, 35) goes a step further, framing the liberal arts as a relic of a bygone era: "The idealized vision of a learned and engaged professor teaching a specialized humanities course to a small group of attentive students is largely a mirage."[9]

Even some liberal education defenders argue that the "economics of scarcity" require that we find "creative options [for] organizing, planning and packaging" liberal education and sending it out over the web (Jansson 2010).[10] This formulation comes from Eric Jansson, the labs director at the National Institute for Technology in Liberal Education.[11] While Jansson (2010) might properly be called a *re*bundler, his enthusiastic review of a 2009 meeting called "Hacking Education," sponsored by a venture capital firm, makes it clear that he joins unbundlers in the conviction that "whatever 'liberal education' is, 'it' can travel over a network." For Jansson, liberal education is susceptible to unbundling and amenable to rebundling because it's an information product that is becoming less scarce as "engaging faculty lectures (with course materials)" become more widely available from online for-profit and nonprofit providers.

Jansson (2010) argues that the future of liberal education lies in packaging and distributing this "style of education" via video conferencing, social media, and gaming. While these technologies—and others that have emerged in the decade since the "Hacking Education" meeting—clearly have a role to play in liberal education, the problem with Jansson's notion is that liberal education is conceived as a thing apart, separate from professional education. This perspective plays into the hands of those who say that liberal education is nice to have, but it's not really necessary and possibly a waste of time.

If we want the liberal arts disciplines to remain viable into the future, focusing exclusively on graduating more liberal arts majors is a mistake. The key to the survival of these disciplines is partnerships with STEM and professional disciplines in order to develop integrative education models in which liberal learning is understood to be integral to higher education and is intertwined with professional education to form a coherent whole.

Indeed, this integration is key to the continued viability of the entire higher education enterprise. Without liberal education, Michael S. Roth (2015, 18) writes, a college education produces people "who are trained for yesterday's problems and yesterday's jobs, [people] who have not reflected on their own lives in ways that allow them to tap into their capacities for innovation and for making meaning out of their experience."[12] Because liberal education "increases our capacity to understand the world, contribute to it, and reshape ourselves" (Roth 2015, 195), it is not supplemental to professional education, but integral to it.

The moral of Jackson Golden's story (featured in the opening of this chapter) is not that liberal arts graduates can be professionally successful. We know that. And in any event, do we really believe that he would have been a failure had he decided on a business major and an anthropology minor rather than the other way around? Jackson's success relies on his ability to integrate liberal learning and professional learning. Under the mentorship of faculty experts, he studied culture and society in order to develop the critical and creative capacities necessary to understand the world and to create a meaningful place for himself in it. At the same time, through study and experience, he gained professional knowledge and skills in business. Importantly, these endeavors intersected and mutually reinforced each other: Jackson studied entrepreneurism through the humanistic and social scientific lenses of anthropology, and he studied culture and society through the lens of entrepreneurism and business activity. In the end, this integration allowed Jackson to make a good living while making a good life.

Integrating institutions to promote the integration of liberal learning and professional learning will require colleges and universities to wrestle with and overcome the pernicious dichotomies that pervade higher education discourse and are instantiated in strict institutional boundaries. Before considering what doing so might look like, we must first confront those dichotomies.

STEM and the Liberal Arts

In 2005, the National Academy of Sciences, the National Academy of Engineering, and the Institute of Medicine were asked by a bipartisan group of members of Congress to produce a report recommending priorities and action steps to enhance science and engineering in the United States. The result was *Rising above the Gathering Storm: Energizing and Employing America for a Brighter Economic Future,* a vigorous, nearly 600-page case for increased federal support for science and technology.[13] Citing the prospect of the United States falling behind in global economic competition, the report sounded the alarm on the future of the country's economic prosperity and national security if it did not make major investments in STEM research and education. The report's four broad recommendations were to increase the talent pool of K–12 science and mathematics educators; to bolster federal support for long-term basic research; to recruit and retain "the best and the brightest" scientists and engineers; and to incentivize innovation. Each recommendation was accompanied by action steps, most of which would require huge investments (for instance, hiring 10,000 science and math teachers and training another 250,000 current teachers—annually). Prioritizing "world-class science and engineering," according to the report, was critical "not simply as an end in itself but as the principal means of creating new jobs for our citizenry as a whole as it seeks to prosper in the global marketplace of the 21st century" (Committee on Prospering in the Global Economy of the 21st Century 2007, 40). While the report cited other public goods, including homeland security, public health, and caring for the environment, these were framed as consequences of economic prosperity. Conspicuously missing among these public goods was democracy, a word that did not appear in the report.

Rising above the Gathering Storm informed debates in Congress, helped shape the policies of both the George W. Bush and Barack Obama administrations, and was instrumental in the passage of the America COMPETES Act of 2007 and its reauthorization in 2010.[14] Many of the report's recommendations have been adopted by policy or passed into law, leading numerous colleges and universities to prioritize STEM education on their campuses.

Six years after the release of *Rising*, the American Academy of Arts and Sciences published *The Heart of the Matter: The Humanities and Social Sciences for a Vibrant, Competitive, and Secure Nation*.[15] Like *Rising*, this report was prepared at the request of a bipartisan congressional group, this time regarding actions that might be taken to "maintain national excellence in humanities and social scientific scholarship and education, and to achieve long-term, national goals for our intellectual and economic well-being; for a stronger, more vibrant civil society; and for the success of cultural diplomacy in the 21st century" (Commission on the Humanities and Social Sciences 2013, 6). The authors positioned this comparatively slender report as a companion to *Rising*, but its tone was markedly different from that of its predecessor. Whereas *Rising* was Hobbesian strident, seeking to stoke fear of competitive failure, *Heart* was Jeffersonian high-minded, invoking our better angels: "as we strive to create a more civil public discourse, a more adaptable and creative workforce, and a more secure nation, the humanities and social sciences are the heart of the matter, the keeper of the republic—a source of national memory and civic vigor, cultural understanding and communication, individual fulfillment and the ideals we hold in common" (9). The goals articulated in the report were comparatively broad: to "educate Americans in the knowledge, skills, and understanding they will need to thrive in a twenty-first-century democracy"; to "foster a society that is innovative, competitive, and strong"; and to "equip the nation for leadership in an interconnected world" (10–12). Insisting that the humanities were "not merely elective, nor are they elite or elitist" (13), the report made a case that the liberal arts were critical to national well-being, competitiveness, and security. The authors offered a number of specific recommendations, including creating a Humanities Teacher Corps to complement a proposed STEM Master Teacher Corps and passing a National Competitiveness Act that would provide funding for the study of international affairs, study abroad programs, and "endangered disciplines" (12). But their ultimate aim was to exhort "parents, teachers, scholars, the media, and the public at-large to join a cohesive and constructive national discussion of these issues" (6). In promoting the values of democracy, the report offered itself as a tool for democratic engagement.

Like *Rising*, *Heart* has been taken up by organizations, agencies, and higher education institutions across the country. Its ideas have shaped conferences, summits, symposia, workshops, humanities festivals, and other events on campuses and in communities; inspired op-eds, blogs, and lectures; informed colleges' and universities' strategic planning processes; and more. The report has served as a basis for discussions across the country and, to some extent, across the world about the value and purpose of the humanities and social sciences. It also inspired a 2014 bill in the US Congress to expand a STEM-focused master teacher program and a request from Congress for a new study of the nation's language education needs. *Heart* has not spurred the same intensity of legislative action as *Rising* has, but it has clearly fulfilled its goal of promoting public discussion.[16]

Together, *Rising* and *Heart* lay out compelling visions of US higher education for the twenty-first century. However, it's important not to treat these reports as salvos from rival camps promoting separate agendas.[17] The liberal arts and STEM should not be conceived as opposing forces, but rather as complementary ones. After all, disciplines associated with both of these formulations find their roots in the classical quadrivium and trivium. The trivium, comprising grammar, logic, and rhetoric, was the basis of classical study, followed by the quadrivium of arithmetic, geometry, music, and astronomy, which in turn led to the study of philosophy and theology. These disciplines were viewed as part of an integrated whole, what some today call the "liberal arts and sciences," and were distinguished from the "practical arts" associated with particular professions, such as medicine.

Fortunately, some emerging frameworks and models refuse sharp distinctions between STEM and the liberal arts. STEAM, for instance, seeks to infuse the arts into STEM education.[18] STIRS (scientific thinking and integrative reasoning skills) is an interdisciplinary, evidence-based framework for undergraduate education championed by the AAC&U, a liberal education association.[19] STS (science, technology, and society) investigates how social, political, and cultural frameworks, perspectives, and methods can help us understand science and technology, as well as how science and technology shape understandings of society, politics, and culture. A variety of fields of study are taking shape at the nexus of STEM and liberal arts disciplines, including the medical humanities or health humanities, the digital humanities, and the computational social sciences.

While some cynics interpret the development of these fields as desperate attempts to make the liberal arts "relevant," these efforts represent a growing understanding that effectively addressing complex challenges, such as resilience, climate change, or cyberterrorism, will require scientific, technological, social scientific, and humanistic perspectives, frameworks, and methods. For instance, urban resilience is both a technical and a human problem. It calls for engineering solutions, such as disaster-resistant infrastructure and barriers to coastal erosion—and also strong communities and sound policies. That's why the Rockefeller Foundation's 100 Resilient Cities (RC) initiative is not just a science and engineering effort, but also emphasizes "civic resilience," or the ability of communities to ensure the well-being of all their people through strengthening inclusive practices, protecting and advancing cultural identities and values, improving communication and access to information among residents, encouraging civic participation, developing more effective governance structures and leaders, and advancing gender and racial equity and justice.[20] The RC recognizes that disasters come in many forms, from earthquakes, fires, and floods to poverty, violence, and political and cultural disenfranchisement. It acknowledges that to address these disasters effectively, we will need to combine scientific and technological thinking with humanistic and social scientific thinking.

As challenges like resilience make clear, it's neither accurate nor helpful to think of STEM as promoting economic prosperity and the liberal arts as promoting democracy. Because scientific, technological, social, and cultural forces and phenomena are bound up in each other, both STEM and the liberal arts have roles to play in promoting individual and community well-being. It's time to get past the unhelpful dichotomies that shape the way we talk about STEM and the liberal arts:

STEM	Liberal Arts
Promotes economic prosperity	Promotes democracy
Narrow, vocational	Broad, general
Makes better employees	Makes better people
Practical, applied	Learning for learning's sake
"Hard" skills (measurable, objective)	"Soft" skills (ineffable, subjective)

These common associations clearly put the liberal arts at a disadvantage: they come off as fuzzy. Vague. Kind of self-indulgent. And yes, "elite and elitist," to invoke *Heart*'s defensive formulation. But STEM disciplines are likewise hamstrung by these associations: they come off as mere job training, uninterested in, say, the human impact and ethical implications of their solutions or in students' holistic well-being or in the common good beyond the strictly economic.

The books I mentioned at the beginning of this chapter, the ones about the professional value of the liberal arts, helpfully undermine any notion of the liberal arts as impractical, ineffable, or soft. But if these books are received as only the latest volley in the STEM vs. liberal arts debate, as merely a brief for liberal arts degrees over STEM degrees, we will have lost an important opportunity to reframe the debate. This is in fact the point of venture capitalist Scott Hartley's (in my view, unfortunately titled) *The Fuzzy and the Techie* (2017). "This book," he writes, "seeks to highlight that the debate has turned on a faux opposition between STEM education and the liberal arts. Indeed, as we evolve our technology to make it ever more accessible and democratic, and as it becomes ever more ubiquitous, the timeless questions of the liberal arts, and their insights into human needs and desires, have become essential requirements in the development of our technological instruments" (Hartley 2017, x).

The time has come to stop pitting STEM and the liberal arts against each other and to start thinking in more complex ways about how all of these disciplines contribute to the kind of holistic education *every* student will need to navigate the demands of our complex world.

Liberal Learning and Professional Learning

Instead of framing this discussion in terms of disciplines, then, we should be talking about learning. We should be talking about how all students need both liberal learning and professional learning—as well as opportunities to integrate them. This formulation does not hinge on disciplines: STEM disciplines can and do contribute to liberal learning, and liberal arts disciplines can and do contribute to professional learning. The student who wants to start her own business might take an English course to sharpen her professional communication skills while the student who is planning a career in the performing arts might take an environmental science course because he has a personal commitment to sustainability.

Let's be clear about these terms. "Liberal" learning does not refer to a partisan political perspective but rather—invoking the word's etymological root (the Latin *liberalis* means "free")—pertains to freedom, tending toward freedom. Liberal learning means freedom of thought, freedom from narrow thinking, parochialism, and bigotry. It entails learning how to be free: to exercise one's independent faculties, think for oneself, and arrive at one's own considered judgments. It's not freedom from tradition, history, or others' judgments, but rather from slavish, unthinking adherence to them. That's why critique is central to liberal learning: it's a means of interrogating claims, their stakes, their consequences, whose interests they serve, and whose they don't. Liberal education engages students in the study of culture and society to help them better understand the world and their possible place(s) in it. So while it resists crude instrumentalism and narrow skills training, it's far from impractical "learning for learning's sake." Liberal education teaches students a range of critical and creative capacities, including contextualizing phenomena, artifacts, and processes within social, cultural, and historical contexts; conducting ethical reasoning; engaging in narrative, imaginative, and speculative thinking; reading, writing, listening, and speaking with confidence, competence, and compassion; and conducting cross-cultural inquiry and analysis.[21] These capacities are central to the study of the humanities and social sciences, but it's also possible—some would argue vital—to teach them in STEM courses and curricula.

Professional learning engages students in developing the knowledge, skills, values, ways of thinking, and behaviors associated with particular occupations: business, education, engineering, nursing, law, computer programming, and so on. This can be accomplished through direct study of those occupations, through applying and transforming prior knowledge and existing skills in professional settings, or through a combination of these. Because professions don't exist in vacuums and because they involve human *and* technological knowledge and skills, both the liberal arts and STEM disciplines contribute to professional learning.

Liberal learning and professional learning should not be opposed to one another; ideally, they are mutually reinforcing. Professions after all exist within societal and cultural milieus and provide contexts for students to bring their liberal learning to bear. Conversely, professional concepts, practices, and the like can be contextualized by the study of society and culture. Professional learning that is *not* informed by liberal learning, particularly the critical perspectives it provides, risks becoming mere skills training. This is a peril John Dewey (1923, 196) recognized nearly a century ago, when he noted that a "school of law, medicine, engineering or theology that teaches only enough science to be a directly practical tool and teaches it only as a subordinate tool or device for material success, and not for the sake of insight into its principles, will not be favorable to culture."[22] He urged all of his colleagues, including his "friends in the professional schools," to work together to produce students who would unite the "purpose and skills of the professional with the breadth and freedom of thought" of the liberally educated (198).

Today, this task seems even more crucial. "As the boundaries between technology and the humanities dissolve," writes Northeastern University president Joseph E. Aoun (2017, 60), "even the engineer needs to consider human interfaces, and even the programmer must learn to be a storyteller. . . . The extension of technology into every aspect of life has very human ramifications that we have to address through politics, economics, law, philosophy, and especially ethics—subjects that must evolve with the growth of AI."[23] All responsible professionals must understand how their work is shaped by and in turn shapes social and cultural forces, and they must be attuned to the political and ethical implications of their practices. As another college president, Amy Gutmann (2015, 16) of the University of Pennsylvania, puts it, "*all* lives and societies will be profoundly shaped by the actions, attitudes, ethos, and ethics of the professions of law, medicine, nursing, business, engineering, and education, as well as the technological and trade disciplines."[24]

Gutmann and Aoun both champion the integration of liberal and professional learning. Gutmann (2015) suggests that "by integrating the liberal arts with a deeper and broader understanding of the professions, universities would better prepare students for facing up to the challenges of their private, professional, and civic lives. Conversely, universities are letting their students and society down when they leave the complex connections between the liberal arts and professions to be made later in life—or not at all" (21). Aoun (2017) proposes an integrative educational model he calls "humanics." This term—a play on "robotics"—reflects the integration of the human and the technological. Aoun argues that in the age of artificial intelligence and automation, higher education must help its students become "robot-proof"—that is, they must learn to leverage capacities that only humans can master. His model includes three "new literacies": (1) technological literacy, which he defines as "knowledge of mathematics, coding, and basic engineering principles"; (2) data literacy, or "the capacity to understand and utilize Big Data through analysis"; and (3) human literacy, which "equips us for the social milieu, giving us the power to communicate, engage with others, and tap into our human capacity for grace and beauty" (55–59). This model applies to all students, no matter their majors, because it helps humans in any field of endeavor to work effectively with machines and not be replaced by them.

Truly integrative educational models like the ones Gutmann and Aoun envision disrupt academic business as usual. Throwing an internship on top of a traditional liberal arts program will not do it. Nor will adding a "soft skills" course or module to an engineering or computer science curriculum. Students need regular opportunities to connect and synthesize what they learn about society and culture with what they learn about professions.

Fortunately, many institutions are beginning to design these kinds of integrative learning opportunities for their students. In liberal arts colleges, for example, we are seeing the development of new educational models called the "practical liberal arts" or the "engaged liberal arts."[25] One particularly interesting example is Mount Holyoke College's "Lynk," a curriculum-to-career program designed to embed career preparation and exploration into every student's liberal arts and sciences education. As faculty members who were involved in the development and implementation of the Lynk have written, the leaders of the initiative "aimed for a cultural shift rather than a small tweak" (Townsley, Packard, and Paus 2015).[26] They imagined their educational model "as something that was not just an add-on that was delivered beyond the faculty—parallel to our regular curriculum—or in one specialized program serving a few students." The Lynk weaves career resources, including internships and community-based research opportunities, throughout the institution, connecting them to the curriculum and making them available to all students. As one might expect, this was a heavy institutional lift, and it encountered resistance, including faculty's fear of vocationalism. Making this change required a patient, comprehensive, institution-wide strategy and years of planning. The key, the authors report, was coordination among the various offices on campus and the faculty. Though they don't use the term, it's clear that institutional integration was required to promote integrative learning at Mount Holyoke.

Moving somewhat in the other direction, community colleges represent an enormous opportunity to integrate liberal learning into professional programs. In fact, community colleges are responsible for more liberal education than any other higher education sector, and they actually award more degrees in the humanities than in vocational/professional fields.[27] But they are primarily identified with vocational and professional learning, and they often segregate liberal and professional learning through what are essentially tracking mechanisms: the liberal arts are stressed for students intending to transfer to four-year institutions, and job training is emphasized for those entering or already in the workforce. Still, many community colleges are involved in exciting multi-institutional collaborations, such as the Student Learning for Civic Capacity initiative and the AAC&U's "roadmaps" project."[28] The challenge moving forward will be to integrate these liberal learning initiatives into professional programs.

One promising model for doing so is a Mellon-funded project at the Community College of Baltimore County (CCBC) designed to "contextualize" composition courses. This initiative uses writing courses to infuse humanities knowledge and skills into the college's curricular pathways: pre–allied health; technology, science, and mathematics; business, law, and criminal justice; arts and humanities; and behavioral and social sciences. (I take up the concept of "pathways" in chapter 6.) Attempting to dispel misconceptions that many students have about the limited relevance of the humanities, the courses begin with a unit called "Humanities and Their Relationship to Other Disciplines and Career Choices." Andrew Rusnak, an associate professor of English at CCBC and the executive director of the Community College Humanities Association, explains how this works in classes he teaches:

> It's really through the contextualized comp courses that I've found a good way to break down these false conceptions and lay the fundamentals of liberal learning and apply them to subjects they aren't applied to in STEM classes for instance. Even though the natural sciences are historically, classically considered part of the liberal arts, they are taught more like applied technology courses, where rote memory becomes the measure of knowledge. I try to convince students that memory is a great skill to have, but you need much more than that to survive as a nurse, an engineer, a chemist, etc. One needs those cognitive skills picked up through liberal approaches to education, critical analysis, creativity and imagination, strategic forecasting, calculated risk, etc. So, we take a liberal approach to technology, biology, chemistry in English comp classes and we discuss and write on the ethics of biotechnology/genetic engineering, nano-tech, and artificial intelligence. The key here I think is to infuse liberal approaches to subject matter that doesn't normally receive liberal approaches because of the siloed culture on the campuses of many CCs [community colleges] and four-years.[29]

It's too early to say what the results of CCBC's contextualized composition program will be, including whether it will shape the courses and pathways students take after their composition course. If it's not implemented carefully, it could amount to little more than adding new content to traditional writing courses—or worse, sacrificing what is often students' only experience of a humanities-based course to career prep. But done right, contextualized composition courses could begin to answer a question posed by another grant program, the Teagle Foundation's Liberal Arts and the Professions: "How can institutions fully integrate and embed the liberal arts into undergraduate preparation for the professions?"[30]

One example of a fully integrated institutional model comes from Olin College, a small engineering college. Founded in 1997, Olin was integrated from the beginning: it was designed around an experimental, "human-focused" approach to engineering. This approach teaches the principles and practices of engineering with attention to social contexts, with the goal of "making a positive difference in the world."[31] The curriculum at Olin consists of three broad, interconnected themes—design and entrepreneurship, modeling and analysis, and systems and control—each of which immerses students in engineering principles, engages them in learning off campus, and challenges them to collaborate with students in other majors. All students complete a concentration in the arts, the humanities and social sciences, or entrepreneurship. Each concentration comprises course sequences with capstones; they are designed to be integrative in their own right and to be integrated with a student's major. Beyond this, Olin offers interdisciplinary courses that "connect engineering, math, and science to arts, humanities, and entrepreneurship. For example, students discover and analyze the historical context of material science in Stuff of History and develop technical solutions in an anthropological context in Engineering for Humanity."[32] With a curriculum it describes as an "interdisciplinary, project-based approach emphasizing entrepreneurship, liberal arts, and rigorous science and engineering fundamentals,"[33] Olin integrates liberal and professional learning throughout students' undergraduate careers.

At Northeastern University, we are redesigning our educational model with inspiration from President Aoun's (2017) concept of humanics. The prototype for this model comes from the College of Social Sciences and Humanities (CSSH) under the leadership of its dean, Uta Poiger. The "experiential liberal arts" is both an educational model and an organizational philosophy through which the college integrates the three parts of its mission: education, research, and outreach.[34] It's designed around three additional integrations: the integration of experiential learning with rigorous classroom study of society, culture, politics, and ethics; the integration of liberal arts capacities (e.g., cross-cultural communication, ethical reasoning) with technological proficiencies (e.g., geocoding, text mining); and the integration of local engagement in Boston with global engagement (C. Gallagher and Poiger forthcoming).[35]

These integrations ensure that students and faculty constantly work with employers and community members in Boston and around the world to bring humanistic and social scientific perspectives, frameworks, and methods to bear on important questions. For many faculty and students, this means crossing disciplinary borders in their research, their teaching, and their learning. The CSSH faculty have collaborated with faculty in professional and STEM disciplines to design minors that integrate liberal learning and professional learning, including one in computational social sciences and another in digital methods, culture, and society. They have also designed combined majors with a range of disciplines, including computer science, which students may combine with criminal justice, economics, English, history, philosophy, political science, or sociology. These programs allow students to apply computational thinking and skills to humanistic and social scientific questions and problems—and to apply humanistic and social scientific methods, frameworks, and perspectives to the study of technology. Combined majors such as these are curricular instantiations of the integration of liberal and professional learning.

Different institutions, different models, same goal: to integrate in the service of integrating liberal learning and professional learning. These colleges and universities are breaking down traditional academic barriers—between classrooms and other learning contexts, between STEM and the liberal arts, between professional and liberal learning—because they recognize that the complex challenges of today's world require integrated, holistic education.

In most institutions, however, liberal learning continues to be considered the exclusive province of liberal arts departments and programs, cordoned off from professional education, which is thought to be the purview of STEM and professional disciplines. Many liberal arts professors prefer it this way, seeing any attention to professional learning as a reflection of the creeping vocationalism of the neoliberal university. At the same time, many faculty in professional schools see liberal education as outside of their sphere of concern—the vaguer subjects and softer skills for which the faculty on the other (usually shabbier) side of campus are responsible. Faculty in the STEM disciplines are often caught in between, some identifying with the liberal arts and sciences and others with particular professions (engineering, computer science). These divisions are both structural and cultural, so challenging them will require changes not only to the organization of the institution, but to the mindsets and behaviors of the people in it. It will mean swimming upstream against institutional history and tradition.

But that current is nothing compared to the permanent whitewater students face as our society and economy continue to churn. To thrive in such conditions, they need more than isolated job skills and more than isolated knowledge about culture and society. They need to develop professional knowledge and skills as part of an evolving understanding of themselves and the culture and society in which they live and work.

What Institutions Can Do

As a small, relatively young school, Olin College is nimbler and more integrative than most. At its inception in 1997, its leadership chose to eschew the traditional departmental structure. Faculty with PhDs teach their specialization, whether anthropology, history, mathematics, design, physics, art, biology, or computer science, but the curriculum is organized to support Olin's three degree programs: engineering (in which students design their own plan of study), mechanical engineering, and electrical and computer engineering. Faculty routinely collaborate across disciplinary lines as they engage students in the college's problem-based educational model.

Older, larger schools are beginning to experiment with integrative reorganization as well. Arizona State University, led by its president Michael Crow, offers one example. This university has undertaken a massive reorganization with the stated goals of combining excellence and access, ensuring meaningful social impact, and generating more interdisciplinary research and education.[36] One of its design principles is to "fuse academic disciplines."[37] Though ASU has retained some colleges and departments, the institution is experimenting with organizing its faculties by broad, interdisciplinary topics. For example, it has formed a School of Human Evolution and Social Change, a School of Social and Family Dynamics, a School for the Future of Innovation in Society, and a School of Earth and Space Exploration. Its "New American University" model, detailed by Crow and co-author William Dabars (2015), is controversial.[38] Defenders claim that it effectively addresses the most intractable problems plaguing higher education, including affordability and accessibility, without sacrificing academic excellence. Critics claim that it erodes disciplinary expertise and departmental authority, that it is too enamored of trendy topics, and that it amounts to little more than belt tightening in the wake of slashed public funding.[39] The jury remains out on this ambitious experiment, but one thing it clearly shows is that even a very large, complex university can move toward a more integrative design.

Whether or not institutions undertake a radical redesign, there are actions they can take to support the integration of liberal learning and professional learning:

- *Motivate and support faculty to work across liberal arts, STEM, and professional boundaries.* From informal workshops and meet-ups to more formal collaborations through research institutes and laboratories, forums can be created for faculty to work together across disciplines—and to involve students in that collaborative work. This transdisciplinary work is critical to integrating liberal and professional learning. Institutions should remove impediments and add incentives for the integration of faculty expertise and should support faculty to take on joint appointments in multiple units, to design co-owned curriculum (such as combined majors and interdisciplinary minors), to mount cross-listed and co-taught courses, and the like.
- *Motivate and support faculty to work with students on the integration of liberal and professional learning inside and outside the classroom.* As

I discussed in chapter 3, many faculty will need support in helping students make connections between classroom learning and learning elsewhere, and that certainly applies to learning in professional contexts. As Olin College recognizes, integrative education requires much of faculty outside the classroom—"from discussing a startup idea over lunch to leading a co-curricular [activity] to helping students develop and teach a new course."[40] This work must be supported, visible, recognized, and rewarded.

- *Create opportunities for collaboration between faculty and career design professionals.* Even colleges and universities with robust career services offices rarely expect disciplinary faculty to interact regularly with the professionals in those offices. This is a missed opportunity. When faculty, advisors, co-op or internship coordinators, and career design specialists work together, they are all in a much better position to help students connect and synthesize what they learn in classrooms with what they learn in professional settings. This could be as simple as providing faculty with information about the kinds of internships or co-ops their students have completed and are interested in or as robust as a full-blown, collaborative curriculum-to-career program like the one at Mount Holyoke.

- *Design curricula that embed liberal learning in professional education and professional learning in liberal education.* Institution-wide general education programs provide an opportunity to fuse liberal and professional learning, as the Community College of Baltimore County example suggests. Institutions can also incentivize and provide models for curriculum innovation at the program level. At Northeastern, for example, the leadership of the College of Social Sciences and Humanities and the College of Computer and Information Sciences provided faculty with encouragement and in some cases institutional resources, such as small grants, to collaborate on co-taught courses, interdisciplinary minors, and combined majors.

- *Forge learning-first partnerships with nonprofits, governmental agencies, community organizations, and businesses in which students can explore their professional interests and learn about professions.* Here, I am extending the recommendation in chapter 3 to "cultivate reciprocal relationships with community and employer partners." While I do not agree with some of my humanities-based colleagues that professional learning is a corrupt feature of the neoliberal university, I recognize that there are dangers in university-corporate relationships. Care must be taken to ensure that students and faculty are not doing the bidding of profit-seeking enterprises and that the critiquing function of liberal learning remains operative as faculty and students engage in these partnerships. It's crucial that partners commit to advancing students' learning, not just give them professional experience or networking opportunities—and certainly students should not be exploited as cheap labor. Institutional resources must be devoted to working directly with these organizations and agencies to ensure that students have meaningful and ethical learning experiences.

What Faculty Can Do

The most important thing faculty can do to promote the integration of liberal learning and professional learning is to not insist on their segregation. Liberal arts faculty who actively discourage students from exploring how their learning could be applied, extended, revised, or challenged in professional settings are not doing their students any more favors than faculty in professional schools who teach a set of technical skills as though they were divorced from how students make sense of and navigate their personal, cultural, and social worlds. Faculty can facilitate their students' integration of liberal and professional learning in the following ways:

- *Cue students to connect and synthesize liberal and professional learning in the classroom.* Not every course or assignment needs to encourage students to look for both liberal and professional applications for the skills or concepts they are learning. But the strategies I explored in previous chapters—engaging students in self-assessment and goal setting early in the semester; prompting connections to other learning experiences during class discussion; designing formal and informal assignments that ask students to make explicit connections to what they are learning or have learned in other contexts; helping students understand the conditions of applicability of what they are learning; and offering students reflective activities that help them solidify and make knowledge and skills available for future use—could make room for such connections. Students' purposes for learning are what matter most, and these should be invited into the classroom. Here are some specific classroom strategies faculty might consider:

- *Ask students to bring prior or current work experiences and professional ambitions to bear during discussions, activities, and assignments in class.* Faculty can solicit information about students' work experiences and professional ambitions and use that information as a backdrop for their engagement with the course material.

- *Solicit from students what they know about how the topic of the course or the profession with which it is associated shapes and is shaped by the broader culture and society.* For example, students in professionally oriented courses might be prompted to consider representations of that profession in popular culture, to pose and examine common ethical challenges that arise in its practice, to research its history, or to study how it involves and impacts particular socioeconomic groups.

- *Arrange for career design professionals or alumni to visit the classroom to talk about professional applications of the skills and concepts associated with the course or major.* Courses in which students are being introduced to majors or in which they are producing capstone work are particularly amenable to such discussions.

- *Mentor and advise students on professional experiences and trajectories.* Faculty can be available to students in formal and informal ways to help them explore, reflect on, and articulate their professional goals and experiences. They might provide advice and feedback during office hours; introduce students to professionals working in their fields of interest; pull together panels of alumni working in those fields; and so on. In all of these encounters, the goal is not just to provide career advice, but to help students explore and deepen their interests, values, and emerging identities.

- *Collaborate with colleagues across the divides between the liberal arts, STEM, and professional fields.* Interdisciplinary colloquia or presentations, teaching centers, research institutes, college- or university-wide committees and initiatives, and the like provide opportunities for rich intellectual engagement across disciplines and also for new pedagogical, curricular, and research projects. In addition, faculty who know other faculty members across the institution have a deep bench of experts to whom they can send students with an interest in another field of study or a specific profession.

- *Engage advisors, career design professionals, service-learning professionals, and other institutional partners.* Virtually every institution employs a range of professionals who help students identify, clarify, pursue, and evaluate their professional interests. These people are a treasure trove of information about how students are—or are not—using what they learn in their classrooms as they build their professional profiles. They are also ready partners for faculty looking to help students explore potential connections between curricula and careers.

- *Participate in partnerships with external organizations.* Disciplinary faculty can play important roles in learning partnerships, including organizing occasional visits to professional or cultural sites where the concepts, knowledge, and skills students are learning in class are practiced; teaching service-learning courses in which students take an active role in organizations and agencies; or creating co-op, internship, or practicum opportunities for students. These opportunities help students contextualize what they are learning in class— and in turn contextualize what they experience outside of class.

Conclusion

While there is some disagreement about how many times today's graduates can be expected to change jobs and careers over their lifetime, it's clear that such shifts are becoming more frequent and that even the most focused, single-minded students are likely to change jobs and careers multiple times.[41] Moreover, as the 2016 election reminded us, we cannot predict the kinds of social and cultural changes that lie ahead. The best way to equip students to navigate constant change is to help them become self-directed, adaptive, integrative learners. Of course they need job skills, but more than that, they need to know how to assess and adapt to ever-shifting terrain as they make a living and make a life.

Faculty are of course key to this effort. To promote integrative learning as I describe it in this book, faculty don't just impart what they know to students. They don't just design meaningful course curricula and learning experiences. They don't just evaluate student work. They do all these things while helping students to integrate their knowledge and skills across classrooms and curricula (chapter 2), across learning contexts beyond classrooms and campus (chapter 3), and even across professional contexts with which they may or may not be familiar (this chapter). Faculty engage their students—and possibly students' other learning partners (faculty colleagues, advisors, career service professionals, employers, alumni)—both inside and outside the classroom. And this is all in addition to the research and service requirements incumbent upon most faculty members.

Is it too much?

Unbundlers argue that it is—that faculty roles should be disaggregated into discrete functions: content development, instructional design, coaching, evaluation, and so on. Seizing on recent advances in educational technology as well as the rise of the contingent faculty labor model, unbundlers call for traditional tenure-track and full-time faculty to be supplanted by teams of part-timers coordinated by digital technologies.

But here's the thing: students' sustained relationships with faculty are critical to their success in and even beyond college. Faculty play many roles inside and outside the classroom: teachers, advisors, mentors, guides, colleagues. Their disciplinary expertise and pedagogical expertise are more critical than ever as students face a world awash in information—and misinformation—and endlessly churning. This is not to say that educational technology cannot play a role—of course it can, and it should. It should be a means of augmenting and extending, rather than replacing, faculty members' expertise within an integrated faculty model, to which I now turn.

CHAPTER 5

HUMANS AND MACHINES

Integrating Faculty Expertise
and Learning Technologies

◢ Amy Farrell, an associate professor of criminology and criminal justice at
Northeastern University, studies how the criminal justice system handles hate
crimes and human trafficking. She has co-authored two books and published an
enviable list of peer-reviewed articles in major research journals, along with many
book chapters and reports. She has won numerous grants, including one for
almost $500,000 from the National Institute of Justice for a project using crime
reports to capture human trafficking. She is a sought-after speaker at
conferences, is active in professional organizations, and has provided expert
testimony to the US House of Representatives Judiciary Committee. She has
served as a consultant for several community organizations, including schools,
and has served on community committees and task forces, including the
Massachusetts attorney general's Interagency Human Trafficking Policy Task
Force. At the same time, she is active within the university, serving as associate
director of Northeastern's School of Criminology and Criminal Justice and on
several college committees.

Farrell sees her research and her teaching as intertwined. In her popular
undergraduate and graduate courses on human trafficking, gender and crime, and
research and evaluation, she not only provides students with access to criminal
justice research, but also invites them to participate in producing it. For instance,
she and student collaborators completed the largest study to date that examines
labor trafficking in the United States (Owens et al. 2014).[1] The Violence and
Justice Research Laboratory (VJRL), which Farrell co-directs, is pioneering "inter-
generational" research teams, in which undergraduates are mentored by graduate
students, and those graduate students are in turn mentored by faculty.[2] In an

Inside Higher Ed profile of the VJRL, Farrell notes that "the lab looks similar to other science labs in that there is shared space and regular collaboration. But students aren't 'using centrifuges or equipment—they're using computers and software packages and talking to each other' " (quoted in Flaherty 2017).[3] The lab is a space where students learn how to conduct cutting-edge research—data mining, crime mapping, and so on—by participating in real research projects.

Describing the nature of the collaboration fostered in the lab, Farrell says that "students still use social media, email, and other digital platforms to communicate with one another (and faculty members) about lab work. But 'there's something to that in-the-moment dynamic, that "Hey, what are you working on" dynamic between people, that improves collaboration' " (quoted in Flaherty 2017). Farrell's commitment to her students and her collaborative mentorship have won national recognition: in 2014, she was honored with the American Society of Criminology's Mentor of the Year Award.[4] ⌐

A my Farrell is the "whole package." High-profile research, effective teaching and mentorship, valuable service to the institution, high-impact community outreach—she does it all. What's more, these activities are interconnected, emerging out of her commitment to making knowledge with and for individuals and communities affected by crime and the criminal justice system. As a result, her sphere of influence is broad, extending across and well beyond the university.

As her comments about the VJRL indicate, it's crucial for Farrell to be present for her students—and for them to be present for each other. Engagement in a physical space matters. That engagement is enhanced by the use of digital tools both for research purposes (geographic information system software for crime mapping, for example) and for the purposes of social connection ("social media, email, and other digital platforms"). Seamlessly integrating her expertise and digital technologies to support student learning in and beyond the institution, Farrell represents a compelling version of the future of higher education.

Yet, if unbundlers and other disruptors have their way, Farrell will be among the last of her kind. Seizing on advances in educational technology and the growing vulnerability of academic labor in light of adjunctification, unbundlers posit a post-faculty higher education system. They seek to disaggregate faculty roles into discrete functions. They propose what Vernon C. Smith (2008, 184–210) calls the "virtual assembly line,"[5] in which different people and machines, connected via digital technology, complete distinct tasks: content development, instructional design, coaching, assessment, and the like. The virtual assembly line is a dream from a management perspective: it leverages digital technologies to control, reduce, and in some instances replace human labor. The human labor that remains is extracted on a piecemeal basis and thus on the cheap and with little likelihood of squabbling over academic content or organizing for improved working conditions.

And this is the point: unbundlers view "traditional" (that is, full-time, professional) faculty as an obstacle to achieving their techno-utopic vision of bringing higher education to the worldwide masses. But the deprofessionalization and disaggregation of faculty only reify and indeed expand social and economic inequality. If faculty members like Professor Farrell do survive in the world of unbundled education, it will be only in our most elite institutions. Students attending those schools—a tiny minority of the college-going population—will work side by side with these faculty to discover and disseminate knowledge. Meanwhile, students without social or economic capital will be relegated to a series of disconnected, discontinuous, short-term educational experiences in which "mentorship," in the form of advising and coaching, is distributed across a variety of paraprofessionals who are unconnected not only from the making of knowledge, but even from the packaging of it. The virtual assembly line, in short, robs students of what we know to be the most important factor to their academic success: relationships with faculty.

The argument I make in this chapter is neither technophobic nor technophilic (see Losh 2014; Davidson 2017).[6] I acknowledge historian of technology Melvin Kranzberg's law that "technology is neither good nor bad, nor is it neutral" (Kranzberg 1986, 547).[7] In other words, the ethical value of technologies is not inherent in them; rather, it resides in the actions of the humans who make and use them. The questions we should be asking of every technology, digital or not, are, What is it used *for*, in whose interests, and with what results? Instead of using edtech to disaggregate faculty, I argue that learning technologies must be put in service of enhancing faculty's disciplinary and pedagogical expertise to best serve their students.

While the adjunctification and unbundling of faculty are well under way, they do not represent a viable long-term strategy for colleges and universities. They may save some money in the short term, but they sacrifice institutions' competitive advantage in the higher education "marketplace." The heart of higher education is the relationships between a faculty member like Farrell and her students. Those relationships are powerful and lasting precisely because of the integrated nature of her roles as a faculty member: as a fully professional disciplinary and pedagogical expert, she is able to fuse the traditional activities of academic labor—research, teaching, and service. She is also able to integrate technologies into her work in ways that serve her goals while remaining fully present for her students. If colleges and universities are to survive and thrive in the years ahead, faculty like Farrell must represent the future, not the past, of higher education.

Careering toward Contingency

"Facing Poverty, Academics Turn to Sex Work and Sleeping in Cars." This sounds like a headline from a trashy gossip magazine, but it appeared in the September 28, 2017, issue of the *Guardian*. The article offers horrific details of what should be a scandal: the desperate, precarious lives of adjunct faculty in the United States. It's estimated that a quarter of these individuals are on public assistance. They rely on food banks and thrift stores. Many adjunct faculty work at multiple institutions and more than sixty hours a week. Those who manage to secure several courses per semester make about $25,000 a year. Given the long hours (there's grading and class planning to do after classes are over), their pay can amount to less than minimum wage. Some of that money will likely go to transportation between the schools at which they teach, and more of it will probably go to pay off student loans—after all, these people have advanced, even terminal degrees.[8]

Early in my career, I was an adjunct for three years. A classic freeway flyer, I taught writing courses at three or four different colleges and universities each term. I would often begin my day with an 8:00 a.m. class and then hold an office hour; drive to another institution, where I would teach two afternoon classes and hold another office hour; and then drive to a third institution and teach a night class. I would arrive home around 10:00 p.m., often with a stack of papers under my arm. I would grade the papers over a reheated dinner, listening to the baby monitor so my wife would not have to get up after her own long day of work and her evening with the baby. I taught multiple classes most days, but on lighter days, I advised a student newspaper for a small amount of extra pay—and of course did more grading. This schedule allowed me to make around $10,000 each semester, an income I supplemented during the summer, when courses were rarely available, by working construction or for a moving company or in a factory.

As the article in the *Guardian* makes clear, conditions are no better for contingent instructors today—they're much worse. Institutions continue to pay shockingly little per course (as low as $1,000), and much of the available employment for those qualified to teach college involves piecemeal work, most often as graders evaluating the work of students whom they do not teach and never meet. Meanwhile, increased student debt loads and the rising costs of health care—which contingent faculty often have to purchase on their own (or go without) since none of their teaching jobs are full time—make their financial existence even more untenable than mine was in the 1990s. And yet the contingent instructor has become, statistically speaking, the norm in higher education. In 1970, 20 percent of postsecondary faculty were contingent; in 2016, that figure was 70 percent (Maxey and Kezar 2016, 7).[9] The percentage of full-time, non-tenure-track faculty today is approaching 20 percent. You can do the math: the full-time, tenure-track professor, once the dominant figure in US higher education, is fast becoming an anomaly.

To be clear, there are some good reasons to hire part-time faculty. As a writing program director at two different institutions, I hired many excellent part-time instructors who brought a wealth of experience and insight from the professional writing and publishing worlds. They liked and excelled at teaching, but it would always be their side gig. Virtually every field has practitioners who make meaningful contributions to students' educational experiences and want to teach only one or two courses per semester. But the part-time ranks are also swollen with aspiring academics vying for the precious few tenure-track positions available each year and with long-term part-timers desperately trying to piece together a living wage. I have hired my share of these individuals too, and most of them are also good teachers. The problem is not that contingent faculty exist or that they can't be effective teachers; it's that higher education has created a system premised on their production and exploitation. Faculty want graduate students in their courses and their labs, and institutions need to have intro courses taught. But once these students earn their degrees, the profession has no place for most of them—certainly not the full-time, tenure-track jobs they desire. They go on "the market," but most of them end up in the only place they *can* end up, given the prevailing practices: in the vast pool of cheap labor that institutions rely on to teach their students.

Some disciplines are actively incorporating "alt-ac" (alternative-academic) career training into their graduate programs, and some institutions have cut back their graduate student admissions. But higher education continues to produce many more people with degrees that qualify them for college teaching than it produces good college teaching jobs—which also means those same institutions are producing more and more bad college teaching jobs. In a number of states, unionization has led to some improvements in part-timers' working conditions and compensation, but in general, contingent instructors are poorly treated and poorly paid. They have little to no job security. They are rarely provided with or have time to take advantage of robust professional development opportunities. They teach highly standardized curricula and courses. They receive little if any meaningful feedback on or evaluation of their teaching. They share crowded offices or cubicles—or are provided no workspace at all. They have little encouragement, motivation, or time to engage in the life of the campus and are excluded from institutional decision-making. As at-will employees, they are denied the protections of academic freedom.

All of this is deprofessionalizing—indeed, dehumanizing—for the individuals who experience it. But students also suffer. A wealth of research demonstrates that instructors' poor working conditions have negative impacts on student outcomes, such as retention, transfer from two-year to four-year institutions, and graduation rates (Maxey and Kezar 2016, 7). Instructors who lack housing and food security, health benefits, and adequate compensation for their labor often, understandably, find it difficult to provide consistently high-quality instruction to their students. Their life challenges, including the fact that they typically teach at multiple institutions, dilute and divide their attention and effort. The lack of collegial and administrative support militates against embedding themselves in the campus community. Their lack of academic freedom discourages them from pursuing truths with their students that might be uncomfortable for those in power.

This last consequence points to the broader social costs of the adjunctification of academic labor. The retreat from academic freedom and tenure ultimately constitutes a retreat from public safeguards. While they are often characterized as personal perks (supposedly ensuring "jobs for life"), academic freedom and tenure are intended to secure free inquiry for the common good. The American Association of University Professors' "1940 Statement of Principles on Academic Freedom and Tenure" is clear on this point:

> Institutions of higher education are conducted for the common good and not to further the interest of either the individual teacher or the institution as a whole. The common good depends upon the free search for truth and its free exposition.
>
> Academic freedom is essential to these purposes and applies to both teaching and research. Freedom in research is fundamental to the advancement of truth. Academic freedom in its teaching aspect is fundamental for the protection of the rights of the teacher in teaching and of the student to freedom in learning. It carries with it duties correlative with rights.

Tenure is a means to certain ends; specifically: (1) freedom of teaching and research and of extramural activities, and (2) a sufficient degree of economic security to make the profession attractive to men and women of ability. Freedom and economic security, hence, tenure, are indispensable to the success of an institution in fulfilling its obligations to its students and to society.[10]

The protections afforded by academic freedom and tenure ultimately redound to society as a whole. The social cost of the shift to the contingent faculty model is the removal of safeguards for "the free search for truth and its free exposition," bulwarks of a democratic society.

Techno-utopic Fever Dreams

It should come as no surprise that unbundlers see an opportunity in the contingent faculty model. In a chapter called "Preparing for the Great Unbundling," Ryan Craig (2015, 118) notes that today, "the central figure in higher education is not the full-time faculty member but rather the part-time non–tenure track adjunct."[11] This is important, Craig adds, because "attempts to galvanize opposition to the changes underway are destined to fall flat. Part-time and adjunct faculty members are primarily interested in more work and steady work. They are likely to be in favor of online programs that have the potential to add enrollment" (118). In other words, academic labor has been weakened to the point that the great unbundling can proceed apace.

Just as Plato's ideal state has no place for poets, unbundlers' techno-utopias have no place for faculty, those pesky denizens of the outmoded hybrid university who don't much care about teaching anyway. I'm not imputing snarkiness here—I'm reporting it. In *The End of College*, Kevin Carey (2015, 149) sneers, "The hybrid university leaves mundane matters like teaching to professors," concluding that "often this leads to a lot of uninspired instruction conducted in blissful ignorance of the principles of learning science."[12] Some unbundlers even believe there is a vast conspiracy to make sure students *don't* learn. In *College Unbound* (2013),

Jeffrey Selingo describes college as "one giant game of favor exchanges between students, professors, and administrators,"[13] while Carey (2015) describes a "mutual disarmament pact among college professors and students: Neither is asked to work very hard, the professors get to focus on the research they care about, and the students all get good grades" (85). These writers do not adduce any evidence, or even examples, to support these claims.[14] It's enough to assert that "traditional" faculty members are impediments to improving higher education.

What *is* the key to improving higher education, according to unbundlers? Technology, of course. And they have some reason to be hopeful, at least from a financial perspective. During the first half of 2015, for example, venture capitalists poured $2.5 billion into edtech companies. This exceeded the total investments for 2014, which had set an all-time record.[15] Clearly, investors are betting big on cracking open a lucrative market. They are counting on private equity funds like Ryan Craig's University Ventures to find the ultimate game-changer, the killer app.

For a while, it looked like massive open online courses (MOOCs) were the answer.[16] The *New York Times* declared 2012 the Year of the MOOC.[17] Harvard, Stanford, MIT, Duke, and other elite universities were leading the charge. Nonprofit ventures like edX and for-profit companies like Coursera and Udacity were revolutionizing higher learning. The gates of higher education were being thrown open to the world, making high-quality learning available to everyone everywhere. Everything was about to change.

But by the end of the year after the Year of the MOOC, the fever had broken. That's when it became clear that the Udacity product that California governor Jerry Brown had purchased for introductory and remedial courses at San José State University was not the silver bullet the state was seeking. In fact, the pass rates for the courses offered by the for-profit company were much *lower* than those of the on-ground courses taught by San José State faculty. Even Udacity's famously brash founder, Sebastian Thrun, was forced to admit that his company's product was "lousy." The contract was canceled.[18]

MOOCs are not always "lousy." They continue to enroll millions of students, and even at a completion rate of only 4 percent, that's still a lot of people who have presumably learned something they wouldn't have otherwise. But they were overhyped. Far from throwing open the gates of higher education to the world's masses, they have served the planet's most advantaged: four out of five students who complete a course already have a bachelor's degree, six in ten are employed full time, and six in ten hail from a developed country.[19]

MOOCs are only one example of the oversold technological solutions to intractable educational challenges. History is littered with disruptive educational technologies—think educational TV or teaching machines—that failed to deliver on overblown promises.[20] Of course, today's disruptors claim that this time it's different: computers and the internet will finally allow us to transform education in fundamental ways. Putting aside the fact that every generation of reformers says this about the technologies of their age, much of today's disruptive discourse follows the historical pattern of thinking of "the situation of teaching as only a signal to be broadcast," as media professor Elizabeth Losh (2014, 5) puts it. In other words, the vast overestimation of the transformative power of technology is at root an overestimation of the importance of content, a misunderstanding of teaching as content delivery, and an underestimation of the importance of human relationships to the educational enterprise.

The latest "game-changer" is adaptive learning, in which computers, using machine learning, serve up learning objects and adjust instruction based on a student's responses. Maybe we don't need faculty at all! Ryan Craig (2015, 91) calls adaptive learning, when combined with competency-based learning, "the killer app of online education." Once again, the hype is overblown. At present, little evidence exists that adaptive learning is effective; it's expensive; it raises privacy concerns; and companies that offer it have not proven their long-term viability. In the hands of effective educators, adaptive learning programs can have diagnostic value and have been shown to help students learn lower-order skills, such as basic mathematics. But as educational technologist Bill Ferster (2014, 167) suggests, the teaching of higher-level skills "has thus far proven immune to technological intervention." Higher-level skills require creative and critical capacities that cannot be programmed or learned by rote or, in behaviorist lingo, by "successive approxima-tions." These skills must be learned through human interaction, which Ferster wryly notes "does not scale very well" (176). Automated technol-ogies and machine learning will surely play increased roles in education at all levels in the years ahead, but they will supplement rather than supplant all-important human relationships. Faculty will remain "robot-proof," in Joseph E. Aoun's (2017) term, in the same way students will: by focusing on the critical and creative capacities that are uniquely human.[21]

The allure of edtech as a democratizing force is understandable: isn't it pretty to think that we can solve the world's problems with a gadget, app, or platform? But while educational technologies have enormous potential to improve—and, yes, extend the reach of—teaching and learning, advances in edtech also tend to reify or even expand social and economic inequality. Leading educators, researchers, and educational technologists at a 2016 summit at the University of California, Irvine, issued just this warning. Their collective research and observations led them to some troubling conclusions: "schools serving privileged stu-dents tend to use the same technologies in more progressive ways than schools serving less privileged students"; "free online learning materials disproportionately benefit the affluent and highly educated"; and "ef-forts to democratize education through technology have often faltered because technologists failed to anticipate broader social and cultural forces[:] institutionalized and unconscious bias and social distance be-tween developers and those they seek to serve" (Reich and Ito 2017, 3).[22] The conclusion is clear: while machines can be powerful tools in the hands of educators, they will not on their own overcome educational injustice. They may even exacerbate it.

Unbundling Faculty

For unbundlers, edtech presents the happy prospect of disaggregating faculty roles, once and for all displacing full-time, fully professional faculty from the higher education enterprise. Ryan Craig (2015, 138–39) describes the disaggregation of faculty roles this way: "Specialist faculty will develop courses. Different faculty will provide instruction. Another group will provide assessment services. Yet another will handle advisement and support." Craig uses the word *faculty* here, but he does not have in mind the kinds of professional educators that word typically connotes. Rather, he is describing a *labor system* that combines the increased use of technology, the unbundling of instructional roles, and heavy reliance on non-instructional staff. This system—Smith's (2008) virtual assembly line—is designed to facilitate the completion of discrete, sequentially ordered tasks: development of subject matter, instructional design, graphic and web design, delivery (networking, technology, etc.), troubleshooting, coaching, mentoring, advising, grading, and course evaluation and improvement. Most of these tasks are taken on by people without educational credentials or experience: instructional designers, web designers, coaches, tutors, contracted assessors, and so on. We can choose to call all of these people "faculty," but to do so is to hollow out that concept.[23]

A form of latter-day Taylorism facilitated by online educational technology, the virtual assembly line is the fullest expression of the neoliberal assault on higher education, which I discussed in chapter 1.[24] It standardizes and commodifies learning, deprofessionalizes and marginalizes faculty, concentrates power in the hands of administrators, and intensifies the precarity of contingent instructors. Individuals perform their tasks separately, without a clear understanding of (or need to understand) the whole process of designing and "delivering" courses. They are carefully monitored and surveilled, and they have little control over their working conditions. While "faculty" are usually called "subject matter experts," the virtual assembly line is not located in academic departments, and course content is determined not according to disciplinary expertise, but rather by managerial fiat and the dictates of instructional design. Ironically, given this system's alleged usefulness for "quality control," standardization makes course improvements difficult and slow. No one in the system has the ability to respond immediately to students' learning needs.

It's important to recognize that while unbundlers are seizing on advances in educational technology to perfect the virtual assembly line, this labor system already exists. Smith (2008) found it among the community colleges he studied more than a decade ago. Maxey and Kezar (2016) find it in many online and for-profit institutions today. The "great unbundling" of the faculty is well under way.[25]

In fact, faculty unbundling has a long history in US higher education. Sean Gehrke and Adrianna Kezar (2015) outline four eras of historical unbundling.[26] First, as the old college model evolved into the university model from the early colonial period through 1860, faculty members morphed from pastoral tutors charged with the holistic development of students into professors charged primarily with imparting knowledge. From 1860 through the 1950s, this shift intensified: faculty came to be associated more closely with specialized disciplinary knowledge, and they were relieved of more and more student-related service/administrative duties, which were absorbed by ascendant student affairs units. From the 1950s through the 1980s, an era that saw an explosion of teaching-focused institutions (including community colleges), teaching came to be unbundled from research, and institutions increasingly relied on part-time, teaching-only faculty for instruction while tenure-track faculty increasingly focused on research. From the 1980s to the present, these developments have intensified, and instruction itself has begun to be distributed across a range of staff (professional and nonprofessional, and predominantly contingent) and technologies, especially but not exclusively in online and for-profit institutions.

As has been the case historically, the unbundling of faculty is being trumpeted today not because it has been shown to improve learning—it hasn't—but rather because it's thought to be an efficient management strategy. However, to date there is little evidence that faculty unbundling results in cost savings (Gehrke and Kezar 2015).[27]

There *is* evidence that students, particularly first-generation and low-income students, "are often disadvantaged and perhaps even harmed by the fragmentation of learning" that results from faculty disaggregation (Gehrke and Kezar 2015, 106). These learners benefit most from close mentorship from professional faculty both inside and outside the classroom. In many cases, unlike their more privileged peers, they lack the resources and support to thrive in an unbundled, do-it-yourself higher education marketplace. On top of this, as Neil Selwyn (2016) suggests, "free market" logic dictates that when these students fail, it will be their own fault: they had the same opportunities as everyone else, and they simply made bad choices. So not only does unbundled, do-it-yourself education exacerbate inequality, robbing our most vulnerable students of the most important contributor to their academic success, but it also exacerbates the pathologizing of those against whom the system is rigged.

Integrating Faculty

We know that meaningful, sustained relationships with faculty, both inside and outside the classroom, are central to postsecondary students' success. A key conclusion of Richard Light's (2001, 85) study of more than 1,600 Harvard students was that "a great college education depends upon human relationships."[28] Students indicated that relationships with faculty were particularly critical. They learned most in classes that were small, were structured, and included writing and feedback on their writing: in short, those that "maximize[d] personal engagement and collegial interaction" (80). They also praised mentored experiences outside of classrooms, where they developed their own projects with the support of faculty (8–9). They especially appreciated faculty "who helped students make connections between a serious curriculum, on the one hand, and the students' personal lives, values, and experiences[,] on the other" (110).

Light's (2001) study relies on self-reported data—what students perceived to be most important to their education—but as higher education researchers Adrianna Kezar and Daniel Maxey (2016, 24) suggest, "a substantial body of research that has been conducted over a span of more than fifty years demonstrates that faculty-student interaction is a key factor in promoting student success—particularly among those students who are most in need of support, such as first-generation college students."[29] High-quality faculty-student interactions have been shown to correlate positively with a range of desired outcomes, including persistence, graduation rates, and academic performance as measured by grades and standardized tests. In fact, "no other factor is reported to have a stronger positive correlation with persistence among students of color than faculty interactions and relationships" (27).

Gehrke and Kezar (2015, 122) point out that advances in neuroscience explain why relationships with faculty are so critical: "learning is more likely to occur when students can make relevant connections to the material in their course with their experiences in their lives and on campus[,] . . . [and] faculty who are more familiar with their students' backgrounds and experiences and have relationships with them are more likely to be able to make these kinds of linkages to ensure that learning is occurring." Integrative learning is facilitated by faculty members who develop holistic relationships with students, support them inside and outside the classroom, mentor them over time, help them build on prior knowledge and make new knowledge available for future use, and connect them with campus, community, and professional opportunities and resources. To be sure, these activities can be augmented by digital technologies, but they are rooted in human relationships. No technology, no matter how advanced, can replicate or replace what faculty offer their students.

The most effective and irreplaceable faculty are those who, like Amy Farrell discussed at the beginning of this chapter, integrate several faculty roles. They intentionally intertwine their teaching, research or creative activity, and service/outreach. Their work in the classroom is complemented and extended by their work outside the classroom. And their physical interactions with their students are complemented and extended by their judicious use of learning and communication technologies.

Unfortunately, faculty like these are becoming increasingly rare. Institutions that still hire on the tenure track tend to recruit a small number of tenure-track faculty with high-profile research and surround them with an army of contingent faculty to do most of the teaching. This may save institutions some money, but it's not good for student learning nor for those contingent instructors—nor, ultimately, for those few tenure-track faculty members, who themselves need the mentorship, support, and collaboration of peers who similarly integrate their faculty roles. Farrell could easily find a (probably better-paying) job doing policy research and consultation, and she could pick up some teaching work if that appealed to her. But she stays at the university because she values the rich relationships she has developed with peers and students.

But if relying on contingent labor saves money, is there any hope that institutions will invest in full-time, fully professional faculty? Actually, it may be their *only* hope. To thrive in an unbundled higher education marketplace, colleges and universities must invest in the assets they possess that alternative providers do not—namely, their professional faculty and their robust learning infrastructures. The value proposition of colleges and universities lies in the integrated nature of the learning experience they offer, and that learning experience relies on meaningful relationships with faculty. *That's* what students and families are really paying for. To date, adopting the contingent faculty model has not hurt these institutions much because most people haven't felt that they have other viable postsecondary options. Students surely are not happy that nearly three-quarters of their instructors are ill-paid, poorly treated, part-time contingent faculty. On some campuses, they rally to support these faculty during Campus Equity Week or National Adjunct Walkout Day, but on the whole, students and their families resign themselves to paying top dollar for education from poorly paid and deprofessionalized faculty. What else can they do? But now that other options *are* becoming available in the marketplace, students and their families will ask why they should shell out huge sums of money and assume risky debt to attend institutions that employ mostly contingent faculty.

So colleges and universities need not just integrated faculty *roles*, but also an integrated faculty *model*. What does this entail? At least three things:

1. *Assembling a predominantly full-time, professional, diverse faculty.*
This is not a pie-in-the-sky demand for tenure for all: there will always be a place for some part-time and nontenured instructors who bring particular kinds of expertise to the institution. Nor do I mean that there shouldn't be different kinds of faculty positions,

some emphasizing teaching more than research and others the reverse. But all faculty positions should include some sort of teaching and some sort of research. Institutions should also consider radically expanding tenure and making the routes to tenure more diverse. But the larger point is that students at any college or university should have access to a faculty that is diverse, secure, well-compensated, academically free, and empowered to participate in institutional decision-making.

2. *Promoting the integration of teaching, research or creative activity, and service/outreach for all faculty.* While faculty profiles may vary, every member should be encouraged to see their work across the traditional spheres of faculty activity as part of a larger whole. Research or creative activity need not result in peer-reviewed scholarship, and service/outreach need not be high profile. What matters is that all faculty engage in some form of these activities and that these activities are mutually reinforcing.

3. *Facilitating the integration of faculty expertise and learning technologies.* In an integrated faculty model, learning technologies are tools for enhancing and extending faculty expertise, not displacing or replacing it. Every faculty member should have access to technologies that they can integrate into their pedagogies and to technical and administrative support. They should not be required to use commercial platforms and courseware products that do not serve their needs as professional educators. The bottom line is that technologies must serve teaching and learning, not the other way around.[30]

These are the key features of an integrated faculty model. It's not one-size-fits-all; individual institutions must strive to achieve it in their own ways, in light of their particular challenges, opportunities, and missions.

What Institutions Can Do

These are my recommendations based on the key features of the integrated faculty model.

Predominantly Full-Time, Professional, Diverse Faculty

Each college and university and each unit within it (college, department, center, etc.) should assemble a diverse faculty that features a robust core of professional educators with job security, good working
conditions, adequate compensation and benefits, academic freedom,
and a significant say in institutional decision-making. Most institutions will retain some small number of part-time, contingent instructors, but all institutions should work toward a primary reliance on full-
time, professional faculty. Making this vision a reality will be a heavy
lift for many institutions. Here are some suggestions:

- *Make full-time faculty a budget priority.* Obviously, different institutions have different resource levels and budget models, but nothing
  is more important to student success and the overall health of the
  institution than the full-time, professional teaching faculty.
- *Consider multiple routes to tenure.* Tenure is a large and complex
  topic, and I cannot treat it adequately here. That said, while it's not
  the only means of securing academic freedom, it's the surest way.
  It allows institutions to recruit and retain the best available faculty
  talent. Like any protection, tenure can be abused, and it's the
  administration's job to ensure this doesn't happen. When properly
  honored, tenure promotes faculty's best, most creative, most
  unflinching work. And as discussed earlier, it promotes the public
  good by safeguarding the pursuit and advancement of truth, however unpalatable it might be to those in power. Tenure is not a
  license to do as one pleases; tenured faculty can be fired for cause
  or under extraordinary circumstances (fiscal exigency, for instance).
  Rather, it's an assurance of inquiry and expression free from cor-
  rupting corporate and political interference. Institutions that
  honor these values should apply them to all facets of faculty work
  and explore various pathways to tenure. Peer review—the sine qua
  non of the tenure process—must be preserved, but peer-reviewed
  research is too narrow a metric by which to evaluate faculty.
  Teaching and service/outreach activities also should be evaluated

for how effectively faculty advance knowledge and impact various constituencies, including of course students. Faculty should be judged holistically on the originality, significance, and impact of their work in all the forms it takes.

- *Ensure academic freedom for all faculty.* Whether or not institutions expand tenure, they must commit to academic freedom for all faculty members across the range of their professional activities. A college or university that does not protect its faculty from corporate or political interference is not advancing the great knowledge project of US higher education and thus is undermining its own mission. Protecting faculty's academic freedom is particularly important in the context of collaborations with external partners, which I have recommended in previous chapters. It's not always easy in the midst of such partnerships to untangle whose interests are being served and for what purposes. That's why I have emphasized learning-first and reciprocal partnerships. Of course partners should benefit from such collaborations. But that benefit should never come at the expense of student learning or academic freedom. If faculty and students are unable to pursue and express hard truths—perhaps truths the partner does not want to hear or confront—then the collaboration is compromised and should be abandoned. The partner can look elsewhere for public relations opportunities.

- *Develop policies and practices that reward research-intensive faculty for their teaching.* Too often, teaching "relief" is used as a reward for research success. Tenure and promotion policies prioritize research over teaching. While some faculty will always be pulled out of the classroom in order to commit time to research or creative activity and to service/outreach, every institution can set the expectation through its work assignments and its promotion and tenure guidelines that teaching is an important part of every faculty member's responsibilities.

- *Set targets for reducing reliance on part-time faculty and increasing reliance on full-time faculty and hold units and the institution accountable for meeting them.* Reducing colleges' and universities' reliance on part-time faculty will not happen on its own. Quite the opposite: it's easy for institutions and programs to increase their part-time ranks slowly over time, often without even noticing they've done so. One contingent faculty member after another is called in to patch a staffing hole, and before you know it, you have assembled a highly useful and inexpensive bullpen to which you turn more and more out of convenience (and for the sake of your budget). It doesn't take malice or even conscious intent to gut the tenure-track and full-time faculty ranks (though I'm sure they help). It does take deliberate effort to rebuild them. Administrators at all levels of the institution can set hiring targets and impose consequences when those targets are not met.

- *Do the same for diversity.* Institutions should engage in an honest, critical self-study to identify racial patterns in who gets hired, promoted, and tenured. We know that nationally the part-time and non-tenure-track (NTT) ranks include more women and people of color.[31] We also know that there are disparities on the tenure track, with fewer women and especially people of color in the higher ranks.[32] These disparities suggest that academic institutions are often not as inclusive as their professed ideals suggest they should be, and this sends a clear and unfortunate message to students about whose knowledge matters and whose doesn't. Institutions should use various strategies to recruit and retain a diverse faculty. Nearly every institution has dedicated resources, often available through an office of institutional diversity.[33] They also have access to active professional communities devoted to institutional diversity, including organizations such as the National Center for Faculty Development and Diversity.[34] While there is always room to innovate—the University of California, Davis, for instance, is experimenting with open searches focused on candidates' contributions to diversity[35]—the problem, typically, is less about knowing what to do than about following through with sufficient energy and commitment.

- *Offer longer-term (three- or five-year) renewable contracts and promotion opportunities for full-time NTT faculty.* One-year contracts or semester-to-semester appointments do not provide the stability and security necessary for most faculty to do their best work. Longer-term contracts demonstrate the institution's commitment to the individual and allow faculty to pursue a professional trajectory that makes sense for them. (Such contracts can accommodate various apportionments of faculty work.) Promotion opportunities provide important milestones of achievement for which faculty members can aim and for which they can be recognized, keeping them professionally engaged and fulfilled.

- *Implement regular and fair evaluations of performance on the basis of those contracts for all faculty.* The evaluation of faculty performance must be driven by peer review, guided by clear and transparent criteria, and aligned with contracted activities. It must provide faculty with formative and summative feedback, reward strong performance, and aim to help all faculty members improve their craft.

- *Commit to shared governance.* This is a sometimes misunderstood phrase among wary faculty and impatient administrators.[36] But it names an honorable and simple principle: administrators and faculty share the responsibility for institutional decision-making. Institutions are stronger and the education they provide is more meaningful and effective when all faculty feel that they are partners in a shared enterprise and have an opportunity to participate in the decision-making processes of the institution.[37]

Integration of Teaching, Research or Creative Activity, and Service/Outreach

- *Expect and support a specified minimal level of research or creative activity for all full-time faculty.* This involves setting clear expectations, dedicating resources, and aligning reward structures. The research or creative activity need not be formal, systematic, published work—though it should be documented and consistent with professional or disciplinary standards. Institutions may consult Ernest Boyer's ([1990] 2016) four-part model of scholarship: the scholarship of *discovery* (original disciplinary investigation);

the scholarship of *integration* ("serious, disciplinary work that seeks to interpret, draw together, and bring new insight to bear on original research"; 82) within and across disciplines; the scholarship of *application* or *engagement* (the use of disciplinary expertise to engage others on and beyond campus); and the scholarship of *teaching* (the systematic study of teaching and learning).[38] Boyer's four types of scholarship are capacious enough to accommodate any active professional mind.

- *Expect and support teaching that leverages faculty's research or creative activity.* In many cases, faculty members' research areas will translate directly into their classrooms, and they can share their own discoveries with students. Faculty whose work does not align directly with their teaching assignments can draw on their experience of the research or creative process. The bottom line is that faculty who engage in knowledge discovery are better able to involve their students in it. Institutions can support faculty in developing programs, courses, and instructional units based on their research or creative activity. They can also incentivize faculty-student research in their program and curriculum design, develop research assistant or fellow programs, create student research grants and awards programs to support faculty-student research, encourage research centers to use student researchers, and so on.

- *Expect and support service/outreach activities that complement and extend faculty's research and teaching.* Service/outreach is often considered the least important of the traditional areas of faculty work, and institutional reward structures reflect that view. Properly understood, however, service/outreach involves making and sharing knowledge and expertise with communities outside of one's normal sphere of influence. Whether it's serving on a department, college, or university committee, offering expert testimony or consultation, sitting on a statewide task force or commission, serving as an officer for a professional organization, or organizing and facilitating community meetings, these activities represent opportunities to extend the significance and impact of faculty's teaching and research or creative activity. As shown in the example of Amy Farrell, wonderful things happen when these three spheres of work mutually reinforce each other. Institutions should place greater emphasis on service/outreach—engagement—and particularly on activities across and beyond campus that are intertwined with faculty's research and teaching expertise.

Integration of Faculty Expertise and Learning Technologies

- *Avoid educational technologies that are pitched as "solutions" to problems with which the institution has long wrestled.* Technologies can and perhaps must be part of solutions to intractable challenges, but they are never themselves *the* answer. Institutions should be especially wary of products that purport to replace rather than support and augment faculty expertise.
- *Involve as many faculty as possible in shaping institutional decisions about technology purchases.* Institutions should empower faculty with expertise to participate in the development of homegrown educational technologies that could be adopted by the institution. Faculty should be invited to meet and consult with vendors that the institution is considering. Institutions should avoid imposing new technologies on faculty without their consultation.
- *Motivate and support faculty to incorporate technology into their pedagogies.* As I suggested in previous chapters, workshops, inquiry groups, symposia, and the like can provide valuable opportunities for faculty to develop as teachers. Faculty who integrate technology can be tapped to showcase their work for colleagues. Institutions can incentivize experimentation with technology-enhanced pedagogies through, for example, professional development opportunities, small grant programs, and reward structures. Among other things, supporting technology-enhanced teaching and learning means creating a culture in which the public sharing of *failed* experiments is valued and rewarded; faculty must be encouraged to take pedagogical risks.

What Faculty Can Do

Predominantly Full-Time, Professional, Diverse Faculty

- *Advocate and organize for faculty positions with job security, good working conditions, adequate compensation and benefits, academic freedom, and decision-making authority.* Faculty standing together across ranks can exert enormous pressure on institutions. Unfortunately, on some campuses, tenured/tenure-track (T/TT) faculty are a major barrier to the professionalization of NTT faculty. Because they view faculty prerogatives as a zero-sum game, they see supporting their colleagues as capitulation to the neoliberal assault on tenure. The truth is closer to the opposite: the fate of T/TT faculty is tied to the fate of NTT colleagues because the attack is not just on tenure, but on academic freedom and on faculty in general. It's critically important for their own sake as well as that of their colleagues that T/TT faculty—a small but powerful group in most institutions—support a strong, professional, unified faculty model.[39]

- *Push the institution to recruit and retain diverse faculty—and participate in efforts to do so.* Here again, the faculty with the most institutional clout can do the most good. But all faculty should use whatever influence they wield to advocate for diversity and inclusion across the institution. When asked to mentor a colleague of color or to attend a conference to recruit first-generation or underrepresented graduate students, they should jump at the chance—and encourage others to do the same. And if the institution is not investing in these kinds of efforts, faculty should push it to do so. Faculty should also practice inclusion in all of their own professional activities.

- *Contribute to the creation of a strong teaching culture.* Whenever possible, faculty should attend pedagogy workshops, talk about teaching with colleagues, participate in the peer review of colleagues' teaching, and so on. It's particularly important that senior research-intensive faculty demonstrate a commitment to teaching and not treat it as a nuisance to be avoided or a burden to be borne entirely by NTT and junior colleagues.

- *Participate in shared governance.* Many faculty complain about the power wielded by administrators on their campuses but are unwilling to participate in shared governance themselves. Faculty have a great deal of power when they serve in the academic/faculty senate, sit on university or college committees and task forces, speak up at town halls, propose new courses and curricula, and the like. Faculty who are active in institutional governance also feel more investment in the institution—even when they are critical of some aspects of it—and can more effectively engage their colleagues, students, and external partners in improving it.

Integration of Teaching, Research or Creative Activity, and Service/Outreach

- *Conduct some form of regular research or creative activity.* All faculty should be engaged in ongoing research or creative projects that are meaningful to them. They should be involved in the processes of inquiry and discovery, following their own curiosities and passions. Their work need not lead to peer-reviewed publication, but it should uphold the standards and traditions of their disciplinary field and profession.
- *Look for and create opportunities to leverage their research or creative activities in their teaching.* Certainly teaching can be made more vivid when faculty bring the results of their own research or creative activity to bear in their work with students. Faculty also gain credibility with students when they do so. But perhaps even more important than the sharing of relevant content is the modeling of the process, the embodiment of the experience of making knowledge. As Richard Light's (2001) research shows, students get the most out of their college experience when they are invited to conduct their own intellectual work under the guidance of experi-

enced faculty mentors. In turn, students can often make valuable contributions to faculty's research programs as research assistants, research team members, and even co-authors of studies.

- *Look for and create opportunities to leverage teaching and research in service/outreach.* Faculty who want to make an impact on their institutions and communities constantly ask themselves: Who can benefit from what I am discovering in my research and teaching? Sometimes this question leads them to disseminate the results of their work in new venues; at other times it leads them to produce knowledge *with* new groups and communities. It's helpful to think of service/outreach not as required diversions from research and teaching, but as opportunities to complement and extend them. Sometimes students can make valuable contributions to these activities. In any case, the faculty who have the richest and most rewarding professional lives, like Amy Farrell, see the spheres of their intellectual and professional work as interconnected opportunities to pursue questions and problems that they care about.

Integration of Faculty Expertise and Learning Technologies

- *Help shape learning technologies.* The purpose of these technologies is to support teaching and learning, so faculty expertise must drive their development. Faculty with technical expertise can work with developers or even develop their own technologies for institutional adoption.[40] Those without this expertise can and should still advise educational technology companies and entrepreneurs because they are the experts in teaching and learning.
- *Participate in the institution's technology planning.* Whenever possible, faculty should accept invitations (or request them if they are not forthcoming) to serve on technology committees, attend vendor presentations, advise administrators on technology purchases, and the like. Faculty must have a strong voice in the institution's technological infrastructure.

- *Experiment with a variety of technologies to achieve teaching and learning objectives.* Whether they are themselves technology innovators, early adopters, regular users, or skeptics, faculty must recognize that both their fields and their students have been transformed by the ubiquity of digital technologies. Fortunately, there is no shortage of professional resources for faculty looking to integrate widely available digital tools and technologies into their pedagogies.[41] Many institutional teaching and learning centers provide guidance and examples as well. The idea is not to overhaul pedagogies in digital form; rather, it's to explore the ways in which new and emerging technologies can provide new insights into one's field and new ways to teach one's students.

- *Share the results of technological experimentation with colleagues.* Pedagogical innovation is contagious. Faculty are more likely to experiment with their teaching when their colleagues do so publicly—that is, when those colleagues share what worked and what didn't when they tried out a new strategy or technology. Faculty should seek and create forums for sharing how the incorporation of certain technologies did and (just as important) did not support their teaching and learning aims.

Conclusion

As unbundlers and other higher ed disruptors continue their search for the technological holy grail, colleges and universities have an opportunity to build and fortify their commitment both to their faculty and to the learning technologies that support their work. Recentering their mission on the people and relationships that promote transformative learning experiences will amplify these institutions' value proposition in an increasingly fractured and confusing higher ed market.

As the new economy requires more and more people to seek alternative credentials—certificates, certifications, licenses, micro degrees, nano degrees—postsecondary institutions have an opportunity to exploit their advantage and radically expand their purview by maintaining their relationships with learners throughout their lives. Unsurprisingly, unbundlers are particularly active in this space: the adult education market and the workforce training market are huge opportunities for non-institutional providers. But as I argue in the next chapter, integrated institutions are well suited to offer both degrees *and* lifelong learning opportunities—and, indeed, to help students integrate these learning experiences in ways that unbundled, do-it-yourself education never can.

CHAPTER 6

NOW AND THEN

Integrating Degrees and
Lifelong Learning Opportunities

◢ Ahmed Habib received his lifetime admission to the university while he was still in high school, and he began using his university-issued digital lifelong learning platform (LLP) to find events and activities he was interested in attending on campus: poetry readings, athletic events, career fairs, and even an all-ages pop-up course on sports and diplomacy, which was organized to coincide with that year's Olympic games.[1] He loved these experiences, but he decided to work and travel after completing high school.

During his time interning for an international health organization in developing countries, Ahmed became interested in the health equity challenges he was witnessing firsthand, and he decided to take an experiential online course in community and public health that he saw in his LLP while still abroad. He was hooked. After two years of work and travel, he returned to the United States and enrolled full time as a health sciences major with a concentration in public health.

On campus, Ahmed completed several courses with the faculty member who taught the Community and Public Health class, Professor Tara Daniels. Together, they reviewed the learning journey that Ahmed had formulated in his LLP. As they looked over the story that he had constructed from his curricular and extracurricular learning experiences, they noticed that while he had a solid academic foundation and some good volunteer and internship experiences in public health, he would benefit from learning in a professional context. So Daniels helped Ahmed land a co-op working with LGBTQ youth—her specialization—in a community health center.

Ahmed's co-op piqued his interest in the issue of access to health services for marginalized populations, and this guided his selection of his remaining courses and his second co-op. He was able to work in a psychiatric hospital, an opportunity recommended to him by his LLP based on data in his learning journey. After graduation, Ahmed took a job as a health educator at a community health center, working with young adults in an addiction, recovery, and wellness program. He found the work rewarding, but he didn't love it the way some of his colleagues did.

A couple of years into this job, Ahmed saw an opportunity pop up on his LLP: an embedded experience in which students or alumni could work alongside a partner practitioner under the guidance of a faculty member who would oversee the learner's exploration of research in the field. To Ahmed, this seemed like a perfect opportunity to try out a possible new career path. He chose an embedded experience with a music therapist who treated patients with dementia in assisted living facilities. Daniels put Ahmed in touch with a faculty colleague in gerontology, who agreed to supervise Ahmed's exploration of research on the impact of music therapy on older adults' depression, agitation, aggression, and cognitive performance. Ahmed worked with the music therapist two nights a week for three months and wrote a literature review, a mini research study, and a final reflection. He learned a lot about music psychology, and the embedded experience solidified his commitment to serving the elderly.

As his gerontology professor pointed out, the embedded experience carried credit toward a graduate certificate in age and aging. Ahmed earned the certificate through online and night courses while working at the community health center during the day. The certificate helped him land a job as a home care specialist working with elderly clients.

Ahmed liked his clients, but he was frustrated by the agency's rote approach to care: its leaders relied on tried-and-true formulas and were not interested in technological innovations in the field. To feed his own curiosity, he took advantage of another opportunity served up by his LLP: a health informatics boot camp offered on five successive Saturdays. He learned about new assistive technologies for older adults, including wearable trackers, monitors, and sensors; voice assistants; and virtual reality. He was entranced. The agency, not so much. His colleagues seemed utterly uninterested in the latest technological advances in their field. Ahmed felt stifled. Day after day, he went through the motions, fearing that he was doing his clients a disservice.

One night when out for drinks, Ahmed told a college friend—a fellow health sciences major—how much he'd loved his boot camp (and how he was coming to hate his job). Meg Moran and a colleague had just launched a tech start-up that developed wearable technologies that tracked and reported biometric data to users and their health providers. They targeted active adults with chronic health problems but were looking to do more with older adults. On the spot, Meg asked if he would be interested in coming on board as a consultant, and on the spot Ahmed agreed.

The company was exciting and fast-paced, and Ahmed's insights into elderly users proved invaluable to the technologists. But because he had worked only in traditional organizations, he felt out of his element. Meg suggested that he look into the university's Social Entrepreneurship Institute, a cohort experience for emerging leaders that offers badges for social entrepreneurship competencies. Ahmed enrolled in three hybrid micro courses facilitated by business professors and social entrepreneurs who were making an impact on their communities.

Ahmed's confidence grew, particularly as a result of his Leading Change course, in which he excelled. While he continued to find the company exciting, he knew that he had leadership potential that could not be realized in Meg's company. So when a major tech company approached him and asked him to lead a team working on developing and testing "smart home" technologies to support lifelong wellness, Ahmed jumped at the opportunity.

Today, Ahmed is a recognized leader in gerontechnology. His team includes engineers, computer scientists, social workers, researchers, and co-op students. He continues to meet with Professor Daniels and to use his LLP to set learning goals, update his learning journey, identify learning opportunities, and network with fellow alums and current students. His field is changing rapidly, but he always knows where to turn to learn more. ∎

Shifting expectations, emerging technologies, multiple career pivots, ever-changing learning needs: this is the reality of work and education in the new economy. "Nontraditional" student enrollments are already closing fast on "traditional" student enrollments in degree-granting colleges and universities,[2] and millions more learners are turning to independent providers for certifications, licenses, apprenticeships, and other educational experiences and credentials. Even as some higher education leaders wring their hands over projected decreases in the supply of eighteen-year-olds with means—those prized first-time, first-year, full-time students[3]—lifelong learning is on the docket for virtually everyone.

The question is, Who is going to provide all this education? I began this chapter with a composite student and a fictional university, rather than an actual example as in previous chapters, because today it's uncommon for people to enter into lifelong learning relationships with a college or university. Most institutions focus on providing two- and four-year degrees for young adults and maybe graduate degrees, which are also mostly geared to younger people. Ahmed's university, by contrast, offers a glimpse of the higher education institution of the future. It's flexible enough to offer Ahmed the variety of learning experiences he needs when he needs them in formats he can fit into his working life. It's credible enough to offer degree and nondegree credentials that both Ahmed and his employers can trust. And it's integrated enough to enter into a lifelong learning relationship with Ahmed, devoting its people (Professor Daniels) and its technologies (the lifelong learning platform) to guiding him on his lifelong learning journey.

Unbundlers have a different vision. They advocate for unbundling institutions and degrees in favor of independent providers offering stackable alternative credentials in a deregulated market. These credentials are purported to be faster, cheaper, and more personalized than traditional degree programs—a boon to those who don't need or want degrees. It's difficult, however, not to be suspicious of this push to provide shorter, narrower, more vocational options to those who are not seen as "college material"—disproportionately people of color and those without financial means—at a moment when the economy is shedding jobs formerly held by those without degrees and adding jobs for those with degrees. Even setting intent aside, the unbundlers' solution creates a second-class education system in which the most vulnerable are forced to take on financial risk by entering into relationships with for-profit entities that offer educational products of dubious value and whose very purpose is to capitalize (on) students' frustrated ambitions (McMillan Cottom 2017).[4]

Of course we need high-quality, reputable options for those who truly don't want degrees, but such options cannot *replace* degrees and should not be used as an excuse to ignore the social and economic inequities that make us believe that we know who the deserving are in the first place or that desiring a college degree is a purely personal and unfettered choice. We cannot blithely say that college is not for them. Degrees are only increasing in value for individuals, families, communities, and employers. The goal should be to radically expand access to degrees *and* to alternative credentials—and to help as many people as possible to integrate learning across a variety of experiences over their lifetime. Accredited, nonprofit colleges and universities—with their assembled faculty experts, their learning infrastructures, and their teaching and learning missions—are uniquely positioned to develop educational models that integrate degrees and lifelong learning opportunities.

The college or university of the future will leverage this competitive advantage through innovation for integration. It will design new learning experiences and credentials while ensuring academic integrity, bearing the risk of innovation so their students don't have to. It will offer flexible, customizable opportunities for learners of all ages. It will guide people to integrate their learning across degree and nondegree opportunities throughout their lifetime. This is the promise of the integrated university—and the focus of this chapter.

Alternative Credentialing

Badges, certificates, licenses, nano degrees, micro degrees—alternative credentialing is booming. More than a quarter of Americans hold a nondegree credential.[5] Foundations and investors are pouring money into alternative credentials. LinkedIn purchased the online learning platform Lynda—essentially a video library that provides certificates of completion for its courses—for $1.5 billion in 2015. Mozilla's Open Badges initiative, with funding from the MacArthur and Gates foundations and the involvement of major companies, such as IBM, Pearson, and Microsoft, has created a web-based platform through which thousands of organizations and employers have awarded millions of badges.[6] The Lumina Foundation is funding the Credentials Engine, a searchable, online credential database. Parchment, an educational transcript service, is developing new forms of digital transcripting to document alternative credentials.[7] Chalk & Wire's MyMantl is helping educational institutions and commercial providers build their own badging programs. Employers themselves are getting into the alternative credentials game, working with the American Council on Education to have their training programs evaluated for academic credit.[8]

Colleges and universities are working in the alternative credentials space as well, for example by offering coding boot camps and badging programs.[9] The Education Design Lab, housed at George Mason University, hosts the 21st Century Skills Badging Challenge, which involves a variety of college and university partners in designing and piloting badges that document twenty-first-century skills, such as critical thinking, resilience, cross-cultural competency, and creative problem solving.[10] The extension schools of the University of Wisconsin, Georgia Institute of Technology, University of California at Davis, University of California at Irvine, University of Washington, and UCLA have created the University Learning Store, an "online marketplace of learning applications and badge assessments that allow learners to earn credentials for a variety of professional skills."[11] The store touts fast, affordable, and industry-aligned credentials. Each learning app and badge costs $25. The catalog is organized into power skills (e.g., business meeting etiquette, communicating professionally by phone), tech skills (e.g., defining project management, managing supply chain risk), career advancement (e.g., communicating and deliberating in work teams, presenting effectively to global audiences), and compliance (HIPAA orientation for physicians' offices and clinics). Modules are taught by a professor, practitioner, or university staff member.

All this activity is no surprise given the increasingly friendly policy context for alternative credentials. Jessie Brown and Martin Kurzweil (2017), authors of *The Complex Universe of Alternative Postsecondary Credentials and Pathways*, summarize some policy developments:

In 2011, the U.S. Department of Education piloted a program enabling students in short-term vocational programs to receive Pell Grants. A 2005 amendment to the Higher Education Act made programs that used direct assessment eligible for student financial aid, but only if learning was translated into credit hours on a student's transcript; and in 2014 the Department of Education began piloting federal financial aid disbursement to competency-based providers. In 2016, the Department of Education selected eight partnerships between alternative providers and traditional postsecondary institutions to participate in the Educational Quality through Innovative Partnerships (EQUIP) program. . . . EQUIP both allows students of the providers to use financial aid for the programs and subjects the providers to additional oversight by their partner institutions and third-party quality assurance entities. (11)[12]

The federal government also has supported alternative credentials through the Health Care and Education Reconciliation Act of 2010, which allocated nearly $2 billion for a grant program to increase the attainment of certificates and other "industry-recognized credentials."[13] This law's support for stackable credentials will likely be amplified in the reauthorization of the Higher Education Act, which may expand access to apprenticeships and other training programs as alternatives to degrees and allow Pell grant recipients to use their aid for short-term credentialing programs.[14]

While the education policy landscape is always dynamic, the federal government is clearly moving to deregulate higher education, and this will create more opportunities for alternative credentials from an ever-wider variety of providers.[15] In addition, alternative credentials are increasingly being positioned by policy makers as alternatives to degrees, rather than as precursors or supplements to them. Education secretary Betsy DeVos has explicitly questioned the value of degrees and called for investment in workforce skills training instead.[16] In this context, it's especially important to ask, Do alternative credentials offer meaningful learning experiences, and are they good investments?

Emerging evidence suggests that in many cases, the answer to these questions is no—and moreover that alternative credentials have the potential to function as a second-class educational tier reserved largely for poor and minority populations. A study of alternative credentials conducted by researchers from the independent firm Ithaka S+R and published by the American Academy of Arts and Sciences finds that "evidence of their efficacy is thin and quality assurance is weak" (Brown and Kurzweil 2017, 4). Little evidence of program effectiveness is available, and the evidence that exists is not promising. The authors express concern that many providers "operate outside any system of quality assurance" (42). The review also finds that "a disappointingly large number of for-profit providers have taken advantage of students by charging high prices, delivering poor outcomes, and making inflated claims about earnings and job placement" (42).[17]

Even more distressing, a study of "stackable credentials" in "career pathways" programs in the health professions finds "noticeable racial disparities in the credential earned" and that "many of the short-term credentials had limited labour market value" (Giani and Fox 2017, 100). Black and white students in the sample had roughly similar rates of earning both very short and short certificates, but only 17 percent of black students went on to earn longer certificates or associate's degrees, while 28 percent of white students did. This disparity is particularly problematic because the study finds that very short and short certificates had zero positive effect on workers' earnings (indeed, students who obtained very short certificates saw *smaller* earnings gains than students who didn't obtain any credentials). According to the study authors, these findings put a damper on the claim that stackable credentials promote economic mobility rather than reinforce economic stratification.

Other data suggest that there are also gender disparities associated with alternative credentials. A 2018 New America study finds that women pay more for nondegree credentials and receive less benefit from them.[18] The gender gap is particularly stark among people who do not have degrees, which suggests that the burgeoning alternative credential market is reinforcing and even exacerbating existing gender-based labor inequities.[19]

While proponents of stackable credentials claim they are godsends for those who don't want to attend college and blame "the higher education monopoly" for effectively forcing them to pursue degrees through what they call "degree inflation,"[20] the truth is that this burgeoning market is a boon both for profit-seeking providers and for employers who wish to forgo the premium they pay for degreed workers and on-the-job training, which can now be outsourced to those for-profit providers, often at employees' expense. Meanwhile, individuals who cannot afford to attend a reputable institution are forced to take on financial risk by turning to unregulated, for-profit providers to purchase credentials of dubious value. They are reduced to mixing and matching fragmented, discontinuous experiences and piecing together a watered-down, vocational education.

The alternative credentials market will continue to evolve, and doubtless these credentials will play a role in many learners' lives in the years to come. It's therefore important to ensure that all learners have access to high-quality nondegree options from reputable providers. But alternative credentials are not suitable replacements for degrees. Indeed, degrees are becoming *more* valuable. If we want higher education to serve as a lever for social and economic mobility, rather than as the engine of inequality it has become, it's imperative that we expand access to degrees for people from all backgrounds.

The Durable Degree

What is a college degree? For unbundlers, it's an overpriced piece of paper that provides little information about its holder. In trying to do too much, the argument goes, a degree delivers too little: "a degree signals not one thing but rather an opaque bundle of many things" (Craig 2015, 99).[21] Ryan Craig likens a degree to a debutante ball—expensive, unrevealing, with a similar "return profile"—and asks, "Will degrees become as impractical and amusing as debutantes?" (98). He seems to think so: he casts degrees (like the one he earned from Yale, about which he regularly reminds his readers) as unaffordable luxuries of a soon to be bygone era—the occasion of a bit of laughable preening by the rich perhaps, but nothing more.

The central problem with degrees, according to unbundlers, is that they are based on seat time rather than acquired knowledge and skills. This critique is rooted in the idea that the Carnegie credit hour is arbitrary. Critics delight in pointing out that the credit hour was never intended to measure student learning but was instead a way of standardizing work units for faculty pensions. Fair enough. But the credit hour is a measure of *contact time* with faculty. The term *seat time* conjures bored, passive students not learning much, but what the credit hour does is assure students a minimum amount of time with pedagogical and disciplinary experts. This is why DeVos's aggressive deregulation campaign has some of the most vociferous critics of the credit hour now defending that embattled metric. For instance, the New America Foundation, whose 2012 *Cracking the Credit Hour* was highly influential in higher ed policy circles, now argues that the credit hour "serves as an important, albeit insufficient, buffer against fraud and abuse."[22]

In chapter 3, I argued that place matters to learning. Time matters too. Learning takes time. To be sure, people learn differently and at different rates. Some will learn more than others. This is always the case in any learning situation. But that is not an argument for abandoning minimum time requirements. All students—who after all are investing their time and money, not to mention their hopes and dreams—should expect to spend time with what we know to be the most important facilitators of their learning: faculty. All students should be taught and mentored by faculty who can take them from wherever they are when they enter a learning experience to wherever they can go while it lasts.

Yet for unbundlers, degrees are little more than scams designed to keep students in school longer than they need to be. Kevin Carey (2015, 140) derides colleges and universities for "simply assert[ing] that the appropriate time period for [an undergraduate degree] is four years."[23] According to Carey (bachelor's degree, SUNY at Binghamton; master's degree, Ohio State), "this is fantastically illogical—Marines don't spend four years on Parris Island—yet everyone goes along with it" (140). He also invites readers to compare the typical four-year time frame for a degree from a college or university with that of Dev Bootcamp, a coding academy "designed to keep people in a formal educational environment for no longer than they need to be. That turns out to be nine weeks, less than universities take off for summer vacation" (141).

Dev Bootcamp, once thought to be revolutionizing higher education, is now defunct.[24] When it was in operation, students were expected to spend nine weeks in an online environment and another nine weeks on campus. I realize this is pointing out the obvious, but nine or eighteen weeks *is* a set period of time. And so is twelve weeks, which is the length of the highly standardized boot camp curriculum on Parris Island.[25] So Carey is inadvertently making my point: learning takes time. Again, people learn at different rates, and that's why in the small print of both Dev Bootcamp and the Parris Island boot camp, recruits are (or in the case of Dev, were) told that they might need to repeat some portions of the curriculum to ensure mastery. The designers of these educational experiences set minimum time periods because they understand that immersion over time with recognized experts is critical to developing the knowledge and skills embedded in the curriculum.

Degrees from accredited colleges and universities work the same way. Typically, a baccalaureate degree consists of a minimum of 120 credit hours, though at many institutions there is considerable variability above that number. Is there something magical about the number 120? No. But there is nothing magical about nine or eighteen or twelve weeks either. These are standard minima based on the professional judgments of those offering the educational experiences (by way of their voluntary participation in accreditation since accrediting bodies set and enforce these minima).

A college degree is an attestation that an individual has undergone the educational experience offered by that institution and attained the knowledge and skills embedded in the institution's course of study. Or better: think of it as an argument. The argument made by the college degree is that the holder has undergone the educational experience offered by that institution and as a result has gained the knowledge and skills embedded in the identified course of study. Accredited institutions do not ask anyone to take these claims on faith; degrees from these colleges and universities are based on articulated learning outcomes, and the faculty formulate their curricula and teach and assess their students vis-à-vis those outcomes. For example, the New England Commission of Higher Education (NECHE) standards are designed to ensure the consistency, integrity, quality, and continual improvement of programs.[26] Among the specific requirements, institutions must

- publish learning goals and requirements for each program (NEASC 2016, 4.2)[27]
- ensure that programs "have a coherent design and are characterized by appropriate breadth, depth, continuity, sequential progression, and synthesis of learning" (4.3)
- ensure that the evaluation of student learning is "based upon clearly stated criteria that reflect learning objectives and are consistently and effectively applied . . . [and] appropriate to the degree level at which they are applied" (4.33)
- regularly review all academic programs, including collecting evidence of student learning and program effectiveness (4.6)
- ensure that faculty uphold academic integrity in evaluating student work (4.44)

The NECHE sets a minimum of 120 credit hours for the baccalaureate and directs institutions to "demonstrate restraint" in requiring hours above that minimum (NEASC 2016, 4.29). At the same time—and this may come as a surprise to those who insist innovation is not possible within an accreditation framework—the NECHE recognizes and accommodates a variety of ways to arrive at the degree-hour requirement: competency-based programs (4.30); direct assessment (4.30); prior and non-institutional learning (4.32, 4.35, 4.37); awarding of transfer credit (4.32–40); shorter-term academic programs (4.45); dual enrollment and distance, correspondence, and continuing education programs (4.46–48); and alternative credentials, such as certificates or badges (4.49). In each instance, the standards direct institutions to adopt measures to ensure high-quality academic programs with adequate academic oversight and appropriate levels of breadth, depth, and rigor of learning. The NECHE's goal is to ensure that innovation is accompanied by quality assurance: the standards allow for alternative forms of learning and credentialing while insisting they meet minimum criteria of academic quality and integrity.

While unbundlers malign accreditation for stifling innovation and serving as a bulwark for the "monopoly" that colleges and universities have on higher education,[28] what accreditation really does is shift the risk of innovation from students and families to institutions. It provides opportunities for institutions to innovate while protecting students by ensuring quality. The accreditation process is not perfect, and it's possible for institutions to approach it as a desultory box-checking exercise. But as I can attest from personal experience both as an accreditation evaluator and as an administrator in institutions undergoing accreditation review, it involves serious and comprehensive self-study and external evaluation, and most institutions use it as a tool for productive soul-searching and significant programmatic improvement. Moreover, accreditation is a highly public process: information about accreditation standards, policies, procedures, and institutional status is readily available from the accrediting bodies.

It's true that the documentation that accredited institutions provide to certify learning—essentially, grades and transcripts—isn't ideal. Grades and transcripts are, as unbundlers and others charge, crude representations of learning. They tell us more than these critics sometimes allow: that in the trained professional judgment of disciplinary and pedagogical experts, the learner has achieved one of several performance levels in the courses listed on the transcript. But it's true that they don't in themselves tell us much about what has been learned, to what extent, or—perhaps most important—what students can *do* with what they have learned. A variety of alternatives to traditional grading have been and are being explored, including mastery-based grading (only passing students once they meet an identified performance threshold); gamified rewards, such as badges and points; rubric-based grading (using a scoring guide to assign adjectives or numbers instead of letter grades); simple pass/fail; distributed assessment using digital portfolios or learning apps; contract grading; and narrative grading or learning records. Institutions are also experimenting with alternative transcripts, including developmental records, twenty-first-century literacy records, cocurricular transcripts, competency-based transcripts, and universal transcripts.[29] As these names suggest, these efforts generally involve documenting students' learning across a variety of contexts.

The initiatives are promising, and they have the potential to promote student learning and make it more visible, but it's not clear that employers will make use of them. Busy employers do not as a rule have time to interact with multimodal ePortfolios or to wade through narrative evaluations or long lists of competencies. One of the virtues of degrees from accredited institutions is that they attest to a variety of things about individuals that employers do not have the time to investigate and evaluate themselves. This points to yet another instance of unbundlers construing strengths as weaknesses. Craig (2015, 99) derides degrees for "signaling" several things about the individual, including specific knowledge and skills, general knowledge and skills, "stick-to-it-iveness," and "the personal benefit of having become educated." But this signaling is precisely the value of degrees to employers. They want to know that the student has gained depth and breadth of knowledge through immersion for a considerable period of time in a learning environment under the mentorship of disciplinary and pedagogical experts. To the extent that employers cannot directly observe and assess the range and depth of candidates' knowledge, skills, and dispositions, they will continue to rely on representations of and attestations to those things by institutions they trust.

But what about the persistent "skills gap" we keep hearing about? First of all, there is evidence that the skills gap is overstated, perhaps even chimerical.[30] Employers raise skill requirements when labor is plentiful, leading to an impression of a skills gap, but then lower the requirements when labor is comparatively scarce.[31] And surveys suggest that employers have a more positive view of higher education than does the general public and that vast majorities of them continue to believe that completing college is "very important" and even "absolutely essential."[32]

In any case, employers continue to require degrees. Sean Gallagher (2016, 165) writes in *The Future of University Credentials*, "little evidence exists that disruptive market forces will wash away universities and their credentials such as degrees any time soon."[33] Gallagher is a proponent of alternative credentials; he welcomes changes to the postsecondary market that would bring about faster, cheaper, more industry-aligned micro and nano credentials. But he recognizes that unbundling the degree is not on the immediate horizon:

> The ability of students to mix and match a series of episodic learning experiences or micro credentials together via a portfolio and present this as a hiring qualification in lieu of a degree is many, many years away—if this vision ever arrives. Few employers foresee this future, and while entrepreneurs and some policy makers are calling for it, our existing higher education system, regulatory environment, and professional communities are not yet organized and structured to facilitate it. (168)

The key phrase here is "in lieu of": employers have little interest in jettisoning degrees in favor of alternative credentials. Indeed, because "sorting through the diversity of new credentials is difficult for hiring executives" (S. Gallagher 2016, 106), the explosion of the credentials market may have the ironic effect of solidifying employers' reliance on degrees from trustworthy colleges and universities. The MOOC innovator Coursera seems to have come to just this conclusion; its CEO, Jeff Maggioncalda, has stated that the company is focused on collaborating with reputable institutions of higher education, "betting squarely on universities—and on the continued relevance, even dominance, of the degree as a master credential."[34]

Individuals and their families also continue to value degrees. Between 2000 and 2015, the percentage of high school completers who immediately attended a two-year or four-year college rose from 63 percent to 69 percent.[35] In terms of total enrolled students in degree-granting postsecondary institutions, there was a 23 percent increase between 1995 and 2005 and another 14 percent increase between 2005 and 2015.[36] Surely a number of factors account for this continual growth, but one is that degrees pay off. The "college wage premium" remains near a record high (S. Gallagher 2016, 40). Individuals with degrees earn on average $1 million more than high school graduates over their lifetime.[37]

This economic disparity is growing in the wake of the Great Recession. A 2016 report from Georgetown University's Center on Education and the Workforce finds that the vast majority of the jobs created during the recovery from the recession have gone to degree holders.[38] Since 2008, individuals with a bachelor's degree or higher have gained 8.6 million jobs, those with an associate's degree have gained 1.3 million jobs, and those with high school diplomas or less have *lost* 5.5 million jobs. From a strictly economic perspective, having a degree is as important as ever and becoming more so.

Either/Or → Both/And

The answer to Ryan Craig's (rhetorical?) question is no, degrees will not go the way of debutantes—at least not in the foreseeable future. If anything, as artificial intelligence continues to reshape the labor force, employers will expect degrees for even more jobs—both because they will need some way to sort through many candidates for fewer positions and because the jobs that remain as automation proceeds will become more complex. To be sure, alternative credentials will have a role to play in supplementing degrees, and they will surely proliferate—edupreneurs and policy makers will ensure that. But treating alternative credentials as a *replacement* for degrees is a recipe for increased social and economic inequality. It leaves the most vulnerable among us to sort through the blooming, buzzing credential confusion that even corporate executives cannot make sense of, encouraging students to participate in potentially "predatory labor market relationships" as they scramble to collect credentials that may or may not be credible or even legible to employers (Mc-Millan Cottom 2017, 174). Meanwhile, those with means, buffered by their economic and cultural capital, matriculate in accredited colleges and universities, receive mentoring and guidance from disciplinary and pedagogical experts, and earn degrees that employers recognize and reward.

Opponents of degrees worry about "credentialism" or "degree inflation." We can all agree that if a job does not require advanced learning, a degree should not be required of applicants. But that's not primarily what we're seeing today. Instead, we're seeing jobs changing as a result of rapidly advancing technologies and, of course, automation. As I've discussed in previous chapters, workers increasingly need what Joseph E. Aoun (2017) calls "robot-proof" knowledge and skills.[39] That's why employers persist in looking for workers who are broadly and deeply educated: individuals with degrees. And that's why lifelong learning opportunities will grow in demand in the coming years.

The real problem with credentialism is that the credential becomes divorced from what it represents. What we should be on guard against is the unmooring of credentials from learning. Credentials then become commodities to be purchased from a vendor and stacked (perhaps in a virtual shopping cart). Their value is determined by the jobs for which they can be exchanged, not the experiences, learning, knowledge, and skills they represent.

Colleges and universities looking to enter the alternative credential space need to think critically about how those credentials will articulate both with each other and with degrees. Essentially mimicking for-profit providers by offering highly commoditized, narrow, one-off credentials is likely to contribute to further educational and social stratification—not to mention damage to the institution's brand. Institutions have an opportunity to leverage their academic bona fides, their learning expertise and infrastructure, and their teaching and learning missions to offer credible, integrated lifelong learning opportunities and credentials.

The key to meaningful lifelong learning, after all, is not the piling up of assorted credentials or even the value of the individual learning experiences that led to those credentials, but rather one's ability to integrate learning experiences across time and space. The notion of stacking credentials is meant to suggest that they somehow fit together, but it invokes the piling up of objects and leads to problematic conceptions of educational experiences as discrete "content blocks." By contrast, the metaphors I invoke throughout this book—"journey," "trajectory," "path"—underscore the importance of integration and continuity.

Let me pause here on the term *pathway*, a buzzword in higher education. This term is particularly popular in community colleges, owing to the work of the Community College Research Center and the American Association of Community Colleges and to the influence of the popular book *Redesigning America's Community Colleges: A Clearer Path to Student Success* (2015).[40] More than 250 colleges are developing some form of "guided pathways," a reform aimed at simplifying and clarifying routes to the successful completion of credentials (Bailey 2017).[41] In one sense, guided pathways are consistent with the arguments I advance in this book: they represent more cohesive educational programs, rather than cafeteria-style offerings, and they promote the integration of academic and student services. They offer some hope that community colleges—which provide more lifelong learning opportunities than any other higher education sector—will lead the way toward institutional integration in the service of integrative learning. At the same time, under the influence of organizations and funders, such as Complete College America and the Gates Foundation, guided pathways have been placed in service of the "acceleration" and "completion" agendas. While these are noble goals in the abstract, they can lead, as critics have pointed out, to simplistic so-called solutions, such as "lowering credit limits for post-secondary general education requirements, structuring students' schedules, standardizing advising requirements, and limiting courses students complete within disciplines to specific 'pathways,'" thereby degrading "disciplinary diversity, student choice, and faculty autonomy" (Kelly-Riley and Whithaus 2017; *see also* Rose 2016).[42] No one should object to removing unnecessary barriers to students' progress and completion, but simply restructuring and standardizing educational experiences will not necessarily lead to and indeed may undermine the kind of integrative learning I describe in this book.[43] There is all the difference in the world between forcing students down a narrow, prefabricated pathway and empowering and guiding them to create their own pathways as intentional, integrative learners.

Recognizing this, colleges and universities of various stripes are beginning to do exciting work to integrate degrees and alternative credentials. Some are integrating credentials directly into degrees, while others are helping students integrate learning across separate but related credentials. So far there has been more movement toward the integration of alternative credentials into degree programs. For example, MIT has developed a program in which the increasingly popular "micro master's" certificate, earned online through edX, can be applied to an accelerated master's degree in supply chain management.[44] Meanwhile, a number of institutions have announced that Google's IT support professional certificate would count toward their information technology degrees.[45]

Another example of integrating alternative credentials into degree programs is the University of California at Davis's sustainable agriculture and food systems major, in which students earn digital badges keyed to core competencies and learning outcomes (e.g., systems thinking, experimentation and inquiry, interpersonal communication, civic engagement, personal development) that fulfill major requirements. These badges become part of an online dashboard or portfolio that displays students' learning and tells their story. In essence, the Davis experiment involves integrating competency-based education and alternative credentialing into a degree program.[46]

Some institutions are going beyond integrating alternative credentials *into* degrees and instead connecting alternative credentials *to* degrees over the course of a learner's lifetime. Two universities' academic plans, both pegged to the year 2025, reflect this ambition. Northeastern University imagines globally connected "networks for lifelong learning and discovery" linking faculty, students, employers, and alumni who live, learn, and work in and across "intercultural hubs for lifelong experiential learning." Learners will craft their own learning pathways, with access both to traditional majors and to alternative learning experiences and credentials, such as project assignments with a professional and other "variable-term experiences that give learners insight into how culture affects professional practice." They will have access to degree and nondegree opportunities throughout their lifetime as members of the Northeastern network.[47]

Stanford University's 2025 vision is called the Open Loop University. The traditional four-years-and-out model is transformed into a lifelong loop-in and loop-out model. Learners will apply for admission whenever they are ready—not necessarily just after high school. Instead of being admitted to a four-year program, they will be provided access to six years of residential learning opportunities, which they can use whenever they wish. Students will maintain relationships with the university throughout their lives, whether they are on campus or not. They will have a standing invitation to loop back in at some point in their lives—to further their education by earning a degree or a shorter-term credential, to take on a special project, to mentor students, and so on.[48]

In a way, Northeastern and Stanford can be said to be "unbundling": instead of focusing only on relatively time-standardized degrees, they aim to offer a suite of opportunities of variable durations from which students can pick and choose. But the promise of both visions is institutional integration for integrative learning. Like Ahmed's fictional university at the beginning of this chapter, the institutions imagined here are coherent and cohesive enough that learners continually turn to them throughout their lives as they craft their learning journeys. The value proposition is that the institutions provide the learning infrastructures, tools, technologies, and sustained relationships with faculty experts and peers that engage students in the kind of integrative learning and thinking that they need to survive and thrive in a complex, ever-changing world.

The realization of visions like these will take much more than compiling a menu of degrees and alternative credentials. The point is not to offer a bunch of credentialing options that can be unbundled and rebundled (or stacked). The point is to offer people the opportunities to integrate learning across these experiences as their learning needs evolve and as they craft their unique learning journeys. This will require institutions themselves to integrate—to synthesize their operations to function as a coherent and cohesive whole, rather than as a conglomeration of assorted units and programs operating more or less independently.

What Institutions Can Do

The most important thing institutions can do to promote the integration of degrees and lifelong learning is to organize themselves to enter into lifelong relationships with learners rather than focusing on offering two- or four-year degrees to recent high school graduates. Some students may wish to earn a shorter-term credential before a degree, while others might earn a degree and then continue their learning journey with additional learning and credentialing opportunities. In all of these cases, colleges and universities should help people connect and synthesize their learning experiences. Here are some specific actions that institutions can take:

- *Develop a suite of lifelong learning opportunities beyond but potentially connected to degree options.* When students enroll in a college or university, they should not think of themselves as customers purchasing a two-year or four-year degree, but rather as members of a learning institution or network who are provided opportunities and resources to author their own learning journey. Institutions can create pathways from which students may choose and invite students to craft their own pathways, putting together educational experiences in ways that suit their learning needs and personal, professional, and civic identities and goals.
- *Explicitly link undergraduate and continuing education offerings.* At many universities, there are two sides of the house: the undergraduate college, serving mostly "traditional" students, and the extension school or continuing education division, serving mostly "nontraditional" or adult learners. Though both operations typically offer degrees—often degrees with identical or similar names—the extension or continuing education division is associated with professional education and workplace training, and it also houses nondegree programs, such as certificates and certifications. The institution's educational offerings are often discrete and fragmented. Institutions can support and reward faculty for working together across these boundaries to develop a range of meaningful

integrative learning experiences and make them available to learners throughout their lives.

- *Implement long-view and wide-view advising.* Too often, advising is confined to helping students fill out their schedules for the next semester, with perhaps some perfunctory discussion of their longer-term goals. Advisors—whether faculty or professional staff—should guide students from the moment they enroll (or subscribe) to consider their postsecondary experience as a learning journey that extends beyond the classroom and the campus (the wide view) and potentially beyond the present credential being pursued (the long view). They should think of themselves as membership counselors who help students reflect on and set goals and then pursue them not just semester by semester or year to year, but throughout their lives.

- *Invest in or develop technologies to extend that type of advising and promote lifelong learning connections.* I have discussed technologies, such as Northeastern's self-authored integrated learning digital platform (see chapter 3), that help students build and maintain their learning networks as they move on and off campus. These technologies need to continue to evolve as learners' needs evolve throughout their lifetime so that they can appropriately guide learners to new opportunities. Here, machine learning will become critically important, as learning platforms adjust to and even anticipate inevitable pivot points in a person's life.

- *Commit significant resources to the improved assessment and documentation of student learning.* It's incumbent on integrated institutions to demonstrate that the learning they promote is superior to what learners could gain by mixing and matching a set of unbundled educational experiences from alternative providers. Too often, institutional assessment is imagined as a compliance activity—a way of meeting accreditation requirements—rather than as an inquiry process through which faculty gather data about student learning and use it to improve programs (which is what accrediting bodies expect in the first place). Institutions must engage and empower faculty, as disciplinary and pedagogical experts, to design and administer valid, reliable, and fair assessments that capture student learning over time and across educational experiences.

- *Establish responsible educational partnerships with employers and other community members.* In previous chapters, I've emphasized the need to ensure that collaborations with employers and community members prioritize learning, promote ethical community engagement, and advance reciprocity. Involving employers in credentialing is particularly fraught. Done poorly, it could amount to providing cheap, watered-down skills training to employees—potentially while funneling federal financial aid money to the employers. On the other hand, if colleges and universities insist on strong faculty oversight and academic review and if the programs meet the quality standards of accrediting bodies, such partnerships could represent a way for postsecondary institutions to maintain control over the credentials market while extending high-quality educational opportunities into the existing workforce. The institution's job is to ensure that the offerings provide robust, integrative learning experiences, not narrow skills training. Colleges and universities should also consider creative ways to partner with community and governmental organizations to promote the organizations' work, the postsecondary institutions' outreach mission, and students' learning. For example, similar to Ahmed's embedded experience, students might gain valuable experience—and perhaps a short-term credential—by working under the mentorship of a sponsoring faculty member in a nonprofit organization and researching the issues that it addresses.

What Faculty Can Do

The most important thing faculty can do to promote the integration of degrees and lifelong learning is to participate actively in their institutions' efforts to develop and connect degrees and alternative credentialing programs. As I point out in chapter 5, unbundlers' arguments against shared governance are given force when faculty fail to participate in it.

As postsecondary credentials continue to evolve and as more and more providers flood an increasingly unregulated market, colleges and universities *will* be working in this space, and it's imperative that the learning experiences they develop are rooted in faculty's disciplinary and pedagogical expertise. Here are some specific suggestions for faculty:

- *Mentor students as they chart their lifelong learning paths.* In previous chapters, I discussed how faculty can help students integrate learning across courses and curricula and between courses and other learning contexts, including professional ones. Here, I'm broadening their remit even further by suggesting that faculty should assist students as they develop their lifelong learning trajectories, as Professor Daniels does for Ahmed. As higher education becomes a lifelong endeavor, each learning experience becomes not an end in itself, a terminus, but instead a step on a lifelong journey of exploration and discovery. Faculty are guides on this journey, assisting learners to perceive or conceive of the next milestone, redraw their map, or reset their compass.

- *Develop degree programs that can incorporate and be supplemented by additional credentials.* Associate's, bachelor's, and graduate degrees can be designed so that students earn certificates, certifications, or badges along the way—or so that these other experiences extend into or from those degrees. Faculty in undergraduate, graduate, and continuing education colleges and divisions should collectively review their offerings and design opportunities for students to connect and synthesize them into learning pathways.

- *Lead assessment efforts to measure and demonstrate student learning.* Many faculty resist assessment, but understood properly, assessment involves the gathering, analysis, and use of information about student learning to inform teaching and learning. Faculty do it every day for both formative (in-process, improvement-focused) and summative (end-point, evaluation-focused) purposes. What faculty really resent, in my experience, are cynical institutional exercises in producing numbers solely to satisfy external accountability requirements. But when led by engaged faculty, assessment can be a powerful tool for collaborative professional development and program improvement. It reveals whether, to what extent, and under what circumstances students are learning what faculty say they want them to learn. It gives faculty an opportunity to adjust their teaching and curricula—and also to demonstrate that the learning experiences they design result in significant student learning. Working with colleagues and taking advantage of institutional, disciplinary, and professional resources,[49] faculty should design assessments that are robust enough to capture the breadth, depth, and, most important, the integration of student learning in and across their programs over time. This will give them the information they need to improve their programs while demonstrating to others the value of the integrated educational experiences they offer.

■ *Partner with employers and other community members to develop learning experiences leading to degrees and alternative credentials.* Some faculty, perhaps especially those in the liberal arts, are hesitant to work directly with employers, fearing that the curriculum will be given over to business interests and higher education will be reduced to workforce training. This is a reasonable fear, but it's more likely to be realized if faculty *don't* engage in these partnerships. Many institutions will move ahead without the thoughtful faculty, perhaps involving only their peers who don't share these concerns. Students will miss out on meaningful and effective integrative learning opportunities in professional and community contexts. It's better if disciplinary and pedagogical experts help shape these partnerships and learning experiences to ensure that they are academically rigorous and integrative—and when they're not, put pressure on the institution to either change the program or pull out of it. Participation in these partnerships is an important way for faculty to exert their institutional prerogatives when it comes to curricular design and pedagogical practices. In doing so, they extend their sphere of influence and their ability to shape learners' trajectories throughout their lifetime.

Conclusion

Alternative credentials should not and will not replace degrees, but they will be a part of many people's lifelong learning journeys in the coming years. About this, there is no question. There *is* a question about whether and to what extent colleges and universities will be involved in the development and implementation of alternative credentials—and how they will distinguish themselves from independent, for-profit providers. While many faculty have reasonable fears about undermining their degree programs or reducing higher education to workforce training, they also have an opportunity to help shape the future of lifelong learning and to keep credentialing moored to learning. As experts in learning and advocates for learners, faculty can ensure that high-quality teaching and learning are not sacrificed on the altar of efficiency and cost savings.

For institutions, the alternative credentials movement represents a threat, to be sure. In the years ahead, we are likely to see increased public subsidies for non-institutional providers, including for-profits, which will likely mean a further erosion of public resources for colleges and universities. But this development also presents an opportunity to leverage the competitive advantages that colleges and universities have over those providers—namely, their assembled disciplinary and pedagogical expertise; their bottom-line mission of serving individuals, communities, and the broader public good rather than, well, the bottom line; and their capacity to offer students the kind of integrative learning experiences they need throughout their lifetime to thrive in a rapidly changing world.

Because this chapter concerns credentials, I have focused primarily on the value of education in the labor market. But a lifelong relationship with a college or university brings many other benefits as well. Ahmed returns to his alma mater for continued mentorship from Daniels. He returns to advance his learning. To draw on other faculty members' expertise. To tap disciplinary and professional networks. To pay it forward by mentoring co-op students. Maybe one day he will take advantage of the university's offerings after retirement.[50] His learning relationship with the institution throughout his lifetime remains rich and multifaceted.

All students deserve this kind of education, and it is on their behalf and on behalf of the better world that they will create that we must strive to make it available to as many people as possible.

CONCLUSION

EDUCATING ESTHER

◢ "Will you read my essay?"

I am in charge of the computer room at the College Essay Boot Camp (CEBC), helping students and their tutors get up and running, troubleshooting computer problems, restocking paper in the printer, answering stray grammar questions. But yes, of course, I will read her essay.

"It's not ready yet," she says and skips off down the hall. I shrug and return to my duties.

I recognize her vaguely. Esther, let's call her.[1] A sort of minor celebrity at one of our partner high schools: a slam poet. She won a state championship or something like that. I am surprised to see her at the boot camp. Isn't she a peer tutor at school? Is she really here to be tutored? On a beautiful autumn Saturday? Most of the Boston high schoolers who come to CEBC—and there have been hundreds since this is our seventh annual event—struggle mightily to put their experiences into words. They have amazing stories of fleeing their war-torn home countries, losing parents to violence and drug addiction, avoiding (or not avoiding) gang life, becoming youth leaders in citywide organizations, and becoming the first in their families to finish high school. But they often don't know how to tell their stories. They have never been asked to tell them. And here is Esther, a gifted storyteller. Maybe she just wanted to visit campus? A lot of high schoolers, many of whom live within walking distance of several colleges and universities, tell us that CEBC is the first time they've ever set foot on a college campus.

For the next three hours, I occasionally stick my head outside the computer room and catch glimpses of her seated at a desk she's pulled from a classroom into the hallway. Now she is hunched over the desk, furiously scribbling, her face pulled tight in concentration. Now she is reading over what she has written, her lips moving, her hands fluttering around her head, fingers wiggling as if she is hearing—no, feeling . . . or feeling for—music. I actually check: nope, no earbuds or headphones. Now she is showing her work to a friend, biting her nails in anticipation of his response. Now she is grasping the pen in her fist and scratching, scratching—crossing out, I assume. Now she's furiously scribbling again. She must have placed something heavy on the paper to hold it still because while she scribbles with one hand, the other cuts through the air as if waving an invisible conductor's baton. Her face is open now, eyes wide, and she is smiling broadly.

As usual, there is a rush on the computer room at the end of the day, and I lose track of Esther. As the last student-tutor pairs finish up, I straighten the computer room. In the other rooms, volunteers are breaking down tables and stacking chairs. I assume Esther has found someone else to read her essay and has joined her friends for what's left of this glorious New England fall day.

By the time I lock up the room, it's past time to leave and getting dark outside. And there she is, essay in hand. "Can you still read it?" she asks, extending the papers toward me. I hesitate just a moment, and she pulls them back, says, "It's okay." No, I'm happy to read it.

"It's just a draft," she says. We sit. I read. She bites her nails.

Esther's essay is a gorgeous, wrenching meditation on the cultural meaning of bead strings in the African village in which she was born. At once a symbol of virginity and sexuality, restriction and movement, the beads came to signify for her a deep desire to breathe deeply, to dance, and to sing. Breaking her bead string, half on purpose, became for her a source of deep shame and at the same time an exertion of power—a reclamation of her body, her gait, and her voice. She sees this potent mixture of shame and power as emblematic of the experience of women and girls not only in Africa but around the world, and she wants to bring this understanding to her future work as a health professional.

I am stunned nearly speechless not only by the musicality of her language, which I expected, but also by the—there's no other word for it—wisdom of this seventeen-year-old. My eyes welling, I quickly give her a couple of notes—"Maybe say a bit more about . . ." "Can you slow this part down?" "This image could be a little sharper"—but I need her to know: "Esther, this is incredibly moving. I can feel this piece."

That broad smile again. "Really?" she asks. "Can you really?" ◣

never did ask Esther why she came to campus that day, but I think her "Can you really?" says it all: she came in search of connection. I later learned that she had been assigned a tutor, but she sought me out as well because I was a faculty member. I think she wanted to know if she could make her words and, by extension, herself make sense here, on a college campus. She wanted to know if she belonged.

What were Esther's hopes and dreams for college? What did she want college to be? I didn't ask her these questions either. I wish I had. But she inspires me to ask, What would college need to be in order to be worthy of her?

Start with the obvious: college would need to be affordable. It would provide Esther with a simple, straightforward financial aid process. It would offer her grants because loans are probably too risky for her immigrant family. The grants would be sufficient to pay for tuition and to feed, house, and clothe her at least until she earned her first degree. The grants would be publicly subsidized both because Esther has shown herself to be eminently worthy of support and because the public good is served by educating her. Esther would reap the benefits of this support, but she would repay it many times over by dedicating her talents and insights to solving the challenges that bedevil our world.

College would guide Esther to develop both generalized understanding and specialized expertise. Maybe she would realize her initial ambition and become a heath professional, or maybe she would be introduced to another area of study that engaged her even more. In any case, she would choose a combination of learning opportunities that would allow her to try on a range of disciplinary and professional ways of thinking and knowing, becoming a competent expert and an informed, responsible, and curious non-expert.

College would give Esther access to exciting classes with expert faculty and student peers on campus, a rich cocurriculum, and the tools necessary to reflect on, validate, track, and synthesize her learning journey across physical and digital learning contexts. She would come to see every experience as a learning opportunity—a chance to build on the knowledge and skills she already has and a chance to lay the groundwork for further learning elsewhere and in the future. She would enter new learning contexts with increasing confidence and competence.

College would help Esther grow as a creative artist, a critical thinker, and a budding professional. She would learn to think for herself, to develop her own convictions. She would develop the critical and creative capacities necessary to critique, appreciate, and participate as an active global citizen in society and culture. At the same time, she would learn the knowledge, skills, values, ways of thinking and knowing, and behaviors associated with professions she wished to explore. She would come to understand these professions in the context of shifting social and cultural landscapes, allowing her to develop the agility and flexibility necessary to successfully navigate dynamic economic conditions. Through the combination of liberal and professional learning, she would reflect on, articulate, and lay the groundwork for the contributions she wished to make to her family, her community, and the world.

College would be a place where Esther could forge the kinds of connections with faculty and peers that she craves. It would introduce her to diverse disciplinary and pedagogical experts who could guide and mentor her both in the classroom and beyond it. She would learn with and from them in multiple modalities across physical and digital spaces. She would interact with peers who would bring their own experiences and perspectives to the great democratic challenge of learning to learn and to live with diverse others.

College would be there for Esther throughout her life, offering her learning opportunities and credentials that would allow her to continue to learn and grow as a person, a citizen, and a professional. It would offer these opportunities in many formats and modalities, allowing Esther to integrate them into her learning journey when and in ways that made sense for her. Esther would always know where to turn for further learning, whether she was looking to make a career or a life course pivot, expand her disciplinary or professional network, or scratch an intellectual itch.

Above all, college would empower Esther to chart her own learning journey as an intentional, integrative, lifelong learner. And it would accompany her on that journey as a constant source of inspiration and support.

■ This is the opportunity that colleges and universities have in the years ahead. Only they have the assembled disciplinary and pedagogical expertise to pull it off. Only they have the necessary learning infrastructure. Only they have teaching and learning as their bottom-line mission, their raison d'être.

To deliver on their value proposition, colleges and universities must integrate themselves. What ails US higher education is not too much bundling but too little integration: the public good is severed from private goods; courses and disciplines are separated from each other; classes and campuses are set apart from the "real world"; liberal learning and professional learning are treated as distinct endeavors; faculty roles are increasingly disaggregated; and degrees for traditional students are segregated from lifelong learning opportunities for nontraditional students. Esther will bring her whole self to college; college must be made whole to serve her well.

Integration will not be easy for most colleges and universities. It will require shifts in mindset and structure. It will involve traversing the boundaries between disciplines, faculty, academic units, the campus and the community, and more. It will mean experimenting with new ways of organizing teaching and learning. It may mean venturing into tricky territory, such as partnering with employers or other community members in the development of alternative credentials.

The challenge is to innovate responsibly, with faculty leadership and academic oversight, while absorbing risks so that families like Esther's will not need to take those risks themselves. Venture capitalists might be happy with a one-in-ten "hit rate," but colleges and universities have a bottom-line responsibility to learners, not to investors and shareholders. Careful deliberation on behalf of learners is a strength, not a weakness, of institutions of higher learning. To be worthy of Esther, colleges and universities must push innovation as fast as, but no faster than, responsible educational practice will allow.

▶ Final question: Can we afford to educate Esther this way?

We could decide that if Esther and her family don't have the funds to pay for college, she should enroll in an apprenticeship or earn a short-term credential. She's smart—maybe she'll be able to determine on her own which credential she needs. Maybe she'll get lucky and find one that she can somehow figure out how to finance herself and that an employer will recognize. Maybe she can avoid being taken advantage of by a provider whose goal is to extract profit from her. Maybe she'll get an entry-level job, and maybe she will earn enough not only to live but to save up for the next credential before the robots take her low- or medium-skill job.

Maybe. But even if all of these pieces fall into place, is this what we want for Esther, knowing that it's not what she wants for herself, knowing that she's qualified and eager to succeed as a college student, and knowing what she is capable of contributing to the world? Is this what we are willing to accept? If it is, are we willing to admit it's because she's black or an immigrant, or because her family doesn't have the money to send her to the kind of institution that more privileged people see as their birthright?

If this were Esther's fate, it would not only be a personal tragedy, but a tragedy for us all. In these challenging times more than ever, we need her talents, her creativity, and her ambitions. We need her to be broadly and deeply educated, to become as agile an integrative learner and thinker as possible, to understand the human and technological features of the complex challenges we all face. College might be Esther's only hope—and she might be ours.

The real question we should be asking is, Can we afford *not* to educate Esther this way?

NOTES

PREFACE

1. Danielle Murad Waiss, a student at Northeastern University, is a participant in a longitudinal study examining students' perceptions of experiential education, global education, and postsecondary writing. The study involves interviews each semester with twenty students from a range of social sciences and humanities majors throughout their entire undergraduate career. Since this is not a research-driven book, I will not use the data from this study in a systematic way here. I make no claims about the generalizability of these students' experiences or insights. Rather, I craft anecdotes and profiles based on data from the study because those experiences and insights nicely frame the issues I address in the book. The study is approved by Northeastern University's Institutional Review Board (#15-10-11). Students' names are real, at the students' request and per IRB permission, unless otherwise indicated.

2. Burnett, Bill, and Dave Evans. 2016. *Designing Your Life: How to Build a Well-Lived, Joyful Life.* Random House.

3. Craig, Ryan. 2015. *College Disrupted: The Great Unbundling of Higher Education.* Palgrave Macmillan / St. Martin's.

INTRODUCTION THE FUTURE OF HIGHER EDUCATION IS INTEGRATION

1. See "Automation and Anxiety." *Economist.* 25 June 2016. https://www.economist.com/news/special-report/21700758-will-smarter-machines-cause-mass-unemployment-automation-and-anxiety.

2. Craig, Ryan. 2015. *College Disrupted: The Great Unbundling of Higher Education.* Palgrave Macmillan / St. Martin's.

3. Ginsberg, Benjamin. 2011. *The Fall of the Faculty: The Rise of the All-Administrative University and Why It Matters.* Oxford University Press; Donoghue, Frank. 2008. *The Last*

Professors: The Corporate University and the Fate of the Humanities. Fordham University Press; Smyth, John. 2017. *The Toxic University: Zombie Leadership, Academic Rock Stars, and Neoliberal Ideology.* Palgrave Macmillan; Schrecker, Ellen. 2010. *The Lost Soul of Higher Education: Corporatization, the Assault on Academic Freedom, and the End of the University.* New Press; Whelan, Andrew, Ruth Walker, and Christopher Moore. 2013. *Zombies in the Academy: Living Death in Higher Education.* University of Chicago Press; Carey, Kevin. 2015. *The End of College: Creating the Future of Learning and the University of Everywhere.* Riverhead Books / Penguin; Selingo, Jeffrey. 2013. *College Unbound: The Future of Higher Education and What It Means for Students.* Amazon Publishing. Kindle edition; Sykes, Charles J. 2016. *Fail U: The False Promise of Higher Education.* St. Martin's.

4. Readings, Bill. 1996. *The University in Ruins.* Harvard University Press; Wilshire, Bruce. 1990. *The Moral Collapse of the University: Professionalism, Purity, and Alienation.* SUNY Press; Anderson, Martin. 1992. *Imposters in the Temple: American Intellectuals Are Destroying Our Universities and Cheating Our Students of Their Future.* Simon and Schuster; Smith, Page. 1990. *Killing the Spirit: Higher Education in America.* Viking.

5. Kerr, Clark. 2001. *The Uses of the University.* 5th ed. Harvard University Press.

6. Buchanan, James M., and Nicos E. Devletoglou. 1970. *Academia in Anarchy: An Economic Diagnosis.* Basic; Freedman, Morris. 1963. *Chaos in Our Colleges.* McKay; Heller, Louis G. 1973. *The Death of the American University, with Special Reference to the Collapse of City College of New York.* Arlington House; Driver, Christopher P. 1972. *The Exploding University.* Bobbs-Merrill; Ulam, Adam Bruno. 1972. *The Fall of the American University.* Library Press.

7. Bass, Randy, and Bret Eynon. 2016. *Open and Integrative: Designing Liberal Education for the New Digital Ecosystem.* AAC&U; Horn, Michael. 2014. "Unbundling and Re-bundling in Higher Education." *Forbes.* 10 July. https://www.forbes.com/sites/michaelhorn/2014/07/10/unbundling-and-re-bundling-in-higher-education/#4a73cd3ec1; Jansson, Eric. 2010. "'Rebundling' Liberal Education." *Inside Higher Ed.* 22 June. https://www.insidehighered.com/views/2010/06/22/rebundling-liberal-education; Large, Larry D. 2015. "Rebundling College." *Inside Higher Ed.* 7 April. https://www.insidehighered.com/views/2015/04/07/essay-calls-rebundling-college-and-its-functions.

8. Veysey, Laurence. 1970. *The Emergence of the American University.* University of Chicago Press.

9. Kamenetz, Anya. 2015. DIY U: *Edupunks, Edupreneurs, and the Coming Transformation of Higher Education.* Chelsea Green.

10. McMillan Cottom, Tressie. 2017. *Lower Ed: The Troubling Rise of For-Profit Colleges in the New Economy.* New Press.

11. Fain, Paul. 2017. "'Too Much, Too Fast'?" *Inside Higher Ed.* 14 December. https://www.insidehighered.com/news/2017/12/14/house-gop-pushes-innovation-and-deregulation-higher-education-act-overhaul; Green, Erica L. 2017. "New Higher Education

Bill Rolls Back Obama-Era Safeguards." *New York Times*. 12 December. https://www
.nytimes.com/2017/12/12/us/politics/house-republican-higher-education-bill-obama
.html?_r=0.

12. My thinking here is influenced by systems theorists such as David Peter Stroh
(2015) and, by way of analogy, by General Stanley McChrystal's (2015) description of
the US Joint Operations Task Force in Iraq in the early 2000s. According to McChrystal, the task force was fighting a nimble, adaptable terrorist network by using a hierarchical, bureaucratic, command-and-control behemoth—and, despite its vastly superior
strength and resources, the task force was losing. In order to better address the complexity of the situation in which it found itself, the task force had to be reimagined as a
"team of teams," a network characterized by "shared consciousness." Everyone needed
to have a "big-picture" understanding of the mission and their role in it because success
"in an interdependent environment requires that every team possess a *holistic understanding* of the interactions between all the moving parts" (141). McChrystal, Stanley,
with Tantum Collins, David Silverman, and Chris Fussell. 2015. *Team of Teams: New
Rules of Engagement for a Complex World*. Portfolio/Penguin. Also see Stroh, David
Peter. 2015. *Systems Thinking for Social Change*. Chelsea Green.

13. First published more than 150 years ago, Cardinal Newman's *The Idea of the University* remains in print and is still widely read and discussed. Newman, John Henry.
1996. *The Idea of the University*. Yale University Press.

14. Newell, William H. 2010. "Educating for a Complex World: Integrative Learning
and Interdisciplinary Studies." *Liberal Education* 96.4 (Fall). https://www.aacu.org/pub
lications-research/periodicals/educating-complex-world-integrative-learning-and-inter
disciplinary.

15. This definition is influenced by the work of Mary Huber and Pat Hutchings (2004)
as well as the "Statement on Integrative Learning" (2004) produced by the AAC&U
and the Carnegie Foundation for the Advancement of Teaching, which maps out several varieties of integrative learning: "connecting skills and knowledge from multiple
sources and experiences; applying theory to practice in various settings; utilizing diverse and even contradictory points of view; and, understanding issues and positions
contextually" (13). AAC&U and Carnegie Foundation for the Advancement of Teaching. 2004. "Statement on Integrative Learning." In *Integrative Learning: Mapping the
Terrain* by Mary Taylor Huber and Pat Hutchings, 13. AAC&U and Carnegie Foundation for the Advancement of Teaching.

16. On low-road and high-road transfer, see Salomon, Gavriel, and David N. Perkins.
1989. "Rocky Roads to Transfer: Rethinking Mechanism of a Neglected Phenomenon."
Educational Psychologist 24.2: 113–42.

17. Nowacek, Rebecca. 2011. *Agents of Integration: Understanding Transfer as a Rhetorical Act*. Southern Illinois University Press.

18. Fain, Paul. 2017. "New Data on Nondegree Credentials." *Inside Higher Ed.* 14 September. https://www.insidehighered.com/news/2017/09/14/feds-release-data-nondegree -credentials-including-certificates-and-licenses.

CHAPTER 1 THE MANY AND THE ONE

1. McMillan Cottom, Tressie. 2017. *Lower Ed: The Troubling Rise of For-Profit Colleges in the New Economy.* New Press.

2. Carey, Kevin. 2015. *The End of College: Creating the Future of Learning and the University of Everywhere.* Riverhead Books / Penguin.

3. Craig, Ryan. 2015. *College Disrupted: The Great Unbundling of Higher Education.* Palgrave Macmillan / St. Martin's.

4. Dorn, Charles. 2017. *For the Common Good: A New History of Higher Education in America.* Cornell University Press.

5. The "common good" was variously defined by these institutions, often in ways that should temper any romanticizing of that concept. South Carolina College (now the University of South Carolina), for instance, put itself in service to the causes of slavery, secession, and regressive codes of honor. Even a school like Smith College was founded by a woman—Sophia Smith—who didn't believe in women's suffrage and held fast to separate-spheres thinking.

6. In *The Higher Learning in America: A Memorandum on the Conduct of Universities by Business Men* (1906), Thorstein Veblen complained about the adoption of business practices in higher education, arguing that the latter "had abandoned its commitment to fostering civic-mindedness through a liberal education and, in its place, adopted a devotion to commercial enterprise" (quoted in Dorn 2017, 115). Howard University alumnus and dean Kelly Miller scolded students for harboring "the mercenary motive" and being "seduced by commercialism." Similarly, sociologist E. Franklin Frazier, also a Howard alum and faculty member, decried students' "narrow and selfish individualism" (both quoted in Dorn 2017, 152).

7. David F. Larabee (2017) takes a net positive view of the ad hoc development of US higher education. *A Perfect Mess: The Unlikely Ascendancy of American Higher Education.* University of Chicago Press. Christopher Newfield (2011) takes a dimmer view, noting that "managing our diversity through stratification" is anti-integrationist (119). *Unmaking the Public University: The Forty Year Assault on the Middle Class.* Reprint ed. Harvard University Press.

8. President's Commission on Higher Education. 1947. *Higher Education for Democracy: A Report of the President's Commission on Higher Education.* US Government Printing Office.

9. See Larabee 2017; Zemsky, Robert, Gregory R. Wegner, and William F. Massy. 2005. *Remaking the American University: Market-Smart and Mission-Centered.* Rutgers

University Press; McMillan Cottom 2017; Davidson, Cathy N. 2017. *The New Education: How to Revolutionize the University to Prepare Students for a World in Flux*. Basic Books; Kirp, David L. 2004. *Shakespeare, Einstein, and the Bottom Line: The Marketing of Higher Education*. Harvard University Press; Newfield 2011. European countries that provide free or highly subsidized higher education include Austria, Denmark, Finland, France, Germany, Norway, Spain, and Sweden.

10. See Cole, Jonathan R. 2010. *The Great American University: Its Rise to Preeminence, Its Indispensable National Role, Why It Must Be Protected*. Public Affairs; Crow, Michael M., and William B. Dabars. 2015. *Designing the New American University*. Johns Hopkins University Press.

11. Carlson, Scott. 2016. "When College Was a Public Good." *Chronicle of Higher Education*. 27 November. https://www.chronicle.com/article/When-College-Was-a-Public-Good/238501. Newfield (2011) argues that a postwar vision of a well-educated, inclusive middle class has come under attack since the 1970s for a reason: "The assault began in earnest just as the American middle class was starting to become multiracial, and as public universities were moving with increasing speed toward meaningful racial integration" (3).

12. Katznelson, Ira. 2006. *When Affirmative Action Was White: An Untold History of Racial Inequality in Twentieth-Century America*. Norton.

13. The school-to-prison pipeline is now well documented. See, for example, Michelle Alexander's (2010) excellent book *The New Jim Crow: Mass Incarceration in the Age of Color Blindness*. New Press. Newfield (2011) reveals one representative data point: in California between 1984 and 2004, per capita "prison expenditures grew 126 percent. That bill was paid in effect from funds for universities, which declined by 12 percent in constant dollars during that period" (91).

14. See Welch and Scott's introduction to Welch, Nancy, and Tony Scott. 2016. *Composition in the Age of Austerity*. Utah State University Press.

15. The term neoliberalism is sometimes used loosely by academics to describe any institutional practices they don't like. Though delving more deeply into this is beyond the scope of the book, I think it's important to trace the particular people, practices, and policies that are eroding the notion of higher education as a public good. For this purpose, Nancy MacLean's (2017) *Democracy in Chains: The Deep History of the Radical Right's Stealth Plan for America* (Viking) is indispensable. MacLean details the influence of Charles Koch and the initiatives and centers he has funded—many of them inside higher education—to launch libertarian, "anti-statist" attacks on public funding for education over the past several decades. The Charles Koch Foundation increased its grants to higher education institutions from $35 million in 2014 to $100 million in 2017. There were Koch-funded programs supporting conservative and libertarian causes at approximately 350 colleges and universities in 2017, though there has been some resistance. See Linskey, Annie. 2018. "Koch Effort at Wellesley Will Be Overhauled after

Public Attention." *Boston Globe*. 28 March. https://www.bostonglobe.com/news/politics /2018/03/27/koch-effort-wellesley-founders-after-public-attention/72BYUzr8Yzq85 CeGVSYfXO/story.html.

16. Davidson (2017, 175) draws on an analysis by the Center on Budget and Policy Priorities. Newfield (2011) notes that according to the State Higher Education Executive Officers association, per-student state allocations hit an all-time low in fiscal year 2005. They ticked up in FY2006, but even then, they were 15 percent below what they had been in FY2001. And then, of course, the Great Recession hit.

17. On public disinvestment in higher education, *see also* Welch and Scott 2016; Newfield 2011; Delbanco, Andrew. 2014. *College: What It Was, Is, and Should Be*. Updated ed. Princeton University Press.

18. Archibald, Robert B., and David H. Feldman. 2017. *The Road Ahead for America's Colleges and Universities*. Oxford University Press, 134.

19. Davidson (2017, 177) suggests as much, pointing in particular to exorbitant presidential salaries.

20. College Board. "Trends in College Pricing." 2016. https://trends.collegeboard.org /sites/default/files/2016-trends-college-pricing-web_1.pdf. In constant 2016 dollars, the annual price of private, nonprofit institutions rose from $10,680 in 1976–1977 to $33,480 in 2016–2017; public four-year schools rose from $2,600 in 1976–1977 to $9,650 in 2016–2017; and public two-year schools rose from $1,190 in 1976–1977 to $3,520 in 2016–2017.

21. The handling of student debt is another tragic feature of this story. In the 1990s and early 2000s, Congress passed a series of laws allowing student loans to be taken over by Wall Street banks, private equity firms, and other private companies. The Obama administration returned some of the responsibility for loan dispersal back to the government, but even so, students face what amounts to modern-day usury. Massachusetts senator Elizabeth Warren and a few others are working on this issue, but the prospects for meaningful reform seem bleak under the Trump administration. As Sara Goldrick-Rab (2016, 5) details in her important book *Paying the Price*, the inverse trend lines of the net price of college (cost of attendance minus grants) and of family income hit lower-income families the hardest. Whereas the net price of college for the average student in the bottom family income quintile in 1990 represented 44.5 percent of their family income, that percentage ballooned to an astounding 84 percent in 2012. These families are, of course, eligible for financial aid, including loans, but even small loan debt can be crippling for people without the means to repay it, especially if they do not finish their degree. Goldrick-Rab notes that most people who default on loans do not carry the six-figure debt we sometimes hear about—those students likely have multiple degrees, often in lucrative fields—but rather left school before completing any degree. She points out that "the amount of debt is inversely correlated with the likelihood of loan trouble—the less college you complete, the less debt you have, but the less likely

you are to repay" (93). *Paying the Price: College Costs, Financial Aid, and the Betrayal of the American Dream*. University of Chicago Press. *See also* Archibald and Feldman 2017.

22. In Goldrick-Rab's (2016) study of 3,000 Pell grant recipients in Wisconsin (lower- and middle-income students), half left school and less than 20 percent finished a bachelor's degree in four years. Goldrick-Rab's surveys and interviews make it clear that a lack of financial means was the primary reason.

23. As Larabee (2017) notes, higher education is contributing to the widening of economic gaps: in 1965, students from families in the top income quartile were seven times more likely to gain a bachelor's degree by the time they were twenty-four years of age than their peers in the bottom quartile; by 2013, they were nine times as likely to do so (108). Derek Bok (2015) similarly reports, "Among students who are academically qualified to do college work, 81 percent of those from high-income families complete a bachelor's degree within eight years, while only 36 percent of qualified low-income students manage to do so" (89). *Higher Education in America*. Princeton University Press. For an economist's view, see Clotfelter, Charles T. 2017. *Unequal Colleges in the Age of Disparity*. Harvard University Press. *See also* Crow and Dabars 2015, chapter 1.

24. Gallagher, Sean. 2016. *The Future of University Credentials: New Developments at the Intersection of Higher Education and Hiring*. Harvard University Press, 40. Archibald and Feldman (2017) soberly note that higher education never has and never will guarantee economic success, but their review of empirical research leads them to conclude that "this is a settled question. Going to college causes economic success" (104). They take up arguments about the "sheepskin" effect—that it's the signaling of degrees that matters, not learning—and conclude that while it's true that degrees pay off in ways that "120 disjointed credits" don't, it doesn't follow that only signaling is at play and that "time spent in a traditional college curriculum is otherwise worthless" (104). In explaining the higher productivity of college graduates, they write that "there is a role for knowledge gains and skills acquisition, as well as signaling" (104–5). I would underscore their use of the word "disjointed"; the value-add may lie precisely in the coherent, holistic experience of a college education, rather than the stacking of random credits. See chapter 6.

25. See Center for Analysis of Postsecondary Education and Employment. 2018. "For-Profit Colleges by the Numbers." https://capseecenter.org/research/by-the-numbers/for-profit-college-infographic.

26. McMillan Cottom (2017, 62) notes that at the time of her writing, only three of the eight presidents of publicly traded for-profit colleges had earned a PhD, while two had only a bachelor's degree.

27. In 2017, the University of Phoenix announced that it would close twenty of its campuses. See Jaschik, Scott. 2017. "Report: 20 University of Phoenix Campuses to Close." *Inside Higher Ed*. 26 September. https://www.insidehighered.com/quicktakes/2017/09/26/report-20-university-phoenix-campuses-close.

28. While we can expect this trend to accelerate under the current administration, it began under President Barack Obama. His Department of Education approved the Educational Quality through Innovative Partnerships program, which for the first time allowed students to access federal financial aid to enroll in programs offered by "nontraditional providers." See Office of Educational Technology. "Educational Quality through Innovative Partnerships (EQUIP)." https://tech.ed.gov/equip.

29. Horn, Michael B., and Andrew P. Kelly. 2015. *Moving beyond College: Rethinking Higher Education Regulation for an Unbundled World.* American Enterprise Institute.

30. *See also* Christensen, Clayton M., and Henry J. Eyring. 2011. *Innovative University: Changing the DNA of Higher Education from the Inside Out.* Jossey-Bass. Jill Lepore (2014) offers a trenchant critique of Christensen's disruption theory as well as Christensen and Eyring's application of it to higher education. "The Disruption Machine." *New Yorker.* 23 June. https://www.newyorker.com/magazine/2014/06/23/the-disruption -machine. She also smartly points out how hard it is to critique disruption—"partly because it's headlong, while critical inquiry is unhurried; partly because disruptors ridicule doubters by charging them with fogyism; and partly because, in its modern usage, innovation is the idea of progress jammed into a criticism-proof jack-in-the-box."

31. Selingo, Jeffrey. 2013. *College Unbound: The Future of Higher Education and What It Means for Students.* Amazon Publishing. Kindle edition.

32. This is the conclusion of Robert Sternberg (2016), a renowned higher education leader and scholar at Cornell University. Sternberg evaluates no fewer than twelve options for bringing down costs—from cutting services to increasing the size of the student body to tinkering with college credits to enhancing online learning options— and determines that while institutions can do some things to control costs, even a combination of these actions will bring only nominal savings. *What Universities Can Be: A New Model for Preparing Students for Active Concerned Citizenship and Ethical Leadership.* Cornell University Press.

33. A 2016 *New York Times* article details the decrepit conditions, resulting from budget cuts, at several institutions in the CUNY system. These include leaking ceilings, a lack of toilet paper, broken desks, bugs and vermin, overcrowded lecture halls, and a lack of books in libraries. As horrifying as these conditions are, they receive far less press than the lazy rivers and climbing walls on elite campuses. See Chen, David W. 2016. "Dreams Stall as CUNY, New York City's Engine of Mobility, Sputters." *New York Times.* 28 May. https://www.nytimes.com/2016/05/29/nyregion/dreams-stall-as-cuny -citys-engine-of-mobility-sputters.html?mcubz=0&_r=0.

34. Archibald and Feldman (2017) note that most of the growth in administrative staff has been staff-professional (i.e., advisors and residence life professionals), not managerial (i.e., academic administrators), and that most of those hires have been in areas that are central to the teaching and learning mission of institutions, such as IT

and student services. They grant that some institutions may spend too much on administrative staff, but they caution that it's "problematic to assume that any cost-increasing addition to the professional staff is unproductive bloat" (81).

35. Goldrick-Rab (2016) also proposes a number of reforms to the financial aid system, including clearer definitions of terms, improved communications to students, emergency aid programs, overhaul of the federal work-study program, and a "maintenance-of-effort" requirement for states, which would have to maintain a certain level of funding for higher education in order to qualify for federal aid. See her chapter 10.

36. While it's clearly not the case that individuals without college degrees cannot be good, engaged citizens, it's nonetheless true that a college education correlates positively with higher levels of political engagement, from voting to participating in campaigns to running for office. Reviewing the available data, Bok (2015) concludes that a "host of . . . studies have confirmed [Thomas] Jefferson's belief in the importance of education to our democracy" (84).

37. Deresiewicz, William. 2015. *Excellent Sheep: The Miseducation of the American Elite and the Way to a Meaningful Life*. Free Press.

38. Armstrong, Elizabeth A., and Laura T. Hamilton. 2013. *Paying for the Party: How College Maintains Inequality*. Harvard University Press. The "party" in Armstrong and Hamilton's title refers to the way many wealthy students experience college—at the expense of the rest of us and particularly non-wealthy students.

39. Arum, Richard, and Josipa Roksa. 2011. *Academically Adrift: Limited Learning on College Campuses*. University of Chicago Press.

40. See Astin, Alexander W. 2011. "In 'Academically Adrift,' Data Don't Back Up Sweeping Claim." *Chronicle of Higher Education*. 24 February. https://www.chronicle.com /article/Academically-Adrift-a/126371. Also see several critical reviews in the February 2012 (63.3) issue of *College Composition and Communication*.

41. Lederman, Doug. 2013. "Less Academically Adrift?" *Inside Higher Ed*. 20 May. https://www.insidehighered.com/news/2013/05/20/studies-challenge-findings-academ ically-adrift.

42. There is some evidence (based on student self-reporting on different instruments) of declines in the amount of time college students spend on educational activities during a given week or day. For an analysis that spans 1961 to 2003, see Babcock, Philip S., and Mindy Marks. 2010. "The Falling Time Cost of College: Evidence from Half a Century of Time Use Data." Working Paper 15954. National Bureau of Economic Research. http://www.nber.org/papers/w15954.pdf. More recent time allocation data are available from the Bureau of Labor Statistics. https://www.bls.gov/tus/charts/students.htm. These data are sometimes used as grist for the student-slamming mill, suggesting to some observers that there is a vast "non-aggression pact" between students and faculty. For a more level-headed analysis, see McCormick, Alexander C. 2011. "It's about Time:

What to Make of Reported Declines in How Much College Students Study." *Liberal Education* 97.1 (Winter). https://www.aacu.org/publications-research/periodicals/its -about-time-what-make-reported-declines-how-much-college.

43. "Seventy Percent of College Students Work while Enrolled, New Georgetown University Research Finds." 2015. Press release. Georgetown University, Center on Education and the Workforce. 28 October. https://cew.georgetown.edu/wp-content/up loads/Press-release-WorkingLearners__FINAL.pdf. According to this study, student workers average nineteen hours per week, and one in four is both a full-time student and a full-time employee. Many students who both work and attend school—as much as 40 percent of students in the CUNY system, for instance—nonetheless struggle with food and housing insecurity. Bauer-Wolf, Jeremy. 2017. "Students without Food." *Inside Higher Ed.* 1 August. https://www.insidehighered.com/news/2017/08/01/study-many -community-college-students-struggle-access-food; National Student Campaign against Hunger and Homelessness. 2016. "Hunger on Campus: The Challenge of Food Insecurity for College Students." https://studentsagainsthunger.org/hunger-on-campus. *See also* Goldrick-Rab 2016, chapter 5; and https://realcollege.org. Real College is an organization doing excellent work bringing awareness to the struggles many college students face, including hunger and homelessness, and challenging dominant conceptions of college students as lazy and entitled.

44. Dorn's (2017) case studies show that college students' misbehavior is a time-honored tradition. In the early nineteenth century, for instance, Bowdoin students engaged in all manner of "high jinks," including "hazing students[,] . . . the burning of the 'Temple' (the college outhouse), and the mock funeral sophomores held each year during which they cremated 'Anna Lytics' (their analytical geometry textbooks) and interred the remains on the college grounds" (21). He also details several student riots and acts of vandalism against faculty members' and administrators' property.

45. These are results from UCLA's Higher Education Research Institute surveys. Wyer, Kathy. 2013. "Survey: More Freshmen than Ever Say They Go to College to Get Better Jobs, Make More Money." http://newsroom.ucla.edu/releases/heri-freshman -survey-242619; Rampell, Catherine. 2015. "Why Do Americans Go to College? First and Foremost, They Want Better Jobs." *Washington Post.* 17 February. https://www .washingtonpost.com/news/rampage/wp/2015/02/17/why-do-americans-go-to-college -first-and-foremost-they-want-better-jobs/?utm_term=.e9b91d710260; Blumberg, Yoni. 2017. "College Students Today Value Education Less and Money More: Study." CNBC. 3 November. https://www.cnbc.com/2017/11/03/college-students-today-value-education -less-and-money-more-study.html.

46. Seeking to understand students' perceptions of experiential education, global education, and postsecondary writing, this study involves interviews with our participants each semester throughout their entire undergraduate career. It is approved by Northeastern University's Institutional Review Board (#15-10-11).

47. Marlen, Estefany. 2016. *I Am Going to College Because* . . . . https://vimeo.com/168101620.

CHAPTER 2 DEPTH AND BREADTH

1. College of Social Sciences and Humanities. N.d. *We Are Human Services.* https://cssh.northeastern.edu/humanservices.

2. At some institutions, many students also complete minors, and these programs can sometimes add coherence to a student's undergraduate experience. However, minors receive relatively little attention in curriculum planning and in the national discourse on higher education, so I leave them to the side in this chapter.

3. Here again my thinking is informed by General Stanley McChrystal's (2015) concept of a "team of teams." In post-9/11 Iraq, McChrystal realized that specialized training can prepare people only for specific actions in response to known and anticipated challenges. What was needed for his Joint Operations Task Force was broader education, which would result in a general understanding of the variety of challenges that could arise (153). This does not mean that everyone needed to be a generalist. SEALs would still need to be able to do their thing, and intelligence analysts would need to do theirs. Specialization remained necessary. McChrystal explains: "We wanted to fuse generalized *awareness* with specialized *expertise*. Our entire force needed to share a fundamental, holistic understanding of the operating environment and of our own organization, and we needed to preserve each team's distinct skill sets" (153). McChrystal, Stanley, with Tantum Collins, David Silverman, and Chris Fussell. 2015. *Team of Teams: New Rules of Engagement for a Complex World.* Portfolio/Penguin.

4. Influential institutional and curricular histories of higher education include Cremin, Lawrence A. 1977. *Traditions of American Education.* Basic Books; Lucas, Christopher J. 2006. *American Higher Education: A History.* 2nd ed. Palgrave Macmillan; Rudolph, Frederick. 1990 (1962). *The American College and University: A History.* Reprint. University of Georgia Press; and Veysey, Laurence R. 1970. *The Emergence of the American University.* University of Chicago Press.

5. Committee of the Corporation and the Academical Faculty. 1828. *Reports on the Course of Instruction at Yale College.* Hezekiah Howe.

6. Committee on the Objectives of a General Education in a Free Society. 1945. *General Education in a Free Society.* Harvard University Press.

7. Louis Menand (2010) reads Harvard's *Red Book* as a Cold War document in the sense that it made a case for general education as a bulwark against perceived intellectual relativism, which could make Americans susceptible to communist ideology. General education would ensure shared understandings and values, i.e., "social glue" (42). *The Marketplace of Ideas: Reform and Resistance in the American University.* Norton. Also see Schneider, Carol Geary. 2010. "General Education 1.0: An Efficiency Overhaul for

the Cold War Curriculum." *Liberal Education* 96.4 (Fall). https://www.aacu.org/pub lications-research/periodicals/general-education-10-efficiency-overhaul-cold-war-cur riculum.

8. In 2004, for instance, the American Council of Trustees and Alumni, a nonprofit organization founded by Lynne Cheney, issued *The Hollow Core*, which argued on the basis of a fifty-institution study that weak "distribution requirements" had replaced a "solid core," thus eroding the value and rigor of general education. Latzer, Barry, 2004. *The Hollow Core: Failure of the General Education Curriculum.* American Council of Trustees and Alumni.

9. Gerald Graff writes extensively about curricula in English studies. See, for example, Graff, Gerald. 2004. *Clueless in Academe: How Schooling Obscures the Life of the Mind.* Yale University Press.

10. Jacobs, Jerry A. 2013. *In Defense of Disciplines: Interdisciplinarity and Specialization in the Research University.* University of Chicago Press.

11. Selingo, Jeffrey. 2014. "The Overworked Bachelor's Degree Needs a Makeover." *Chronicle of Higher Education.* 16 June. https://www.chronicle.com/article/The-Over worked-Bachelors/147105.

12. Herk, Monica. 2015. "Fixing Our Broken Colleges: Competency-Based Education and Reauthorizing the Higher Education Act." Committee for Economic Development. 15 May. http://www.ced.org/blog/entry/fixing-our-broken-colleges-compe tency-based-education-and-reauthorizing-the.

13. Adams, Susan. 2014. "The 10 Skills Employers Most Want in 2015 Graduates." *Forbes.* 12 November. https://www.forbes.com/sites/susanadams/2014/11/12/the-10-skills -employers-most-want-in-2015-graduates/#1ed4827b2511.

14. AAC&U. 2015. "Falling Short? College Learning and Career Success." https:// www.aacu.org/leap/public-opinion-research/2015-survey-falling-short.

15. Aoun, Joseph E. 2017. *Robot-Proof: Higher Education in the Age of Artificial Intelligence.* MIT Press.

16. Gallup and Purdue University. 2014. "Great Jobs, Great Lives: The 2014 Gallup-Purdue Index Report." https://www.luminafoundation.org/files/resources/galluppurdue index-report-2014.pdf.

17. Jacobs (2013, 93) notes, for instance, that Penn State has no fewer than twenty-one separate, specialized research centers devoted to the interdisciplinary area of homeland security.

18. http://www.bennington.edu/academics/areas-of-study; http://gallatin.nyu.edu; https://www.hampshire.edu/academics/areas-of-study.

19. Flaherty, Colleen. 2016. "Plato in Marketing Class." *Inside Higher Ed.* 24 May. https://www.insidehighered.com/news/2016/05/24/champlain-college-touts-benefits -interdisciplinary-four-year-general-education.

20. https://www.champlain.edu/academics/academic-divisions/core-division.

21. https://www.champlain.edu/academics/undergraduate-academics/core-curriculum/core-in-year-4-capstone.

22. "LaGuardia Community College." 2017. In *Rising to the LEAP Challenge: Case Studies of Integrative Pathways to Student Signature Work*, ed. Peden, Wilson, Sally Reed, and Kathy Wolfe, 23–26. AAC&U.

23. http://www.eportfolio.lagcc.cuny.edu.

24. http://www.northeastern.edu/core.

25. The special issue of *Peer Review* titled "Faculty Leadership for Integrative Liberal Learning" (Fall–Winter 2015) is a useful primer and offers a variety of models.

26. Gallagher, Chris W. 2007. *Reclaiming Assessment: A Better Alternative to the Accountability Agenda*. Heinemann.

27. I have been critical of what sometimes passes for "outcomes assessment" in higher education. Gallagher, Chris W. 2012. "The Trouble with Outcomes." *College English* 75.1 (September): 42–60. At the same time, I have led assessment efforts at my institutions and consulted for other institutions on theirs, and I believe that assessment of student learning is critical to program and institutional improvement efforts.

28. https://www.aacu.org/value/rubrics/integrative-learning.

29. Nowacek, Rebecca. 2011. *Agents of Integration: Understanding Transfer as a Rhetorical Act*. Southern Illinois University Press.

30. Ambrose, Susan A., Michael W. Bridges, Michele DiPietro, Marsha C. Lovett, and Marie K. Norman. 2010. *How Learning Works: Seven Research-Based Principles for Smart Teaching*, 117–20. Jossey-Bass.

CHAPTER 3 INSIDE AND OUTSIDE

1. On transfer as recontextualization, see Nowacek, Rebecca. 2011. *Agents of Integration: Understanding Transfer as a Rhetorical Act*. Southern Illinois University Press.

2. Carey, Kevin. 2015. *The End of College: Creating the Future of Learning and the University of Everywhere*. Riverhead Books / Penguin.

3. "Learning by doing. That's experiential learning at Kent State." https://www.kent.edu/experiential-learning.

4. "Experiential learning is any learning that supports students in applying their knowledge and conceptual understanding to real-world problems or authentic situations." University of Texas, Austin. Faculty Innovation Center. https://facultyinnovate.utexas.edu/experiential-learning.

5. "Experiential learning is a process through which students develop knowledge and skills and values from direct experiences outside a traditional academic setting." University of Colorado, Denver. Experiential Learning Center. http://www.ucdenver.edu/life/services/ExperientialLearning/about/Pages/WhatisExperientialLearning.aspx.

6. The institutional definitions of experiential education that I have cited do not, of

course, exhaust the plethora of understandings of the term in the vast literature on the subject or in the professional organizations devoted to it (the National Society for Experiential Education and the Association for Experiential Education). For a comprehensive overview of theories and practices, definitions, foundations, history, models, critiques, and social and political issues associated with experiential education, see Warren, Karen, Denise Mitten, and T. A. Loeffler, eds. 2008. *Theory and Practice of Experiential Education*. Association for Experiential Education. For a general introduction and discussion of active learning, problem-based learning, project-based learning, service learning, and place-based learning, see Wurdinger, Scott D., and Julie A. Carlson. 2009. *Teaching for Experiential Learning: Five Approaches That Work*. R&L Education. David A. Kolb's 1983 *Experiential Learning: Experience as the Source of Learning and Development* (2nd ed., Pearson, 2015) continues to be highly influential. John Dewey's 1938 *Experience and Education* remains, in my view, the most important book on the topic. In *The Collected Works of John Dewey: The Later Works of John Dewey, 1925–1953*, vol. 13: *1938–1939*. Free Press.

7. Dewey, John. 1916. "Democracy and Education." In *The Collected Works of John Dewey: The Middle Works of John Dewey, 1882–1953*, vol. 9: *1916*. Free Press.

8. Lave, Jean, and Etienne Wenger. 1990. *Situated Learning: Legitimate Peripheral Participation*. Cambridge University Press. Lave and Wenger, the foremost proponents of situated learning theory, draw heavily both on Dewey and on Soviet psychologist Lev Vygotsky.

9. Brown, John Seely, Allan Collins, and Paul Duguid. 1989. "Situated Cognition and the Culture of Learning." *Educational Researcher* 18.1 (January–February): 32.

10. The influential American Council on Education and Credly, a digital credentialing company, announced in 2017 a digital credentialing system that evaluates workplace training programs for academic credit. https://www.acenet.edu/news-room/Pages/ACE -Credly-Launch-New-Digital-Credential-Program-to-Recognize-Workforce-Train ing.aspx. One indicator of the rise of PLA is the establishment of a new academic journal devoted entirely to it: *Prior Learning Assessment Inside Out*.

11. Zhenghao, Chen, Brandon Alcorn, Gayle Christensen, Nicholas Eriksson, Daphne Koller, and Ezekiel J. Emanuel. 2015. "Who's Benefiting from MOOCs, and Why." *Harvard Business Review*. 22 September. https://hbr.org/2015/09/whos-benefiting-from -moocs-and-why.

12. Overall, the online education market continues to grow, but it's unstable, and some of the biggest online providers, such as the University of Phoenix and Ashford University, have seen precipitous enrollment drops. Straumsheim, Carl. 2017. "'Volatile' but Growing Online Ed Market." *Inside Higher Ed*. 2 May. https://www.insidehigher ed.com/news/2017/05/02/report-finds-growth-volatility-online-education-market.

13. Hawthorn, Christopher. 2015. "Google's New Headquarters Design Takes Trans-

parency to New Levels." *Los Angeles Times.* 3 March. http://www.latimes.com/enter
tainment/arts/la-et-cm-new-google-headquarters-mountain-view-20150303-column
.html.

14. "Google for Startups Campus." https://www.campus.co.

15. Levy, Steven. 2017. "One More Thing: Inside Apple's Insanely Great (or Just In-
sane) New Mothership." *Wired.* 16 May. https://www.wired.com/2017/05/apple-park
-new-silicon-valley-campus/.

16. Useem, Jerry. 2017. "When Working from Home Doesn't Work." *Atlantic.* November. https://www.theatlantic.com/magazine/archive/2017/11/when-working-from
-home-doesnt-work/540660.

17. One meta-analysis of 225 studies found that students are 1.5 times more likely to
fail in courses that feature traditional lecturing versus those that feature active learning.
Freeman, Scott, Sarah L. Eddy, Miles McDonough, Michelle K. Smith, Nnadozie
Okoroafor, Hannah Jordt, and Mary Pat Wenderoth. 2014. "Active Learning Increases
Student Performance in Science, Engineering, and Mathematics." *Proceedings of the
National Academy of Sciences* 111.23 (10 June). http://www.pnas.org/content/111/23/8410.

18. City University of New York. 2016. "A Plan for Experiential Learning." https://
www.cuny.edu/news/publications/ExperientialLearning.pdf. Prepared in response to a
New York state goal of making "experiential/applied learning" available to all CUNY
and SUNY students as well as a state directive to consider the feasibility of making this
kind of learning a graduate requirement, this report identifies, tracks, and documents
experiential learning opportunities (ELOs) across the system. One of the important
findings of the committee is that "at every college, CUNY faculty members play a
critical role in making experiential learning available and meaningful for students. In
fact, many faculty members consider ELO[s] a pivotal part of the student experience at
CUNY, and view their own involvement in supporting experiential learning an important component of their work" (8). While the report is limited by a narrow definition of
experiential learning as necessarily taking place "beyond the classroom" (4), it cites
"classroom integration" (11) as an area of future emphasis.

19. http://guttman.cuny.edu/academics/summer-bridge-program.

20. http://guttman.cuny.edu/category/experiential-learning.

21. Fleming, Nancy P., and Mark S. Schantz. 2010. "The Odyssey Program at Hendrix College." *Directions in Teaching and Learning* 124 (Winter): 75–80.

22. Hku, Teli. 2016. "The Results of Integrating a MOOC into On-Campus Teaching."
edX. 9 February. https://blog.edx.org/integrating-a-mooc-into-on-campus-teaching.

23. https://sail.northeastern.edu.

24. For an excellent overview of the opportunities and challenges of community engagement, see Gardinier, Lori. 2016. *Service-Learning through Community Engagement.*
Springer.

25. Guttman Community College. 2018. "2nd Annual Global Learning Summit Engages Participants." 26 January. http://guttman.cuny.edu/2018/01/26/2nd-annual-global-learning-summit-engages-participants.

CHAPTER 4 A LIFE AND A LIVING

1. This profile was constructed from a "student pathway" narrative posted by Northeastern University's College of Social Sciences and Humanities: https://www.northeastern.edu/cssh/shared-content/pathway/jackson-golden.

2. http://grandslambaseball.squarespace.com. There are also public websites and YouTube videos about Grand Slam Baseball.

3. Marcus, Jon. 2017. "How the Humanities Can Train Entrepreneurs." *Atlantic*. 20 September. https://www.theatlantic.com/education/archive/2017/09/how-the-humanities-can-train-entrepreneurs/540390; Hipps, J. Bradford. 2016. "To Write Better Code, Read Virginia Woolf." *New York Times Sunday Review*. 21 May. https://www.nytimes.com/2016/05/22/opinion/sunday/to-write-software-read-novels.html?_r=0; Sharma, Piyush. 2017. "60 Famous, Successful People and the One Thing They Have in Common." *MensXP*. 18 July. http://www.mensxp.com/work-life/leadership/38230-60-famous-successful-people-and-the-one-thing-they-have-in-common-the-liberal-arts.html; Berr, Jonathan. 2017. "Does a Liberal Arts Degree Lead to Low Pay? Not Necessarily." *MoneyWatch*. 29 August. https://www.cbsnews.com/news/a-liberal-arts-degree-low-pay-not-necessarily; Anders, George. 2016. "Good News, Liberal-Arts Majors: Your Peers Probably Won't Outearn You Forever." *Wall Street Journal*. 11 September. https://www.wsj.com/articles/good-news-liberal-arts-majors-your-peers-probably-wont-outearn-you-forever-1473645902; Grasgreen, Allie. 2014. "Liberal Arts Grads Win Long-Term." *Inside Higher Ed*. 22 January. https://www.insidehighered.com/news/2014/01/22/see-how-liberal-arts-grads-really-fare-report-examines-long-term-data; Morad, Renee. 2017. "Why Mark Cuban Believes Liberal Arts Is the Future of Jobs." *Forbes*. 28 February. https://www.forbes.com/sites/reneemorad/2017/02/28/why-mark-cuban-believes-liberal-arts-is-the-future-of-jobs/#6df7de3f7a92; Ward, Marguerite. 2017. "Google Exec, Mark Cuban Agree That These College Majors Are the Most Robot-Resistant." *CNBC*. 21 April. https://www.cnbc.com/2017/04/21/these-college-majors-are-the-most-robot-resistant.html.

4. Hartley, Scott. 2017. *The Fuzzy and the Techie: Why the Liberal Arts Will Rule the Digital World*. Houghton Mifflin Harcourt; Madsbjerg, Christian. 2017. *Sensemaking: The Power of the Humanities in the Age of the Algorithm*. Hachette; Stross, Randall. 2017. *A Practical Education: Why Liberal Arts Majors Make Great Employees*. Redwood Press; Anders, George. 2017. *You Can Do Anything: The Surprising Power of a "Useless" Liberal Arts Education*. Little, Brown.

5. Nussbaum, Martha. 2010. *Not for Profit: Why Democracy Needs the Humanities*.

Princeton University Press. *See also* Altschuler, Glenn. 2015. "How to Save the Liberal Arts from Extinction." *New Republic*. 8 April. https://newrepublic.com/article/121492 /how-save-liberal-arts-extinction; Flaherty, Colleen. 2016. "Saving the Liberal Arts." *Inside Higher Ed*. 20 May. https://www.insidehighered.com/news/2016/05/20/scholars -consider-how-save-liberal-arts.

6. For a smart analysis of the last ten years of data on majors in the humanities, see Schmidt, Ben. 2018. "The Humanities Are in Crisis." *Atlantic*. 23 August. https://www .theatlantic.com/ideas/archive/2018/08/the-humanities-face-a-crisisof-confidence/56 7565.

7. Between 2008–2009 and 2013–2014, computer and information sciences (+46%), engineering and engineering technologies (+29%), and health professions and related fields (+65%) saw significant increases in degrees conferred, while foreign languages, literatures, and linguistics (−4%) and philosophy and religious studies (−4%) experienced decreases in degrees conferred. Taking a slightly longer view, between 2004–2005 and 2014–2015, English language and literature/letters dropped in terms of both number of degrees conferred (54,379 to 45,847) and percentage of all degrees conferred (3.8% to 2.4%), and the same is true, though less dramatically so, for philosophy and religious studies, which went from 11,584 (0.8% of total degrees) in 2004–2005 to 11,072 (0.6% of total degrees) in 2014–2015. Meanwhile, engineering increased in terms of both raw numbers (64,707 to 97,858) and percentage of total degrees conferred (4.5% to 5.2%). Business too saw growth in the raw number of majors (311,574 to 363,799), though its share of total degrees conferred dipped slightly (21.6 percent to 19.2 percent). National Center for Education Statistics. N.d. "Fast Facts." https://nces.ed.gov /fastfacts/display.asp?id=37; National Center for Education Statistics. N.d. "Digest of Education Statistics." https://nces.ed.gov/programs/digest/d16/tables/dt16_322.10.asp ?current=yes.

8. Herk, Monica. 2015. "Fixing Our Broken Colleges: Competency-Based Education and Reauthorizing the Higher Education Act." Committee for Economic Development. 15 May. http://www.ced.org/blog/entry/fixing-our-broken-colleges-competen cy-based-education-and-reauthorizing-the.

9. Carey, Kevin. 2015. *The End of College: Creating the Future of Learning and the University of Everywhere*. Riverhead Books / Penguin. To be fair, Carey is not an opponent of the liberal arts per se—in liberal arts colleges, at least. Carey, Kevin. 2014. "A Liberal-Arts College That Gets It Right." *Chronicle of Higher Education*. 10 February. www .chronicle.com/article/A-Liberal-Arts-College-That/144651.

10. Jansson, Eric. 2010. "'Rebundling' Liberal Education." *Inside Higher Ed*. 22 June. https://www.insidehighered.com/views/2010/06/22/rebundling-liberal-education.

11. The NITLE is an independent nonprofit organization housed at the Council on Library and Information Resources in Washington, DC.

12. Roth, Michael S. 2015. *Beyond the University: Why Liberal Education Matters.* Yale University Press. Kindle edition.

13. Committee on Prospering in the Global Economy of the 21st Century. 2007. *Rising above the Gathering Storm: Energizing and Employing America for a Brighter Economic Future.* National Academies Press.

14. Members of the 2005 Rising above the Gathering Storm Committee. 2010. *Rising above the Gathering Storm, Revisited: Rapidly Approaching Category 5.* National Academies Press. This second report acknowledged the gains, but at the same time expressed concern that the United States was not doing enough and that our European counterparts were doing more along the lines suggested by the original report than the United States was doing.

15. Commission on the Humanities and Social Sciences. 2013. *The Heart of the Matter: The Humanities and Social Sciences for a Vibrant, Competitive, and Secure Nation.* American Academy of Arts and Sciences.

16. Commission on the Humanities and Social Sciences. 2015. *The Heart of the Matter around the Country.* American Academy of Arts and Sciences.

17. Members of the Commission on the Humanities and Social Sciences (2015, 7), reflecting on their drafting of *Heart*, noted that they

> did not want to position the disciplines against each other in a new competition for shrinking governmental support. . . . Nor were we strictly interested in boosting the statistical profile of the humanities and social sciences—for example, by increasing the number of undergraduates who major in these disciplines. We simply wanted to remind students, parents, teachers, researchers, and the public that their personal and professional lives, as well as the intellectual life of the nation, are deepened and strengthened by their daily interactions with the humanities and social sciences.

18. See, for example, Rhode Island School of Design's STEM to STEAM framework: http://stemtosteam.org.

19. See the *Peer Review* special issue on STIRS: 18.4 (Fall 2016).

20. http://www.100resilientcities.org.

21. The AAC&U, the foremost professional organization devoted to liberal education, defines liberal education as

> an approach to learning that empowers individuals and prepares them to deal with complexity, diversity, and change. It provides students with broad knowledge of the wider world (e.g., science, culture, and society) as well as in-depth study in a specific area of interest. A liberal education helps students develop a sense of social responsibility, as well as strong and transferable intellectual and practical skills such as communication, analytical and problem-solving skills, and a demonstrated ability to apply knowledge and skills in real-world settings. (https://www.aacu.org/leap/what-is-a-liberal-education)

Readers may also be interested in journalist and CNN personality Fareed Zakaria's *In Defense of Liberal Education* (Norton, 2015), in which he argues that the great value of liberal education lies in teaching students how to write, how to speak, and how to learn.

22. Dewey, John. 1923. "Culture and Professionalism." In *The Collected Works of John Dewey: The Middle Works of John Dewey, 1882–1953*, vol. 15: *1923–1924*. Free Press.

23. Aoun, Joseph E. 2017. *Robot-Proof: Higher Education in the Age of Artificial Intelligence*. MIT Press.

24. Gutmann, Amy. 2015. "What Makes a University Education Worthwhile?" In *The Aims of Higher Education: Problems of Morality and Justice*, ed. Brighouse, Harry, and Michael McPherson, 7–25. University of Chicago Press.

25. Wagner College: http://wagner.edu/academics/undergraduate; Bates College: https://www.bates.edu/catalog/the-college. For several other examples of liberal arts colleges incorporating practical and professional emphases, see Anft, Michael. 2017. "From Liberal Arts to Making a Living." *Chronicle of Higher Education*. 22 October. www.chronicle.com/article/From-Liberal-Arts-to-Making-a/241510.

26. Townsley, Eleanor, Becky Wai-Ling Packard, and Eva Paus. 2014–2015. "Making the Lynk at Mount Holyoke: Institutionalizing Integrative Learning." *Peer Review* 16.4–17.1 (Fall–Winter 2015). https://www.aacu.org/peerreview/2014-2015/fall-winter/townsley. *See also* https://www.mtholyoke.edu/lynk/how-lynk-works.

27. Nine million students were enrolled in two-year colleges in 2015–2016; that's 39 percent of the total undergraduate population in the United States. Of all undergraduates who completed a degree that year, 49 percent had attended a community college at some point in the prior ten years. These figures are from the Community College Research Center at Columbia University and are based on National Center for Education Statistics data. https://ccrc.tc.columbia.edu/Community-College-FAQs.html. This site also provides data and analysis on student demographics, including race, income, and first-generation status. On humanities degrees, see Humanities Indicators, a project of the American Academy of Arts and Sciences. https://www.humanitiesindicators.org/content/indicatorDoc.aspx?i=10807.

28. Teagle Foundation. N.d. "Student Learning for Civic Capacity." http://www.teaglefoundation.org/Grants-Initiatives/Grants-Database/Grants/A-Larger-Vision/Student-Learning-for-Civic-Capacity; Community College National Center for Community Engagement. N.d. "Student Learning for Civic Capacity Project." http://ccncce.org/projects/student-learning-for-civic-capacity-project; AAC&U. N.d. "Developing a Community College Student Roadmap." https://www.aacu.org/roadmap.

29. Rusnak, Andrew. 2018. Personal communication. 18 September.

30. Teagle Foundation. N.d. "Liberal Arts and the Professions." http://www.teaglefoundation.org/Grants-Initiatives/Current-Initiatives-Listing/Liberal-Arts-and-the-Professions/RFP.

31. http://www.olin.edu/academics/curriculum.

32. http://www.olin.edu/academic-life/experience.

33. http://www.olin.edu/about/at-a-glance.

34. https://www.northeastern.edu/cssh/undergraduate.

35. Gallagher, Chris W., and Uta G. Poiger. Forthcoming. "Integrating the Experiential Liberal Arts at Northeastern University." In *Redesigning Liberal Learning: Innovative Program Design for 21st Century Undergraduate Education*, ed. Pope-Ruark, Rebecca, Philip Motley, and William Moner. Johns Hopkins University Press.

36. https://newamericanuniversity.asu.edu.

37. https://newamericanuniversity.asu.edu/about/design-aspirations.

38. Crow, Michael M., and William B. Dabars. 2015. *Designing the New American University*. Johns Hopkins University Press.

39. John Warner has published critical blog posts in *Inside Higher Ed*; see, e.g., Warner, John. 2015. "ASU Is the 'New American University'—It's Terrifying." *Inside Higher Ed*. 25 January. https://www.insidehighered.com/blogs/just-visiting/asu-new-american-university-its-terrifying.

40. http://www.olin.edu/faculty.

41. Young, Jeffrey R. 2017. "How Many Times Will People Change Jobs? The Myth of the Endlessly-Job-Hopping Millennial." *EdSurge*. 20 July. https://www.edsurge.com/news/2017-07-20-how-many-times-will-people-change-jobs-the-myth-of-the-endlessly-job-hopping-millennial.

CHAPTER 5 HUMANS AND MACHINES

1. Owens, Colleen, Meredith Dank, Amy Farrell, Justin Breaux, Isela Banuelos, Rebecca Pfeffer, Ryan Heitsmith, Katie Bright, and Jack McDevitt. 2014. "Understanding the Organization, Operation, and Victimization Process of Labor Trafficking in the United States." Urban Institute. 21 October. https://www.urban.org/research/publication/understanding-organization-operation-and-victimization-process-labor-trafficking-united-states.

2. https://web.northeastern.edu/irj/violence-and-justice-research-laboratory.

3. Flaherty, Colleen. 2017. "Social Science Lab Rats." *Inside Higher Ed*. 26 July. https://www.insidehighered.com/news/2017/07/26/interdisciplinary-social-sciences-lab-northeastern-u-challenges-prevailing-norms-lab.

4. To learn more about Farrell, see https://cssh.northeastern.edu/people/faculty/amy-farrell.

5. Smith, Vernon C. 2008. "The Unbundling and Rebundling of Faculty Roles in E-Learning Community College Courses." PhD diss., University of Arizona.

6. Losh, Elizabeth. 2014. *The War on Learning: Gaining Ground in the Digital University*. MIT Press; Davidson, Cathy N. 2017. *The New Education: How to Revolutionize the University to Prepare Students for a World in Flux*. Basic Books.

7. Kranzberg, Melvin. 1986. "Technology and History: Kranzberg's Laws." *Technology and Culture* 27.3: 544–60.

8. Gee, Alastair. 2017. "Facing Poverty, Academics Turn to Sex Work and Sleeping in Cars." *Guardian.* 28 September. https://www.theguardian.com/us-news/2017/sep/28/adjunct-professors-homeless-sex-work-academia-poverty.

9. Maxey, Daniel, and Adrianna Kezar. 2016. "The Current Context for Faculty Work in Higher Education: Understanding the Forces Affecting Higher Education and the Changing Faculty." In *Envisioning the Faculty for the Twenty-First Century: Moving to a Mission-Centered and Learner-Centered Model,* ed. Kezar, Adrianna, and Daniel Maxey, 3–22. Rutgers University Press.

10. American Association of University Professors. 1940. "1940 Statement of Principles on Academic Freedom and Tenure." https://www.aaup.org/report/1940-statement-principles-academic-freedom-and-tenure.

11. Craig, Ryan. 2015. *College Disrupted: The Great Unbundling of Higher Education.* Palgrave Macmillan / St. Martin's.

12. Carey, Kevin. 2015. *The End of College: Creating the Future of Learning and the University of Everywhere.* Riverhead Books / Penguin.

13. Selingo, Jeffrey. 2013. *College Unbound: The Future of Higher Education and What It Means for Students.* Amazon Publishing. Kindle edition.

14. I have pointed out in previous chapters that unbundlers have a curious habit of generalizing from an *n* of one—themselves. Occasionally, they will collect additional "data," as when Carey (2015, 163) "got on the phone and talked with a half dozen MIT students about the class. For the most part, their experience was just like mine." Although they claim to be proponents of "data-driven" education, unbundlers offer scant data, and what little they offer has been collected in remarkably ad hoc ways.

15. Selwyn, Neil. 2016. *Is Technology Good for Education?* Wiley.

16. Ferster, Bill. 2014. *Teaching Machines: Learning from the Intersection of Education and Technology.* Johns Hopkins University Press.

17. Pappano, Laura. 2012. "The Year of the MOOC." *New York Times.* 2 November. https://www.nytimes.com/2012/11/04/education/edlife/massive-open-online-courses-are-multiplying-at-a-rapid-pace.html.

18. Davidson (2017) offers a fuller rendition of this story in chapter 4 of *The New Education.*

19. Zhenghao, Chen, Brandon Alcorn, Gayle Christensen, Nicholas Eriksson, Daphne Koller, and Ezekiel J. Emanuel. 2015. "Who's Benefiting from MOOCs, and Why." *Harvard Business Review.* 22 September. https://hbr.org/2015/09/whos-benefiting-from-moocs-and-why.

20. Cuban, Larry. 1986. *Teachers and Machines: The Classroom Use of Technology since the 1920s.* Teachers College Press; Cuban, Larry. 2001. *Oversold and Underused: Computers in the Classroom.* Harvard University Press; Ferster 2014.

21. Aoun, Joseph E. 2017. *Robot-Proof: Higher Education in the Age of Artificial Intelligence.* MIT Press. An interesting experiment along these lines is the University of Michigan at Ann Arbor's M-Write program, which combines automated peer review processes and automatic text analysis to provide feedback to students on their writing-to-learn in large-enrollment courses. The program, which was designed by faculty in the Gayle Morris Sweetland Center for Writing, provides feedback to students on their writing. The idea is that faculty in large-enrollment courses cannot provide tailored feedback to every student, and this program fills that need. There is skepticism in my field of writing studies about the use of computers to "read" and especially to evaluate student writing; see "Professionals against Machine Scoring of Student Essays in High-Stakes Assessment." 2013. http://humanreaders.org/petition. But Michigan's program, spearheaded by Anne Gere, a leader in the field, is designed to supplement rather than supplant instruction. It provides only feedback on writing-to-learn tasks, for instance; it is not a grading tool. Gere has also been clear that the goal of the program is not to improve students' writing, but rather to improve their learning of the content of the course *through* writing. Still, M-Write is controversial, and it is worth watching as research on its implementation becomes available. See Straumsheim, Carl. 2017. "More Writing through Automation." *Inside Higher Ed.* 10 July. https://www.insidehighered.com/news/2017/07/10/university-michigan-prepares-test-automated-text-analysis-tool; Brown, Jessica Leigh. 2017. "How U of Michigan Built Automated Essay-Scoring Software to Fill 'Feedback Gap' for Student Writing." *EdSurge.* 6 June. https://www.edsurge.com/news/2017-06-06-how-u-of-michigan-built-automated-essay-scoring-software-to-fill-feedback-gap-for-student-writing.

22. Reich, Justin, and Mizuko Ito. 2017. *From Good Intentions to Real Outcomes: Equity by Design in Learning Technologies.* Digital Media and Learning Research Hub.

23. This question of how we define "faculty" is at the heart of the controversy involving Western Governors University, the best-known provider of competency-based education. In September 2017, a US Department of Education audit by the inspector general found the online, nonprofit institution to be out of compliance with Title IV requirements because more than 50 percent of its courses were found to be "correspondence" rather than "distance" courses. Correspondence courses involve students completing assigned work and taking exams at home using materials provided by the institution, while distance courses additionally "use technologies to support regular and substantive interaction between students and their instructors." The inspector general found that fewer than 50 percent of WGU's courses met the latter definition and ordered it to repay $713 million in federal financial aid. The audit found that faculty are primarily responsible for course content and do not interact sufficiently with students to warrant the "distance education" label. The leaders of WGU argued that mentors should "count" as faculty and that the inspector general was applying outdated educational policies and interpretations to a twenty-first-century educational model. As

widely expected, the Trump administration rejected the inspector general's finding in early 2019. But the audit raised the larger question of whether unbundled faculty models can provide adequate faculty-student interactions. See Office of Inspector General. 2017. "Western Governors University Was Not Eligible to Participate in the Title IV Programs: Final Audit Report." US Department of Education. https://www2.ed.gov /about/offices/list/oig/auditreports/fy2017/a05m0009.pdf; Fain, Paul. 2017. "Federal Audit Challenges Faculty Role at WGU." *Inside Higher Ed.* 22 September. https://www .insidehighered.com/news/2017/09/22/education-depts-inspector-general-calls -western-governors-repay-713-million-federal; Kamenetz, Anya. 2017. "Who Is a College Teacher, Anyway?" National Public Radio. 28 September. https://www.npr.org /sections/ed/2017/09/28/553753020/who-is-a-college-teacher-anyway-audit-of-online -university-raises-questions; Kreighbaum, Andrew. 2019. "No Penalty for Western Governors." *Inside Higher Ed.* 14 January. https://www.insidehighered.com/news/2019/01/14 /trump-administration-rejects-inspector-generals-critical-audit-findings-western.

24. Smith (2008) credits David F. Noble with predicting nearly two decades ago both the unbundling of the faculty and the results it would bring, including the commodification of learning and the deprofessionalization of the faculty. Noble, David F. 2002. *Digital Diploma Mills: The Automation of Higher Education.* Monthly Review Press.

25. The virtual assembly line could also be said to have a predecessor in late nineteenth- and early twentieth-century correspondence schools, which employed "scores of women sitting five abreast at desks check[ing] student work in assembly line fashion, who turned it over to instructors to double-check" (Ferster 2014, 28, quoting Thomas Foster, founder of International Correspondence Schools).

26. Gehrke, Sean, and Adrianna Kezar. 2015. "Unbundling the Faculty Role in Higher Education: Utilizing Historical, Theoretical, and Empirical Frameworks to Inform Future Research." In *Higher Education: Handbook of Theory and Research*, vol. 30, ed. Michael B. Paulson, 93–150. Springer.

27. *See also* Neely, Patricia W., and Jan P. Tucker. 2010. "Unbundling Faculty Roles in Online Distance Education Programs." *International Review of Research in Open and Distance Learning* 11.2 (May). https://files.eric.ed.gov/fulltext/EJ895745.pdf.

28. Light, Richard J. 2001. *Making the Most of College.* Harvard University Press.

29. Kezar, Adrianna J., and Daniel Maxey. 2016. "Recognizing the Need for a New Faculty Model." In *Envisioning the Faculty for the 21st Century*, ed. Adrianna J. Kezar and Daniel Maxey, 23–42. Rutgers University Press.

30. While many faculty are skeptical of edtech—and from my perspective they come by that skepticism honestly, given the penchant of disruptors and administrators to foist highly hyped new technologies on them without consultation—surveys suggest that they are increasingly embracing learning technologies in their classrooms and are warming to online teaching. They remain dissatisfied with commercial platforms and courseware products, and they want better tools for teaching hybrid and "flipped"

courses as well as more administrative support. These are the conclusions of a 2017 *Chronicle of Higher Education* report on various faculty surveys. The surveys show that more than 70 percent of faculty members prefer a teaching model that mixes online and face-to-face features. Nearly two-thirds support the increased use of technology in education. Of those who teach online, 70 percent say their teaching is improved by the experience. McMurtrie, Beth. 2017. "Why Faculty Members Still Aren't Sure What to Make of Educational Technology." *Chronicle of Higher Education*. 9 November. www .chronicle.com/article/Why-Faculty-Members-Still/241729. *See also* Lederman, Doug, and Lindsay McKenzie. 2017. "Faculty Buy-In Builds, Bit by Bit: Survey of Faculty Attitudes on Technology." *Inside Higher Ed.* 30 October. https://www.insidehighered .com/news/survey/faculty-buy-builds-bit-bit-survey-faculty-attitudes-technology. For a critique of reports on faculty attitude surveys, see Bali, Maha. 2017. "Seeking Integrity in EdTech Research—Again." *Chronicle of Higher Education*. 1 November. http://www .chronicle.com/blogs/profhacker/seeking-integrity-in-edtech-research-again/64497.

31. TIAA Institute. 2016. "Taking the Measure of Faculty Diversity." https://www .tiaainstitute.org/publication/taking-measure-faculty-diversity.

32. National Center for Education Statistics. N.d. "Fast Facts." https://nces.ed.gov /fastfacts/display.asp?id=61.

33. In many cases, institutional diversity programs have grown out of National Science Foundation ADVANCE grants designed to promote the advancement of women in academic STEM careers. See https://www.nsf.gov/funding/pgm_summ.jsp?pims _id=5383.

34. https://www.facultydiversity.org.

35. Flaherty, Colleen. 2018. "Open Searches and Diversity." *Inside Higher Ed.* 5 November. https://www.insidehighered.com/news/2018/11/05/uc-davis-holding-eight-fa culty-searches-focused-candidates-contributions-diversity.

36. See Olson, Gary A. 2009. "What Exactly Is 'Shared Governance'?" *Chronicle of Higher Education*. 23 July. https://www.chronicle.com/article/Exactly-What-Is-Shared /47065.

37. The AAUP has collected a wealth of resources on shared governance: https:// www.aaup.org/our-programs/shared-governance/resources-governance.

38. Boyer, Ernest L. (1990) 2016. *Scholarship Reconsidered: Priorities of the Professoriate.* 2nd expanded ed. Jossey-Bass.

39. Fortunately, there are efforts in this direction. See the fall 2018 special issue of the Modern Language Association journal *Profession*, especially Betensky, Carolyn, Seth Kahn, Maria Maisto, and Talia Schaffer. 2018. "Common Good, Not Common Despair," which reports on the activities of an organization called Tenure for the Common Good. https://profession.mla.org/common-good-not-common-despair.

40. For instance, writing studies experts Jeff Grabill, Bill Hart-Davidson, and their

colleagues at Michigan State University have developed some robust software that reflects disciplinary understandings of writing. http://opendrawbridge.com.

41. For example, there are open-access, peer-reviewed journals, such as *Hybrid Pedagogy*, which explores the interaction of critical pedagogy and digital pedagogy, and the *Journal of Interactive Technology and Pedagogy*, which is concerned with "critical and creative uses of digital technology in teaching, learning, and research." The Institute for Distributed Creativity's *Learning through Digital Media* (2011) features a variety of faculty testimonials from across disciplines. It includes short essays on the pedagogical uses of social bookmarking, video annotating and editing, open-source community sites, and media production. Scholz, R. Trebor, ed. 2011. *Learning through Digital Media: Experiments in Technology and Pedagogy.* Institute for Distributed Creativity. Another resource is the multiauthored, multidisciplinary blog ProfHacker, which features brief introductions to new technologies by smart colleagues who have test-driven them, short how-to guides on software programs and apps, reading suggestions for the tech curious, and think pieces about hot-button issues, such as the status of the digital humanities. Formerly hosted by the *Chronicle of Higher Education*, ProfHacker is now at http://profhacker.com.

CHAPTER 6 NOW AND THEN

1. Though I have drawn elements of his story from various students and alumni I have known, Ahmed is not a real person. The names of his professors and co-workers are pseudonyms.

2. In 2016, according to the National Center for Education Statistics, of the 20.5 million students enrolled in degree-granting institutions in the United States, more than 8 million were age twenty-five or over. https://nces.ed.gov/programs/digest/d14/ch_3.asp. By 2025, of the 23 million students enrolled, more than 9.5 million will be age twenty-five or over, bringing nontraditional students to 41 percent of total enrollment.

3. Despite occasional alarmist media stories about the bottom falling out of undergraduate enrollments, the data cited in these stories present a mixed picture. According to the Western Interstate Commission for Higher Education (WICHE), "the nation is projected to produce fewer high school graduates in all of the 10 graduating classes between 2013 and 2023, compared to the highest recorded number of graduates in 2013. . . . While the country is projected to see three years of growth between 2024 and 2026, this will be a short-term increase as the average size of graduating classes between 2027 and 2032 is expected to be smaller than those in 2013." WICHE. 2016. "Number of High School Graduates across America Leveling Off; Minority Grads Rising, to Be Near Majority Soon." 6 December. https://www.wiche.edu/news/knocking-at-the-college-door-9th. The commission notes that some regions will see increases while others

see decreases. Meanwhile, the National Center for Education Statistics reports that "between 2000 and 2015, total undergraduate enrollment in degree-granting postsecondary institutions increased by 30 percent (from 13.2 million to 17 million). By 2026, total undergraduate enrollment is projected to increase to 19.3 million students." NCES. 2017. "Undergraduate Enrollment." https://nces.ed.gov/programs/coe/pdf/Indicator _CHA/coe_cha_2017_05.pdf.

4. McMillan Cottom, Tressie. 2017. *Lower Ed: The Troubling Rise of For-Profit Colleges in the New Economy*. New Press.

5. Fain, Paul. 2017. "New Data on Nondegree Credentials." *Inside Higher Ed*. 14 September. https://www.insidehighered.com/news/2017/09/14/feds-release-data-nondegree -credentials-including-certificates-and-licenses.

6. https://openbadges.org.

7. Editors of Inside Higher Ed. 2015. *Extending the Credential* (booklet). https://www .insidehighered.com/booklet/extending-credential.

8. McKenzie, Lindsay. 2018. "Valuing Learning, Wherever It Occurs." *Inside Higher Ed*. 22 February. https://www.insidehighered.com/news/2018/02/22/higher-ed-group -seeks-key-role-alternative-credential-landscape.

9. Northeastern University's Level is one example. https://www.leveledu.com.

10. Blumenstyk, Goldie. 2016. "2 Projects That Promote Alternative Credentials Reach Key Milestones." *Chronicle of Higher Education*. 19 September. https://www.chronicle .com/article/2-Projects-That-Promote/237823. For information on the 21st Century Skills Badging Challenge, see http://eddesignlab.org/badgingchallenge.

11. http://universitylearningstore.org.

12. Brown, Jessie, and Martin Kurzweil. 2017. *The Complex Universe of Alternative Postsecondary Credentials and Pathways*. American Academy of Arts and Sciences.

13. Giani, Matthew, and Heather Lee Fox. 2017. "Do Stackable Credentials Reinforce Stratification or Promote Upward Mobility? An Analysis of Health Professions Pathways Reform in a Community College Consortium." *Journal of Vocational Education and Training* 69.1. https://www.tandfonline.com/doi/abs/10.1080/13636820.2016.1238837 ?journalCode=rjve20.

14. Harris, Adam. 2017. "What You Need to Know about the GOP Bill to Bring Sweeping Changes to Higher Ed." *Chronicle of Higher Ed*. 1 December. https://www .chronicle.com/article/What-You-Need-to-Know-About/241947.

15. Trump's Department of Education has paused Obama-era regulations that punished poor-performing for-profit colleges and that offered loan forgiveness to defrauded students. It is also eyeing changes to safeguards enshrined in accreditation procedures, a requirement that distance programs ensure "regular and substantive interaction" between students and instructors, and the credit hour. Protopsaltis, Spiros, and Clare McCann. 2018. "Misguided Effort to Dismantle Federal Protections." *Inside Higher Ed*. 16 April. https://www.insidehighered.com/views/2018/04/16/risks-trump-ad

ministrations-next-push-deregulate-higher-education-opinion; Stratford, Michael. 2018. "What's Next on DeVos' Regulatory Chopping Block?" *Politico*. 30 March. https://www.politico.com/newsletters/morning-education/2018/03/30/whats-next-on-devos-regulatory-chopping-block-154849. In early 2019, the administration released details of its deregulatory plans. Camera, Lauren. 2019. "DeVos' Deregulatory Higher Education Agenda." *US News and World Report*. 7 January. https://www.usnews.com/news/education-news/articles/2019-01-07/devos-deregulatory-higher-education-agenda.

16. Kreighbaum, Andrew. 2017. "Is DeVos Devaluing Degrees?" *Inside Higher Ed*. 28 November. https://www.insidehighered.com/news/2017/11/28/devos-says-us-has-emphasized-four-year-degrees-expense-work-force-training.

17. While their proponents claim that shorter-term credentials are inexpensive alternatives to degrees, they can be pricey. Coding boot camps, for example, can run in excess of $20,000—and this does not include lost earnings from missed work time. Some alternative credentials might be quite good, but given the short duration and unclear return on investment, these kinds of programs ask learners to assume considerable risk, especially when the provider is not well known.

18. Tesfai, Lul, Kim Dancy, and Mary Alice McCarthy. 2018. "Paying More and Getting Less: How Nondegree Credentials Reflect Labor Market Inequality between Men and Women." New America. 13 September. https://www.newamerica.org/education-policy/reports/paying-more-and-getting-less/paying-more-and-getting-less.

19. Fain, Paul. 2018. "Men Benefit Most from Nondegree Credentials." *Inside Higher Ed*. 13 September. https://www.insidehighered.com/news/2018/09/13/new-data-gender-gaps-benefits-nondegree-credentials.

20. For instance, the authors of *Dismissed by Degrees*—a 2017 white paper produced by Accenture (a business strategy and consulting firm), Grads of Life (a national campaign to support youths who are neither working nor in school), and Harvard Business School—argue that degree inflation, the phenomenon of employers requiring degrees for positions that did not previously require them, is harming US businesses and barring "middle-skilled Americans" from the middle class. They recommend that employers prioritize competencies and experience over degrees in hiring processes and that they partner with high schools, vocational and community colleges, and workplace training programs to offer shorter-term, customized training. Fuller, Joseph B., and Manjari Raman. 2017. *Dismissed by Degrees*. Accenture, Grads of Life, and Harvard Business School.

21. Craig, Ryan. 2015. *College Disrupted: The Great Unbundling of Higher Education*. Palgrave Macmillan / St. Martin's.

22. Laitinen, Amy. 2012. *Cracking the Credit Hour*. New America Foundation and Education Sector; Bass, Jared Cameron, Amy Laitinen, and Clare McCann. 2018. "The Department of Deregulation: DeVos' New Regulatory Agenda to Roll Back Protections for Students." New America. 30 March. https://www.newamerica.org/education

-policy/edcentral/the-department-of-deregulation. For a similar argument, see Reed, Matt. 2018. "Defending the Bad against the Awful." *Inside Higher Ed.* 1 April. https://www.insidehighered.com/blogs/confessions-community-college-dean/defending-bad -against-awful.

23. Carey, Kevin. 2015. *The End of College: Creating the Future of Learning and the University of Everywhere.* Riverhead Books / Penguin.

24. Carey seems to have a penchant for negatively contrasting "traditional" education with overhyped educational reforms whose bubbles are about to burst. First MOOCs and then boot camps. Dev Bootcamp shut down in December 2017 after announcing that it could not make its business model work. Iron Yard, another popular provider, quickly followed suit. While close to 100 coding boot camps remain in operation as of this writing, they do not appear to be the game-changer they were touted to be.

25. US Marine Corps. N.d. "Training Summary by Week." http://www.mcrdpi.ma rines.mil/Recruit-Training/Training-Summary-By-Week.

26. NECHE was formed in a 2018 reorganization of the New England Association of Schools and Colleges (NEASC).

27. NEASC. 2016. "Standard Four: The Academic Program." https://cihe.neasc.org /standards-policies/standards-accreditation/standards-effective-july-1-2016#standard _four.

28. See, for instance, Carey, Kevin. 2012. "The Higher Education Monopoly Is Crumbling as We Speak." 12 March. *New Republic.* https://newrepublic.com/article/101620 /higher-education-accreditation-mit-university.

29. Mintz, Steven. 2017. "Reimagining the College Transcript." *Inside Higher Ed.* 12 January. https://www.insidehighered.com/blogs/higher-ed-gamma/reimagining-college -transcript.

30. In an article in the *National Association of Colleges and Employers Journal*, Edwin Koc surveys various economic trends and concludes that "despite the employer-based assessments [to the contrary], there is no credible supporting evidence of a national skills gap." Koc, Edwin. 2018. "Is There Really a Skills Gap?" *NACE Journal.* 1 February. https://www.naceweb.org/talent-acquisition/trends-and-predictions/is-there-really -a-skills-gap.

31. O'Brien, Matt. 2019. "The Skills Gap Is Fixed, Because There Was No Skills Gap." *Washington Post.* 14 January. https://www.washingtonpost.com/business/2019/01/14/skills -gap-is-fixed-because-there-was-no-skills-gap/?noredirect=on&utm_term=.9a932 04f4690.

32. Bauer-Wolf, Jeremy. 2018. "Public May Not Trust Higher Ed, but Employers Do." *Inside Higher Ed.* 28 August. https://www.insidehighered.com/news/2018/08/28/survey -business-leaders-believe-students-are-learning-skills-not-those-needed.

33. Gallagher, Sean. 2016. *The Future of University Credentials: New Developments at the Intersection of Higher Education and Hiring.* Harvard University Press.

34. Quoted in Lederman, Doug. 2018. "Look Who's Championing the Degree." *Inside Higher Ed.* 6 March. https://www.insidehighered.com/digital-learning/article/2018/03/06/coursera-purveyor-moocs-bets-big-university-degrees.

35. National Center for Education Statistics. N.d. "Fast Facts." https://nces.ed.gov/fastfacts/display.asp?id=51.

36. National Center for Education Statistics. N.d. "Fast Facts." https://nces.ed.gov/fastfacts/display.asp?id=98.

37. Carnevale, Anthony P., Ban Cheah, and Andrew R. Hanson. 2015. "The Economic Value of College Majors: Executive Summary." Georgetown University, Center on Education and the Workforce. https://cew-7632.kxcdn.com/wp-content/uploads/The-Economic-Value-of-College-Majors-Exec-Summ-Web.pdf.

38. Carnevale, Anthony P., Tamara Jayasundera, and Artem Gulish. 2016. "America's Divided Recovery: College Haves and Have Nots." Georgetown University, Center on Education and the Workforce. https://cew.georgetown.edu/cew-reports/americas-divided-recovery.

39. Aoun, Joseph E. 2017. *Robot-Proof: Higher Education in the Age of Artificial Intelligence.* MIT Press.

40. Bailey, Thomas R., Shanna Smith Jaggars, and Davis Jenkins. 2015. *Redesigning America's Community Colleges: A Clearer Path to Student Success.* Harvard University Press. *See also* Jenkins, Davis, Hana Lahr, and John Fink. 2017. *Implementing Guided Pathways: Early Insights from the AACC Pathways Colleges.* Community College Research Center.

41. Bailey, Thomas R. 2017. "Guided Pathways at Community Colleges: From Theory to Practice." *Diversity and Democracy* 20.4 (Fall). https://www.aacu.org/diversitydemocracy/2017/fall/bailey.

42. Kelly-Riley, Diane, and Carl Whithaus. 2017. "Editors' Introduction." *Journal of Writing Assessment* 10.1. http://journalofwritingassessment.org/article.php?article=115; Rose, Mike. 2016. "Reassessing a Redesign of Community Colleges." *Inside Higher Ed.* 23 June. https://www.insidehighered.com/views/2016/06/23/essay-challenges-facing-guided-pathways-model-restructuring-two-year-colleges.

43. I do not want to be read as dismissing the importance of completion rates, especially for marginalized populations. Approximately 60 percent of students who pursue a bachelor's degree ultimately complete one. White, Asian, and high-income students complete at greater rates than black, Hispanic, and low-income students. Commission on the Future of Undergraduate Education. 2017. *The Future of Undergraduate Education: The Future of America.* American Academy of Arts and Sciences, 4. One promising model is the City University of New York's Accelerated Study in Associate Programs (ASAP), which has had remarkable success helping low-income students attain an associate's degree by alleviating financial burdens (meeting their full financial needs, providing transit passes, etc.), improving advising and support, and quickly addressing

academic underpreparedness. Students attend full time (since part-time students are far less likely to complete their degrees) and are expected to earn their degree in three years. ASAP students have significantly outperformed their control-group peers on persistence, three-year graduation, and transfer rates to four-year colleges. For more information on ASAP, see Commission on the Future of Undergraduate Education 2017, 34.

44. https://micromasters.mit.edu; Straumsheim, Carl. 2017. "MIT Deems Micro-Masters a Success." *Inside Higher Ed.* 26 July. https://www.insidehighered.com/news /2017/07/26/mit-deems-half-online-half-person-masters-program-success; Thomason, Andy. 2015. "MIT Unveils 'MicroMaster's,' Allowing Students to Get Half Their Degree from MOOCs." *Chronicle of Higher Education.* 7 October. https://www.chronicle .com/blogs/ticker/mit-unveils-micromasters-allowing-students-to-get-half-their -degree-from-moocs/105615.

45. Fain, Paul. 2018. "Google Curriculum, College Credit." *Inside Higher Ed.* 26 September. https://www.insidehighered.com/digital-learning/article/2018/09/26/growing -number-colleges-partner-google-offer-credit-its-new-it. It remains to be seen whether students will be guided to integrate their learning across the certificate and degree programs or if this initiative simply amounts to institutions giving credit. This experiment, involving as it does a credential offered by an external partner that is not an educational organization, deserves close scrutiny.

46. Filmer, Ann. 2014. "Digital Badge System Helps Students Develop Skills." University of California at Davis, College of Agricultural and Environmental Sciences. 9 January. http://www.caes.ucdavis.edu/news/articles/2014/01/groundbreaking-digital-badge -system-for-sustainable-agriculture-program-2; Fain, Paul. 2014. "Badging from Within." *Inside Higher Ed.* 3 January. https://www.insidehighered.com/news/2014/01/03/uc-daviss -groundbreaking-digital-badge-system-new-sustainable-agriculture-program#sthash .ZANX1bRj.dpbs.

47. "Academic Plan: Northeastern 2025." 2016. http://www.northeastern.edu/academic -plan/plan.

48. "Stanford 2025: Open Loop University." N.d. http://www.stanford2025.com/open -loop-university.

49. Most institutions have teaching and learning centers that offer an array of assessment resources. Many disciplinary organizations and professional accrediting bodies have developed assessment models appropriate to their domains. General assessment resources are available from organizations such as the AAC&U; see https://www.aacu .org/resources/assessment-and-value.

50. I am thinking here of lifelong learning institutes and institutes for learning in retirement of the sort Harvard (http://hilr.harvard.edu), Duke (https://learnmore.duke .edu/olli), and other institutions offer. The popularity of these programs demonstrates

the enduring appeal of colleges and universities as places where people throughout their life can gather to learn with and from faculty and peers.

CONCLUSION EDUCATING ESTHER

1. Esther is a real person, though Esther is not her name. She is now a student at an Ivy League university.

INDEX

68, 116; and faculty disaggregation, 133; mapping, 68; pluralism in, 65

Dabars, William, 115
data literacy, 109
Davidson, Cathy N., 31, 38, 40, 44, 124
debt: of adjuncts, 125, 126; from alternative credentials, 153; default on, 34, 188n21; and emphasis on private good, 24; and for-profit providers, 34; and noncompletion, 32; privatization of, 188n21; risks from loans, 179, 181; and social inequality, 32–33
degrees: and alternative credentials, 154, 156, 162, 165–75; degree inflation, 158, 166; devaluing of, 158–60, 163; as durable, 158–65; overproduction of, 127; and political engagement, 191n36; as signaling, 163, 189n24; standards, 38, 161–62; as valued, 59–60, 163–66. *See also* M+GE+E=D model
democracy, xiv, 29, 40, 45, 73, 102–3, 105, 129
depth. *See* breadth/depth in higher education
deregulation, 1, 2, 7, 9, 34–37, 156, 159
DeVos, Betsy, 156, 159
Dewey, John: on experiential learning, 14, 76–77, 78–79, 81, 88, 91–92, 94–95; on professional learning vs. training, 107–8
dismantling. *See* unbundling
distance courses, 161, 204n23, 208n15. *See also* online courses
distributed assessment, 163
distribution model for general education, 52, 55–56
distribution requirements, 7, 49, 52–57, 63–65
diversity of faculty, 139, 141, 145
divisions, program, 3, 11–12, 14
Dorn, Charles, 26–29, 182n44
dual enrollment, 57, 161
Duke University, 130, 212n50

edtech: adaptive learning, 7, 131–32; completion/pass rates, 81, 130–31; costs of, 37–39; design of, 88–89, 91; Esther example, 180; faculty interest in, 205n30; faculty's role in integration, 38, 138, 144, 147–48; and faculty unbundling, 120, 121, 130–34; integra-

tion strategies, 144, 147–48; and lifelong learning, 171; limits of, 131–32, 204n23; machine learning, 131–32, 171; purpose of, 124–25, 138, 147; and rebundling liberal arts, 99–100; resources on, 148; selection of, 144, 147–48; and social inequality, 132; unbundling role, 7, 37–39, 79–81, 128, 130–34
Educational Quality through Innovative Partnerships (EQUIP), 156, 190n28
edX, 130, 168
electives. *See* M+GE+E=D model
employers: and alternative credentials, 158, 163, 164, 166, 172; campuses by, 82; employment rates, 34; experiential learning role, 89–90, 93–94; and liberal arts, 97–99, 100, 113, 114, 116–17, 119, 120; lifelong learning role, 172, 174; valuing of higher education, 8, 59–60, 163–64, 166
engaged liberal arts, 109
enrollments: dual, 57, 161; in liberal arts, 98; media coverage of, 207n3; nontraditional, 152–53; traditional, 152–53, 164–65
Esther, 21, 177–82
experiential learning: vs. classroom learning, 73–76; defined, 75; examples of, x–xiv, 72–73, 84–88, 90–91, 171; faculty's role in, 76, 86, 87–88, 90, 91–94, 197n18; forms of, 84–85; need for integration, 74–75, 76–77, 79–84; opportunities (ELOs), 197n18; strategies for, 88–94; theory of, 76–79; ubiquity of, 18, 74–75, 78, 79, 84, 94–95; unbundlers' emphasis on, 74–75, 79
experiential liberal arts, 112–13
expertise, 61, 62, 65, 67, 193n3
extension education. *See* continuing education

faculty: breadth/depth in learning role, 66–71; as critical to integrative learning, 16; and curriculum design, 53, 67, 68; disaggregating, 12, 120, 123–25, 129–35, 181; diversity of, 139, 141, 145; divisions in, 3; edtech integration role, 138, 144, 147–48; edtech interest, 205n30; as entrepreneurs, 13; experiential learning role, 76, 86, 87–88, 90, 91–94, 197n18; at for-profit providers, 34, 134;

historically black colleges and universities, 27, 31

Horn, Michael B., 35–37

housing insecurity, 182n43

humanics, 108–9, 112–13

human literacy, 109

hybrid courses, 205n30

hybrid model, 24–25

IBM, 82, 154–55

institutional decision-making, 139, 142, 144, 145, 146, 147–48, 172–73

institutional support: for breadth/depth, 65–66; for experiential learning, 88–91; for integrating faculty model, 138–44; for integrating liberal arts, 114–17; for lifelong learning, 170–72

integrative learning: as bidirectional, 73; challenges to, 5, 11–12, 181–82; defined, 5, 13, 15; vs. interdisciplinarity, 15, 50; need for, xiii–xiv, 5–6, 181–82; overview, 5–6, 10–15; as term, 11, 15. *See also* alternative credentials; breadth/depth in higher education; classroom learning; experiential learning; liberal arts; lifelong learning; private good; public good

interaction in learning, 76, 81, 83, 88, 92, 94–95

interdisciplinarity, 15, 50, 61–62

international baccalaureate (IB), 57

Iron Yard, 210n24

Jansson, Eric, 99–100

job changes, 119–20

job skills: advantages of liberal arts, 100; at community colleges, 110; emphasis on, 1, 8, 58; in history of education, 24–25, 28, 51; skills gap, 163–64; skills training vs. professional learning, 107–8; students' focus on, 40, 41, 42; and value of degrees, 165, 166

Kajimoto, Masato, 86–87

Kelly, Andrew P., 35–37

Kerr, Clark, 2, 12–13

Kezar, Adrianna, 134, 135, 136

Koch, Charles, 187n15

Kurzweil, Martin, 155–56

LaGuardia Community College, 63–64, 68

learning: effect of faculty-student engagement on, 136–37; as more than skill acquisition, 8–9; prompting students about, 70; retirement learning, 175–76; students' interest in, 43; time for, 83, 159–60; transfer, 15, 69–70, 77. *See also* classroom learning; experiential learning; integrative learning; learning transfer; liberal education; lifelong learning; professional learning

learning technology. *See* edtech

learning transfer, 15, 69–70, 77

lectures, 80, 83–84, 86, 197n17

liberal arts: criticism of, 99–100; development of, 51; enrollments, 98; government policy, 102–3; humanics, 108–9, 112–13; integration, need for, 100–101, 106–14; integration examples, 96–97, 104, 109–13, 114, 116; integration strategies, 114–19; media interest in, 97–99, 105–6; vs. STEM, 98–99, 101–6

liberal education: Esther example, 180; in history of education, 24–25; and professional learning, 107–8, 181; as term, 106–7

lifelong learning: examples, 150–52, 153, 169, 173, 175–76, 180–81; integrating, 154, 166–67, 168–74; need for, 153, 166, 181; pathways, 167–68, 170; platforms, 150–52; and risk, 181–82; strategies for, 170–74

LinkedIn, 154

literacy: "new," 109; records, 163

living expenses, 39

loans, 31, 32–33, 34, 125, 179, 181, 188n21

Lynda, 154

Lynk, 109–10

M+GE+E=D model: alternatives to, 57–58, 62–65; development of, 17, 25, 51–52; as fragmented, 18, 49–50; integrative learning with, 52–57, 62–65

machine learning, 131–32, 171

majors: alternatives to, 63, 64, 66; as central concept, 50–51, 52; combined, 113; integrative learning across, 56–57; integrative learning within, 53–54; liberal arts enrollments, 98. *See also* M+GE+E=D model

Marlen, Estefany, 44
Maxey, Daniel, 134, 135
McChrystal, Stanley, 185n12, 193n3
McMillan Cottom, Tressie, 9, 20, 24, 33–34,
  37, 44, 153, 166
mentoring: and experiential learning, xi, 90,
  93; by Farrell, 122, 123; in liberal arts integration, 118–19; in lifelong learning, 169,
  173, 176; modeling by, 146–47; of other faculty, 145; and student success, xiii, 20, 38,
  84, 96, 120, 135, 136, 159; and unbundling,
  124, 133, 134–35
Michigan State University, 27, 206n40
"micro master's," 87, 168
minors, 193n2
MIT (Massachusetts Institute of Technology), 87, 130, 168
MOOCs (massive open online courses), 7,
  38, 79–81, 86–87, 130–31, 164
Mount Holyoke College, 109–10, 116
Mozilla, 154–55
"multiversity," 12–13
M-Write, 204n21
MyMantl, 155

National Science Foundation, 14, 206n33
neoliberalism, 9, 31–32
Neuman, Martha, 47–49
New America Foundation, 159
New England Commission of Higher Education (NECHE), 161–62
Newman, Cardinal, 13, 25
nonprofits, partnerships with, 89–90, 93–94,
  116–17
Northeastern University: Esther example,
  177–82; experiential learning program, 87–
  88, 91, 171; faculty example, 122–23, 125;
  general education at, 64–65; liberal arts
  integration, 112–13, 116; and lifelong learning, 168–69; reasons for attending, 42–44
NUpath, 64–65
NYU's Gallatin School of Individualized
  Study, 63

Obama administration, 102, 188n21, 190n28,
  208n15
Odyssey program (Hendrix College), 85–86

Olin College, 112, 114, 116
online courses: access to, 80–81; cost of, 38;
  design and infrastructure of, 88–89, 91, 93;
  growth in, 196n12; integration, need for,
  74–75, 79–84; MOOCs, 7, 38, 79–81, 86–87,
  130–31, 164; reliance on staff vs. faculty, 134
Open Badges, 154–55
Open Loop University, 169

Parchment, 155
partnerships: cautions about, 117, 140; for experiential learning, 89–90, 91, 93–94; for
  liberal arts integration, 116–17, 119; for
  lifelong learning, 172, 174
pathways, 110–11, 167–68, 170
peer reviews: automated, 204n21; faculty, 139,
  142, 145
Pell grants, 31, 43, 156
people of color: faculty, 141; students, 37, 136,
  153–54, 157, 211n43
physical spaces for learning, 39, 82–83, 89, 93,
  94, 180
pluralism, curricular, 65
Poiger, Uta, 112
policy, education, 16, 101–3, 155–56. See also
  deregulation
portfolios, 63–64, 67, 163
practical liberal arts, 109
prior experience, 78, 118, 161
prior learning assessment, 78, 161
privacy and adaptive learning, 131
private good: emphasis on, 24, 26, 30–40, 181;
  in history of higher education, 24–29; as
  reinforcing public good, 23, 44, 45–46;
  students' interest in, 40–42, 44
privatization of student debt, 188n21. See also
  for-profit providers; unbundling
professional development, 90, 115, 127, 144,
  145–46, 174
professional learning: defined, 107; Esther
  example, 180; integrating with liberal arts,
  100–101, 106–14, 117–19; vs. liberal learning, 181; vs. skills training, 107–8. See also
  alternative credentials; STEM
ProfHacker, 206n41
public good: and academic freedom, 128–29,
  139, 140; defined, 186n5; erosion of idea,

23–24, 30–40; Esther example, 179, 180, 182; and financial aid, 39–40, 179; and for-profit providers, 33–34, 37; in history of higher education, 24–29; and liberal arts, 102–3; and lifelong learning, 175; as reinforcing private good, 23, 44, 45–46; and STEM, 102; students' interest in, 42, 44

quadrivium, 51, 103–4

race: faculty diversity, 141; and perception of public good, 30–31. *See also* students of color
Reagan, Ronald, 31
Real College, 182n43
rebundling, 3–4, 99–100
Red Book, 51–52
reflective activities, 70, 92, 118
requirements. *See* credit-hour requirements; distribution requirements
research, 134, 138, 140, 142–43, 146–47
Resilient Cities (RC), 104–5
retirement learning, 175–76
Rising above the Gathering Storm, 101–2, 103
risks, financial, 158, 162, 179, 181–82, 209n17
robots, 9, 19, 109, 132, 166, 182
Rusnak, Andrew, 111

SAIL (self-authored integrated learning), 87–88, 171
salaries: administration, 38; faculty, 38, 39, 125, 126, 127, 128, 145; students, 157, 165
Samtani, Riddhi, 22–23, 24
San José State University, 130
scheduling, 66, 167
Schneider, Carol Geary, 56
scholarship, model of, 142–43
Selingo, Jeffrey, 7, 58, 130
service learning programs, 84, 86, 93, 119
Servicemen's Readjustment Act, 29, 30
service/outreach, faculty, 122–23, 138, 139–40, 143–44, 147
short-form courses, 4–5, 83, 161
situated learning theory, 77, 80–81
skills. *See* job skills; thinking skills
Smith, Vernon C., 124, 133, 134

Smith College, 27, 186n5
social inequality: and alternative credentials, 153–54, 157–58, 165–66; and debt, 32–33; and edtech, 132; and for-profit providers, 9, 37; and graduation rates, 33; and unbundling, 9, 37, 124, 134–35
South Carolina College, 186n5
Southern New Hampshire University, 7
specialization, 14, 49, 56, 98
staff: experiential learning role, 85, 88, 90, 93; growth of, 190n34; liberal arts role, 116, 118, 119; lifelong learning role, 171; and unbundling, 133, 134
Stanford University, 130, 169
STEAM (science, technology, engineering, arts, and math), 104
STEM (science, technology, engineering, and math): integration, need for, 100–101, 106–14; integration examples, 104, 109–13, 114, 116; integration strategies, 114–19; vs. liberal arts, 98–99, 101–6
STIRS (scientific thinking and integrative reasoning skills), 104
STS (science, technology, and society), 104
students: and adjunct faculty, 128, 136–37; assessment of, 70, 78, 92, 117, 161, 163; depictions of, 40–41; and faculty unbundling, 133, 134–35; first-generation, 9, 134–36; food/housing insecurity, 182n43; goal setting, 70, 92, 117; interest in private/public good, 40, 41, 42, 44; job changing by, 119–20; pranks by, 41; reasons for attending, 42–44; role in integrative learning, 16–17; self-assessments, 70, 92, 117; time spent by, 181n42; working, 41
students of color, 37, 136, 153–54, 157, 211n43
SUNY (State University of New York), 197n18

teaching: as complex endeavor, 8–9; vs. content delivery, 131; in integrated faculty model, 138, 139–40, 142–43, 145–47; separation from research, 134. *See also* faculty-student engagement
technological literacy, 109
tenure, 128–29, 136, 137–40, 141, 145
text analysis, automated, 204n21

thinking skills: and breadth/depth of learning, 61–62; employers' need for, 8, 59, 166; Esther example, 180; need for flexible, 3
time for learning, 83, 159–60
transcripts, 162–63
transfer, learning. *See* learning transfer
transfers between schools, 57, 128, 161
trivium, 51, 103
Trump administration, 34, 156
tuition, 32, 34, 39–40

UCLA (University of California at Los Angeles), 155
Udacity, 130
unbundling: criticism of traditional model, 35–36, 49–50, 57–58, 99–100, 158–60, 163; as customization, 10; defined, 2, 6; and deregulation, 7, 34–37; as disruptive innovation, 11, 36–37; edtech emphasis, 7, 11, 37–39, 79–81, 130–34, 148; experiential learning emphasis, 74–75, 79; and faculty, 120, 123–25, 129–30, 132–35; fragmentation from, 2, 4–5; generalizations in, 41, 80, 203n14; history of, 134, 205n24; and lifelong learning, 149, 153; overview of, 1, 2–3, 6–9; portrayals of students, 41; private good emphasis, 24, 25, 36–37; and social inequality, 9, 37, 124, 134–35; and venture capital, 37, 130, 154

unionization, 127
University Learning Store, 155
University of California, Davis, 141, 155, 168
University of California, Irvine, 155
University of Maryland University College, 7
University of Michigan, 204n21
University of Phoenix, 196n12
University of Virginia, 31
University of Washington, 155
University of Wisconsin, 155
University Ventures, 6, 130
urban resilience, 104–5
US Department of Education, 156, 190n28, 204n23

venture capital, 37, 130, 154
virtual assembly line, 124, 133–34

Waiss, Danielle Murad, x–xiv
Western Governors University (WGU), 204n23
Western Interstate Commission for Higher Education (WICHE), 207n3
women: and alternative credentials, 157; faculty, 141; and social inequality, 37; STEM grants, 206n33
women's colleges, 27
workplace training credits, 196n10